NORTHERN

by the same author

for Children
AXE-AGE, WOLF-AGE: A SELECTION FROM THE NORSE MYTHS
(André Deutsch)
BEOWULF (Oxford University Press)
THE CALLOW PIT COFFER (Macmillan)
THE DEAD MOON (André Deutsch)
THE EARTH-FATHER (Heinemann)
THE FIRE-BROTHER (Heinemann)
THE FOX AND THE CAT: ANIMAL TALES FROM GRIMM (Andersen)
THE GREEN CHILDREN (Macmillan)
GREEN BLADES RISING: THE ANGLO-SAXONS (André Deutsch)
HAVELOK THE DANE (Macmillan)
KING HORN (Boydell)
THE PEDLAR OF SWAFFHAM (Macmillan)
THE SEA STRANGER (Heinemann)
STORM (Heinemann)
Awarded the Library Association's Carnegie Medal
STORM AND OTHER OLD ENGLISH RIDDLES (Macmillan)
THE WILDMAN (André Deutsch)
WORDHOARD (*with Jill Paton Walsh*) (Macmillan)

Poems
THE DREAM-HOUSE (André Deutsch)
THE RAIN-GIVER (André Deutsch)
TIME'S ORIEL (Hutchinson)
WATERSLAIN (Hutchinson)
THE BATTLE OF MALDON AND OTHER OLD ENGLISH POEMS
(*translations; with Bruce Mitchell*) (Macmillan)
BEOWULF (*translation; with Bruce Mitchell*) (Macmillan)
THE EXETER BOOK RIDDLES (*translations*) (Folio/Penguin)

Mythology
THE NORSE MYTHS (André Deutsch)

Travel
PIECES OF LAND: JOURNEYS TO EIGHT ISLANDS (Gollancz)

as Editor
THE ANGLO-SAXON WORLD (Boydell and Brewer)
THE FABER BOOK OF NORTHERN FOLK-TALES (Faber and Faber)
THE FABER BOOK OF NORTHERN LEGENDS (Faber and Faber)
FOLK-TALES OF THE BRITISH ISLES (Folio/Faber and Faber)
THE OXFORD BOOK OF TRAVEL VERSE (Oxford University Press)
RUNNING TO PARADISE: AN INTRODUCTORY SELECTION OF THE POEMS
OF W. B. YEATS (Macmillan)
WINTER'S TALES 14 (Macmillan)
WINTER'S TALES FOR CHILDREN 3 (Macmillan)

NORTHERN LIGHTS

Legends, Sagas
and Folk-tales

edited by
Kevin Crossley-Holland

Illustrated by Alan Howard

faber and faber
LONDON · BOSTON

First published in 1987
by Faber and Faber Limited
3 Queen Square, London WC1N 3AU

Printed in Great Britain by
Mackays of Chatham Ltd, Kent

All rights reserved

Selection and introductory material
© Kevin Crossley-Holland 1987
Walter and Hildegund © Jennifer Westwood, 1977
Wayland Smith © Penelope Farmer, 1977

This book is sold subject to the condition that it shall not,
by way of trade or otherwise, be lent, resold, hired out
or otherwise circulated without the publisher's prior consent
in any form of binding or cover other than that in which
it is published and without a similar condition including this
condition being imposed on the subsequent purchaser.

British Library Cataloguing in Publication Data

Crossley-Holland, Kevin
  Northern lights: legends, sagas and
  folk tales.
  I. Title
  823'.914[F]   PR6053.R63

ISBN 0–571–14809–3

for
PHYLLIS HUNT

Contents

Foreword	vii
Sources and Acknowledgements	xi

HEROIC LEGENDS

Dietrich of Bern	3
Walter and Hildegund	12
The Curse of Andvari's Ring	26
Beowulf Fights the Dragon	32
Wayland Smith	42
How Sigurd Awoke Brynhild upon Hindfell	55

SAGAS

The Burning of Bergthorsknoll	71
Gestumblindi's Riddles	80
Thorstein Staff-Struck	89
The Hauntings at Frodriver	98
The Expedition of Thorfin Karlsefni	106
Authun and the Bear	118
The Battle of Stamford Bridge	126

FOLK-TALES

The Pleiades	135
How Some Wild Animals Became Tame Ones	138
The Three Heads of the Well	142
Why the Sea is Salt	147
The Bremen Town Musicians	151
The Wizards of the Vestmanna Isles	156
Jorinde and Joringel	160
A Stork is not always a Stork	164

Tom Tit Tot	166
The Enchanted Apple-tree	171
The Elf Maiden	174
The King o' the Cats	179
Little Annie the Goose-girl	182
The Dead Man's Nightcap	186
The Herd-boy and the Giant	188
The Black Bull of Norroway	193
The Ghost and the Money-chest	197
Mr Miacca	200
The Woman of the Sea	202
Johnnie in the Cradle	205
Peter Bull	207
The Juniper Tree	212
Toller's Neighbours	221
Door Prayer at Evening	225
Bibliography	226

Foreword

One mellow evening when I was nineteen, I was sitting in a stationary punt listening to a portable wireless (deplorable, I know) and revising for a retake of my Anglo-Saxon exams. To pass meant that I would be able to stay up, young and in love and at Oxford; to fail meant the almost unbearable prospect of expulsion from paradise. And I was going to fail.

This was when fate intervened. I was attacked by a swan—a music-hating, Anglo-Saxon-hating swan. Thinking as no Anglo-Saxon would have done discretion the better part of valour, I leaped for the river bank and ripped a cartilage in my right knee. Several trainee medical students stretched me out and jumped on it a bit. Then for the next two weeks I was laid up in the children's ward of an Oxford hospital, safe from the seductions of the city below, almost my only bedside reading Sweet's *Anglo-Saxon Primer* and *Anglo-Saxon Reader*.

During those days I got a tenuous grip on Old English grammar, but this was also the moment when my eyes and ears opened to the quite thrilling way of seeing and saying shared by the early Germanic peoples. How is one to characterise this Northern viewpoint and voice? Only with great difficulty, and only with recourse to generalisations. Yet even today something of it survives like a powerful undercurrent. If I were simply to mention the Ring cycle of Richard Wagner and J. R. R. Tolkien's *The Lord of the Rings*, the ecstatic light in the pictures of Emil Nolde and the verse of W. H. Auden, would we be able to agree that their work has something in common?

When I edited *The Faber Book of Northern Legends*, I wrote that the most pronounced strains in the make-up of the Germanic heroic peoples, as revealed through their prose and poetry, were "fatalism, courage, loyalty, superstition, cunning, melancholy, a sense of wonder, curiosity about all that's new"; while the *Irish Press* reviewer spoke of how that book's ice-bright stories had "a hardness, clarity, zest and immediacy". Perhaps these are the right sort of directions to look in.

This new anthology, *Northern Lights*, draws material from *The Faber Book of Northern Legends* and *The Faber Book of Northern Folk-Tales* in an attempt to show something of the unity as well as the variety (no anthology is much good if it is not various) of the Northern vision. Its constituents are heroic legend, saga and folk-tale. Myth is not represented here because my own retelling of the Norse myths, *Axe-Age, Wolf-Age*, is readily available.

The Germanic tribesmen who settled in North-Western Europe—the Angles and Saxons and Frisians and Jutes and Franks and Burgundians and Goths and Ostrogoths and Huns and many another!—were illiterate. They relied on the story-telling poet to act as their memory. He knew the stories about larger-than-life men and women (and monsters) who had won fame for good or evil, he knew stories that illustrated great daring or great foolhardiness, great love or great treachery, and with them he regularly educated and entertained his lord's followers. Changing as they passed from teller to teller, place to place and generation to generation, these heroic legends constituted a kind of history actual and imaginary of the early North-West European tribesmen. Old English poetry contains many allusions to them and also boasts in *Beowulf* the earliest surviving heroic poem; other legends were ultimately written down in Denmark and Iceland while the great medieval German poem, *Nibelungenlied*, contains traditions that must already have been known in North-West Europe for at least one thousand years.

During the twelfth and thirteenth centuries, there was quite extraordinary literary activity in Iceland. The inhabitants, of mixed Irish and Viking descent and thought to number no more than 50,000 at any one time, produced a magnificent crop of both prose and poetry. The Icelandic sagas are prose narratives. Racy and witty and shrewd, they are the precursors of the modern novel, telling of the lives, loyalties, dilemmas and feuds of individuals and families. There are sagas about kings and saintly bishops, historical sagas, sagas about the Viking exploration and settlement of Greenland and the eastern seaboard of Northern America. To read them is to get caught up in the momentum of fine stories and to learn much about the ideals and attitudes and day-to-day lives of a most remarkable people.

And so to the folk-tales. Here are the stories which (and the like of which) were told beside hearths all over North-Western Europe throughout the slow centuries before our own—stories which were finally written down by the great army of collectors who converted folklore from a hobby into a science during the nineteenth century. Some of them, explaining how things came to be ("The Pleiades" and "How Some Wild Animals Became Tame Ones" and "Why the Sea is Salt") approach the borders of myth. Some move easily between worlds, as does a child's mind. And some are concerned with home truths and derive, as Peter Vansittart noted when reviewing *The Faber Book of Northern Folk-Tales* in *The Times*, from peasant lore: "One must take nothing for granted, respect bargains, animals, and the old, work hard, fear winter, suspect the rich. Even the impossible has to be achieved."

My two earlier anthologies were published ten and seven years ago. At that time, if I may appropriate a few words from King Alfred, "so general was the decay of learning in England that there were very few on this side of the Humber . . . and I believe there were not many beyond the Humber" who were seriously interested in promoting a greater awareness of North-West European myth, legend and folk-tale. The concentration on the Classical world was formidable.

But things have begun to change. Those "few" who have all along been devoted to the northern world have seen the tide start to turn. Appreciably more schools (above all primary schools) are giving substantial time to projects centred on the Anglo-Saxons and the Vikings, to local history and to continuities (think only of our language, laws, coinage, the look of our land), in pursuit of a sense of belonging. The Northern world has been well served, too, by major exhibitions occasional (such as The Domesday Book) and continuous (such as Jorvik) and by prime time television series on The Vikings and Sutton Hoo.

In so far as it goes, this activity bodes well, but it still does not go very far. I hope *Northern Lights* will be thought useful on two counts: firstly as a repository of some marvellous stories and secondly as a kind of anchorage. It matters not a fig whether we are of North-West European or Caribbean or Indian or African parentage, nor whether our skins are black, blue, green or white. The fact is that if we happen to live in North-West Europe, we are likely to be stirred and moved and better earthed by listening to the voices of our predecessors, by reading the stories partly shaped by our own landscapes, our climate, our keen light, and the cold seas that surround us.

Walsham-le-Willows July 1986

Sources and Acknowledgments

"Dietrich of Bern" is taken from *German Hero-Sagas and Folk-Tales* (1958) by Barbara Leonie Picard, reprinted by permission of Oxford University Press. "Walter and Hildegund" © Jennifer Westwood 1977 was written specifically for *The Faber Book of Northern Legends*, and is reprinted by permission of the author. "The Curse of Andvari's Ring" is taken from *Myths of the Norsemen* (1960) by Roger Lancelyn Green and reprinted by permission of Penguin Books Ltd. "Beowulf Fights the Dragon" comes from my own translation of *Beowulf* (1968), and is reprinted by permission of Deborah Rogers Ltd. "Wayland Smith" © Penelope Farmer 1977 was written specifically for *The Faber Book of Northern Legends*, and is reprinted by permission of the author and Deborah Owen Ltd.

"The Burning of Bergthorsknoll" is taken from *Njal's Saga* (1960) translated by Magnus Magnusson and Hermann Pálsson, and is reprinted by permission of Penguin Books Ltd. "Gestumblindi's Riddles" are translated by N. Kershaw (Nora Chadwick) in *Stories and Ballads of the Far Past* (Cambridge University Press, Cambridge, 1921). "Thorstein Staff-Struck" and "Authun and the Bear" both come from *Eirik the Red and other Icelandic Sagas* (1961) selected and translated by Gwyn Jones and reprinted by permission of Oxford University Press. "The Expedition of Thorfin Karlsefni" comes from *The Norse Discoverers of America: The Wineland Sagas* (1921) translated by G. M. Gathorne-Hardy and is reprinted by permission of Oxford University Press.

"The Bremen Town Musicians" comes from *About Wise Men and Simpletons—Tales from Grimm* translated by Elizabeth Shub (Hamish Hamilton, London, 1972). "The Wizards of the Vestmanna Isles" and "The Dead Man's Nightcap" come from *Icelandic Folktales and Legends* by Jacqueline Simpson (B. T. Batsford, London, 1972). "Jorinde and Joringel" was translated by Hildegund Kübler and Kevin Crossley-Holland for *The Faber Book of Northern Folk-Tales* and is © Hildegund Kübler and Kevin Crossley-Holland 1980. 'A Stork is not Always a Stork" comes from *Scandinavian Legends and Folk-Tales* (1956) retold by Gwyn Jones and is reprinted by permission of Oxford University Press. "The Ghost and the Money Chest" and "Door Prayer at Evening" come from *Ghosts, Witchcraft and the Other World* by Alan Boucher (Iceland Review Library, Reykjavik, 1977). "The Woman of the Sea" is taken from *The Princess Splendour and Other Stories* retold by Helen Waddell and edited by Eileen Colwell © Longman Young Books 1969, and is reprinted here by kind permission of Mary Martin. "Johnnie in the Cradle", collected by Hamish Henderson, is reprinted from *A Dictionary of British Folk-Tales* edited by Katharine Briggs (Routledge and Kegan Paul, 1970–1). "The Juniper Tree" is taken from *Animal Stories* by Walter de la Mare (Faber and Faber, London, 1939) and reprinted by permission of the Literary Trustees of Walter de la Mare and the Society of Authors as their representative.

Acknowledgments are due and gladly given to the holders of copyrights listed above for their permission to include material in this anthology. All the other stories in this book are out of copyright; the authors and, where appropriate, the translators are credited at the end of each tale.

When I edited *The Faber Book of Northern Legends* and *The Faber Book of Northern Folk-Tales*, I wrote of my editor Phyllis Hunt's own knowledge of this field, and of her patience, support and discernment. Let me record them again here and add to them the dedication of this phoenix selection.

HEROIC LEGENDS

Dietrich of Bern

In the early days, south of Germany, a king named Dietmar ruled over the Amelungs in the little kingdom of Bern. His elder brother, Ermenrich, was lord of a mighty empire, but Dietmar was content enough with the love and the loyalty of his Amelungs and he acknowledged no man as his master.

His great pride was his son Dietrich, a bold and handsome child, who soon grew tall and strong beyond his years. When he was five years old, his father gave him into the keeping of Hildebrand, the greatest warrior in those parts, that he might train the boy in battle-craft and feats of arms. And so skilled was his teaching and so eager was the boy to learn, that by the time he was twelve, Dietrich was as strong and able as any warrior of twice his years. From the first day that he saw him, Dietrich loved and honoured Hildebrand, and they were firm friends for all their lives.

When Dietrich had grown to be a youth, there came to the king's house one day word of two giants, Grim and his sister, Hilde, who were ravaging the land and killing all who tried to withstand them; King Dietmar immediately set out with his warriors to slay them. but though he searched his kingdom from end to end, the giants had learnt of his coming and had hidden themselves too well, high up in the mountains, and he could not find them. Dietmar returned home, discouraged and angry, and, immediately, the giants came out of hiding and began to plunder farms and villages once more.

Dietrich said to Hildebrand, "Let us go alone, just you and I, and search out these monsters in their lair. Who knows, we might have the luck that was denied my father."

So Hildebrand and young Dietrich set off; but for a long time their search seemed hopeless. And then one day, in the mountains, Dietrich chanced to catch one of the dwarf folk who lived beneath the earth.

"Keep a fast hold of him," said Hildebrand. "He may well be a friend of the giants, and can tell us where they are."

But the dwarf swore that he was no friend to the giants, who had done him and his kind much wrong. "I am Elbegast, the lord of the mountain dwarfs," he said. "If you are foes of Grim and Hilde, then you are friends of mine." And he promised to lead them to where the giants might be found. "But," he said, "you will never slay them without the help of a weapon forged by the dwarfs. For the dwarfs are the finest swordsmiths of all."

So he gave to Dietrich the sword Nagelring, which had no equal in the world. Then, early one morning, he took Dietrich and Hildebrand by a hidden path to where they could see the giants' footprints, huge tracks upon the dewy grass, leading to the hollow mountain where they lived. "Good luck be with you both," said Elbegast. "And may Nagelring prove trusty."

Dietrich and Hildebrand followed the footprints to the great cave where the giants were hidden; but, as they reached the mouth of the cave, Grim heard them and rushed forth like a mountain tempest, brandishing above his hideous head a burning log snatched up from his fire. With this huge cudgel he struck at Dietrich again and again; and had Dietrich not been quick and light upon his feet, he would have been dead in a very little time. But not a chance did Dietrich have to strike a single blow with Nagelring in return, for he needed all his strength and wits to avoid the giant's blows and the sparks which flew from the smouldering log.

Hildebrand would have gone to his aid, had not Hilde, hearing the sounds of the combat, come from an inner cave, and before he could strike at her with his sword, she had caught him up in her two arms and crushed him to her as though she would break all his bones.

Hildebrand struggled in vain in her grip. Closer and closer she clasped him until he thought that death was surely near, and with

his little remaining breath he gasped out, "Dietrich, help me, or I am dead."

Dietrich heard, gave a swift glance round and saw how it was with his friend and, made desperately bold by his fears for Hildebrand, he leapt right over the flaming club as it was swung at him again and brought Nagelring down with all his strength upon the giant's head, splitting his thick skull. Then he turned to Hilde, and before she could fling down Hildebrand to defend herself, he had slain her too.

When he was a little recovered and could speak once more, Hildebrand smiled and said, "I taught you all I know of skill at arms, yet it seems you have surpassed me and could now teach me much."

All the people of Bern rejoiced when they heard that the giants were slain and would trouble them no longer, and King Dietmar was more than ever proud of his son, who had acquitted himself so well on his first adventure.

But soon after, to the great sorrow of the Amelungs, King Dietmar died, and so young Dietrich became king in Bern.

A few years passed and then one day Dietrich learnt of a third giant, Sigenot, more terrible by far than the others, who had entered Bern and was slaying cattle and people alike in vengeance for the death of his kinsfolk Grim and Hilde.

Dietrich called for Nagelring to be brought to him. "I will go to the mountains and slay this Sigenot," he said.

Everyone who heard him, save Hildebrand, cried out, "You must not go. He is too terrible. Not even an army could withstand him."

But Hildebrand said, "You shall not go alone, for I will go with you, my king."

"No," said Dietrich, "for he is only one. One warrior against another, that is the law of fair combat. Two against one is the coward's way. You taught me that yourself."

"Then go alone," said Hildebrand, "and may good fortune go with you. If you have not returned when eight days are passed, I will go after you to free you if you are a prisoner, or to avenge you if you are dead, or to die myself at the giant's hands." They embraced, and Dietrich went.

He tracked Sigenot to a cave in the mountains, and there he came face to face with him; and Sigenot was even taller and broader than Grim had been. With a roar he took up his great club and strode to where Dietrich stood. "You are Dietrich, for no one else would be bold enough to come to me alone," he said. "Now shall my kinsfolk be avenged." And he swung his club above his head.

As he had done with Grim's flaming brand, Dietrich darted here and there to avoid the mighty blows of the club; at the same time giving stroke after stroke with Nagelring, until it seemed as though he might, in spite of the giant's huge bulk, be the victor in their combat. But then, dodging quickly to one side, he came beneath a tree, and as he raised Nagelring high above his head with both his hands to strike at Sigenot once more, the blade caught in the overhanging branches and, before he could free it, Sigenot's club had crashed down upon his helmet and he fell senseless to the ground.

With a great shout of triumph, Sigenot snatched up Dietrich in his arms, flung him over his shoulder, and strode off to his cave; and there, in the darkest corner of the cave, he cast him down into a pit of serpents.

When the eight days were passed and Dietrich had not returned, Hildebrand armed himself, took sword and shield, and rode for the mountains. There he spied the giant's tracks, leading to his cave, and there he found Dietrich's horse wandering alone; and there, too, he saw Nagelring caught fast in the branches of the tree. "So Dietrich is dead," he thought. "Well, I can but avenge him or die too." And he took a firm hold of his sword and went forward to the cave.

Sigenot saw him approaching and came out, swinging his great club. "You are Hildebrand," he shouted. "First I catch the young one and now I catch the old one. Truly, Grim and Hilde will be well avenged." And eagerly he rushed upon Hildebrand.

The combat lasted many hours. In his rage, Sigenot tore up young trees to serve as weapons, and heaved up rocks and stones to hurl at Hildebrand; but with skill Hildebrand evaded all his blows, until he was too spent and the giant's mighty strength proved too much for even his endurance and, like Dietrich, he was felled by Sigenot's club. Sigenot slung him over his shoulder, took his sword as a victor's prize, and strode back to the cave, shouting his triumph till the mountain echoed.

He flung Hildebrand to one side of the cave and the sword to the other and went off to find a chain that he might bind his senseless captive. But the force of the fall brought Hildebrand back to himself and he sat up, dazed and battered, and looked about him. The cave was wide and light enough, though in its farther corners no daylight reached, and Hildebrand saw his sword lying where Sigenot had flung it. He staggered to his feet and took it up and hid himself behind a pillar of rock until the giant should return.

When Sigenot came back, rattling and clanking the chains he had fetched, he gave a roar of anger at seeing Hildebrand gone from where he had left him lying. Then he saw him hidden in the shadow behind the rock and rushed at him, and their combat was begun anew.

But Hildebrand was very weary, and step by step he had to give way to the furious giant, and slowly he was forced deeper and deeper into the cave where the light was bad and he could hardly see to avoid the giant's blows. He felt that his strength was going fast, and he could not fight much longer. "Now Dietrich will never be avenged," he thought, "and in a very little while I, too, shall be dead." And Sigenot, seeing him weaken, laughed till the cave rang. "In a moment now, good Grim and Hilde will be avenged," he cried.

But Dietrich, who had been listening to the shouts of fighting from the cave above him, heard the shout of triumph and called out, "Is it you, Hildebrand, come as you promised? I have been waiting for you."

At the joyful knowledge that Dietrich was not dead, Hildebrand felt himself the equal of ten giants; his strength returned for one last mighty effort and a moment later Sigenot was lying vanquished on the floor of the cave, and Hildebrand struck off his head.

"Where are you, Dietrich?" he called into the shadows.

"I am here, in the pit of serpents at the very end of the cave. I have killed many of them, and eaten some for food; but there are still scores left alive, so help me out with all the speed you can."

With ropes lowered into the pit, Hildebrand drew him out, and

Dietrich of Bern

as the friends embraced, Dietrich laughed and said, "After all, you are still my master and can teach me much in the matter of fighting skill. For you overcame Sigenot, but I was overcome by him."

For many years after that, Dietrich ruled well and wisely, and he gather about him a little band of skilled warriors from all corners of the world, who had come to him in Bern, drawn by his fame. Yet always his most loved comrade was Hildebrand.

But Dietrich was not destined to rule in peace for all his days. There came a time when his uncle, the Emperor Ermenrich, urged by evil counsellors, cast greedy eyes upon his nephew's little kingdom, and he sent messengers to Dietrich demanding tribute from him and his lords. Now, Dietrich, like his father Dietmar before him, had never paid tribute to any man, and he and his lords were indignant.

"Tell your master," the Amelungs said to the messengers, "that we pay our tribute to our rightful lord, King Dietrich, and to no other."

"And tell my uncle the emperor," said Dietrich, "that if he wants his tribute, he must come and fetch it for himself; and we will pay him with our spearheads and the sharp edges of our swords."

The angry emperor gathered together a great army and marched against Bern. But Dietrich did not wait to be attacked. At the head of his Amelungs he rode out to meet him; and so unprepared for his coming was the emperor that he was taken by surprise; and Dietrich, falling upon his camp before sunrise one morning, won a victory and checked his advance. Though it was no great victory, it cheered the Amelungs and gave them courage for the dark days they knew must lie ahead.

From the emperor's camp Dietrich took much booty, which he sent back to Bern in the charge of Hildebrand and five of his most trusted warriors: old Amelolt, Sigeband, Helmschrott, Lindolt and Dietlieb of Styria; and with them was Hildebrand's young nephew Wolfhart. But on the way to Bern they were ambushed and taken captive, and only Dietlieb escaped to bear the news to Dietrich.

The emperor was planning to attack again; every day more warriors joined him, sure of his eventual victory; and many, even, of Dietrich's own men deserted him, believing that Bern was lost.

But bitterest of all to Dietrich was the knowledge that his trusted friends, and among them Hildebrand, were in the emperor's hands.

Dietrich still had certain of the emperor's lords whom he had taken captive when he had attacked his uncle's camp, and he sent to Ermenrich with an offer to exchange these men for Hildebrand and his five comrades.

But the emperor sent back scornfully, "Do as you will with your captives, I care nothing for them. For my part, I intend to hang your warriors unless I have your word that you will give me Bern, and that you and those who still wish to call you king will go from the land with you, on foot and leaving all they possess."

In his first anger at Ermenrich's reply, Dietrich thought, "I have no hope of victory in battle against his might. Yet he shall at least see how the Amelungs can die. And they would rather die than deign to live dishonoured on her terms." But then he thought how, if he fought and died gloriously with the few men who remained to him, he was condemning to a shameful death, unfitting to any warrior, his good friends: Sigeband, Helmschrott, old Amelolt, Lindolt, rash young Wolfhart, and Hildebrand—above all, Hildebrand. And he knew that he could not do it.

He sent to Ermenrich, agreeing to his demands, and Hildebrand and the others were freed. Together, on foot, leading their horses and taking no possessions with them, Dietrich and Hildebrand and their friends left Bern; and with them went those warriors who chose exile with their king rather than service under the emperor: and out of all the Amelungs, there were only three and forty of them.

They wandered northwards to Bechlaren, beside the Danube, where Rudiger held lands from King Etzel* of the Huns. Rudiger had been a comrade of Dietrich in former days, and he welcomed him kindly and gave him arms and gifts, for he was a good and loyal friend. He gave Dietrich hope, also, for he told him to go to King Etzel and ask his aid. "He is a mighty king and has many warriors to serve him from all the lands of the world. And though he is a heathen, he is no foe to Christian men. He may well give you help

---

* Etzel is the name given in legend to Attila, King of the Huns, who appears in the next story.

in your fight against the emperor. If not today, then at some later time, when he is in a mood to do so."

So Dietrich and his few faithful Amelungs went to Hunland to King Etzel's court, and he received them kindly, for he had heard—as who had not—of the prowess and the sad fate of Dietrich. And in time he gave help to Dietrich, and men to fight for him; and in time, too, Ermenrich died and Dietrich returned to Bern and was welcomed by his people. But of the three and forty Amelungs who had gone into Hunland with him, only one—old Hildebrand—returned home with him, for the others had all by mishap been slain at Etzel's court.

Dietrich became not only king of Bern once more, but his uncle, Ermenrich, having had no other heir, he succeeded to the emperor's lands, and ruled them to the end of his days, honoured by all.

retold by BARBARA LEONIE PICARD

Walter and Hildegund

The dark, trackless forest of Mirkwood spread like a creeping stain on the edges of habitation. It was the boundary between the familiar and the alien: this side the farms and fields of the settled Germanic kingdoms; on the other the endless green plains of Hunmark, land of the nomads.

Great herds of horses had roamed there, the herdsmen following them with their tents in both summer and winter, but now the rolling plains were strangely empty, left to the play of the wind and the crying curlew. And in Hunmark for this state of things there was only one explanation...

A rumour came out of Mirkwood that the Huns were mustering for war, and hard on its heels rode men who with their own eyes had seen Attila's war-host. It was numberless, they said, as the stars in the sky or grains of sand on the shore; and it had already crossed the Danube.

The news ran like wildfire, yet it could scarcely outrun the great horde of the Huns, who came sweeping on like a plague, cutting a swathe of death and destruction. Behind them columns of smoke rose up in thin black spirals away to the edge of sight.

There was no defence against them, and now they had crossed the Rhine, and now the earth shook with the tramp of horses, and a forest of iron spears shone through the fields like a bloody sunset. Attila was at the gate.

King Gibich of the Burgundians was in his palace at Worms when the news reached him. He was celebrating the birth of his only son, Gunther, and calling a halt to the feast, he asked his counsellors what to do.

"Resistance is useless," they told him. "All we can do is ask for terms. We must send them a hostage, and gold as tribute. Better that than lose our lives."

Gibich agreed to this. "Now as to the hostage," he went on. "My own son Gunther is too young to be taken from his mother. Whom shall we send in his place?"

The counsellors' choice fell on Hagen, a boy of eleven or twelve who was nobly born and seemed likely to become a great leader when he was older. Envoys took him with the gold to the Hunnish camp, where Attila, being a good judge of money and men, saw fit to accept them.

When they heard what Gibich had done, the other, less powerful kings decided to follow his example. They thought: "We needn't be ashamed of becoming subject-nations if the Burgundians, for all their wealth, have had to do it"; and bought themselves treaties. But they paid a higher price for peace than Gibich, because they had no excuse not to send their own children as hostages.

Hereric rode into the Huns' camp in person, his little daughter Hildegund before him on the saddle, he was so loath to part with her until the last possible moment. And shortly after that, an ambassador from Aquitaine brought the heir of King Albhere, Walter, not much more than ten years old.

Now Hereric and Albhere were allies, and when Hildegund was born they had promised their children to each other in marriage. It was little more than a year since they had solemnized their betrothal, and Walter and Hildegund both took the memory of it into exile.

Attila meant to be kind to his hostages, and gave it out at court that they were to be brought up as his own children. He sent Hildegund to the Queen, to live in the women's quarters, while he trained the boys himself. So the children met seldom, yet whenever they did it was always with affection. They made no other friends.

As if their harsh Tartar features were not frightening enough, the faces of the warriors had been scarred when they were children, so that the hair would grow only in long thin straggling moustaches. They were as devilish as they looked. But the three hostages very soon learnt to hide their disgust, and their terror, and their passionate longing for home, behind a bland mask of contentment, so that Attila if he had been asked would have said that they were happy.

As Hildegund grew older, the Queen taught her how to run Attila's household, as she would her own daughter, and she proved so willing and quick to learn that Queen Helche began to rely on her more and more, and finally left everything to her, even giving the painted chests that were Attila's treasury into her keeping.

All this time, Walter and Hagen were being trained in warfare together. They were never apart, and it was not long before they swore vows of friendship to each other.

Attila's two sons had been killed in battle when they were only boys, and Walter and Hagen had come to fill the gap this had left in his affections. When they reached manhood and proved themselves to be great warriors, he was as proud of them as if they had been his own, and made them his lieutenants.

And so it was a bitter pill for him to swallow when the court woke one morning to find that Hagen was missing. Word had come the day before that Gibich was dead, and that Gunther, the moment he was acclaimed as king, had broken the treaty. Some said that Hagen had run away because he thought he would be killed in reprisal.

"How could he have thought that?" Attila said. "He must have known I'd never kill him. I looked on him as my son."

The Queen, who saw further than most, said: "Hagen wasn't afraid. He simply took his chance to go back to his people."

"After all I've done for him?" raged Attila. "I brought him up as a prince—and then to leave me for a puppy so careless of his life that he broke the treaty with us like a straw!"

"But Gunther is a Burgundian," she said, "and we are aliens. So beware, Attila. The one who had half your heart has fled from you without a backward look: the other may do the same."

"How can I prevent it?" Attila asked.

Helche said: "Let Walter choose himself a wife from among our Hunnish princesses. Then he will not want to leave."

But when Attila made him this offer, the young man turned it down as tactfully as he was able. "Don't make me do it, little father! What sort of leader shall I be with a family to consider? Let me stay as I am!"

This was the sort of argument that Attila understood, and he was only too willing to listen. But Hagen's flight had made Walter chafe at his own long exile, and he too had been making plans.

Not long after this, Walter put down a revolt against the rule of the Huns by one of their subject tribes. When he returned to the citadel, he went straight into the hall to report to Attila, and afterwards made his way to the royal apartments to change his clothes and rest.

There he came on Hildegund, sitting by herself. He asked her to fetch him some wine, and as he gave back the cup he touched her hand lightly and said: "When are we going to be married?"

She did not know what to answer. She had almost come to believe that he only loved her as a sister, for he had said not one word that encouraged her to think otherwise. Now she said: "Why ask such a question? Do you think that I don't know you're going to marry one of the princesses?"

"That isn't so," Walter said. "Surely I don't need to *tell* you that I love you? If I haven't shown it, it's only because we are so seldom alone together. I'm sick of exile, and I might have got away when we were fighting on the borders, if I'd left you behind. Will you come with me, Hildegund?"

Hildegund said in a low voice: "I was only four years old the first time I saw you, and I have loved you ever since more than anything in the world. Where you go, I will go, and endure any hardship. What do you want me to do?"

Making sure that no one was coming, he said quietly: "You must get hold of everything for our journey—the workmen are so used to taking their orders from you that they will not question you. We need four pairs of shoes each, fish-hooks and some line, food for a few days so we can make good speed until we are over the border, and a little wine in case we run into trouble. Last of all, I want you to get two fairly big boxes, and fill them full of gold from Attila's treasury. Can you do all this?"

"I can do it," Hildegund answered. "But why must we steal

their gold? It's dishonourable enough to break the treaty and run away, after all their kindness."

"You must forget their kindness," said Walter. "However fond of us he seems, Attila is a savage who would not scruple to take our lives if it suited his purpose. Your first loyalty, and mine, has to be to our own people. Now that the Burgundians have broken free, they will be looking round for allies, and our fathers can't afford to reject their advances. But they won't act while we are here.

"As for the gold, gold is kingship. The power of a king resides in his treasure. If we take Attila's gold, we diminish him and he will be less able to take revenge.

"And so I will not go home empty-handed, but like the heroes of old will bring a treasure to my people."

About a week later, Walter gave a feast to celebrate his victory. Attila's great hall with the painted beams was shot through with gleams of splendour it did not know by day, as the firelight glinted on war-gear hung around the walls, and on the golden cups on the tables.

When they had finished eating, the women returned to their apartments, and the tables were cleared. Then Walter had the servants bring in huge bowls of wine he had taken as loot, and asked Attila to launch the evening's carousal.

There was nothing Attila liked better. With a laugh, he raised his cup, and swilled the wine down like ale, and called for more; and he and all his men began to vie with each other in drinking.

Only Walter did not drink but plied them with more and more wine until they were sodden, not one left awake, not even a servant.

They lay just as they had fallen late into the next day, Attila sprawled askew in his great carved chair, the other revellers on the floor among the rushes and scattered cups and dogs still foraging for titbits. Not till the burnished light of evening came slanting low through the door did Attila awaken. His men still lay snoring like hogs, but he could not see Walter among them. He stumbled out of the hall to his private quarters, head pounding, calling for Walter as he went to keep him company in his misery. But Walter was not to be found.

Walter and Hildegund

Nor, so it shortly appeared, was Hildegund.

The Queen came in, outraged and indignant. "Why didn't you do as I said, and get him safely married? Now he's gone and your gold has gone too. As for Hildegund—oh, what a fool I was to think that I could trust her!"

Attila said nothing. In the whole of his career he had never been so gulled. He could not eat, he could not sleep, but tossed in his bed all night, pulled this way and that by grief and fury. But by next morning the fury was uppermost, and he swore to give his weight in gold to the man who brought him Walter in shackles, yet there was not one of the Huns who would do it for him: they knew Walter too well of old.

As for Walter and Hildegund, as soon as everything was quiet, they got ready to leave the citadel. They loaded Walter's warhorse, Lion, with their bundles and the gold. Then they set out, Walter in front, spear in hand, while Hildegund came behind, leading Lion by the bridle.

All night long they journeyed, but as soon as the sun was up they hid in the woods and waited for darkness; and with darkness they went on. And so they passed like shadows over the land till they were clear of Attila's horse-runs. After that, they travelled by day.

By day or by dark, Walter never slept but only dozed fitfully, leaning on his spear, keeping watch while Hildegund rested.

When they had finished the food they brought with them, they snared birds, fished in streams, or gathered berries, careful to avoid any habitation and keeping always to the woods and the desolate places.

Forty days or so later, when all but their last pairs of shoes were worn into holes, and they felt themselves stretched thin as threads for weariness, they saw against the setting sun the russet hills of the Rhineland. Early next evening they came down to the Rhine, and turned northward along the bank for a little way, to look for some means of crossing over.

King Gunther was sitting at dinner the next night with Hagen at his right hand when two fish dressed with pungent herbs were set on the plate in front of him. "*These* didn't come out of the Rhine!" he exclaimed as soon as he tasted them, and immediately sent for the cook to inquire where he got them.

"I bought them in the market this morning," answered the cook, "from an old ferryman who works down the river, a mile or two below the town. But he didn't say where they came from."

The ferryman was fetched and questioned. He said: "I was on the farther bank yesterday evening, waiting for custom, when along came this tall young man and a girl who was leading a warhorse, and on the horse's back were two big stout wooden boxes, which every now and then gave out a clinking sound—and I said to myself, 'That's gold.' I took them across the river, horse and all, and they gave me the fishes as payment."

Hagen could scarcely wait for the old man to finish before he burst out: "This is welcome news! This must be Walter coming home from Hunmark."

"Not so," said Gunther. "It is the gold my father paid Attila coming home to me."

And shoving the table back with his foot, he hurried out of the hall, buckling his armour on as he went, and calling for his horse to be saddled and bridled. He picked a band of twelve men to go with him on his mission, and Hagen was one.

Now Hagen was in a dilemma. "What shall I do?" he thought. "I am bound to Walter by oaths of friendship, but Gunther is the lord to whom I have sworn allegiance. Where does my loyalty lie—Walter or Gunther? It's plain that Gunther intends to take the gold by force if he has to. I must make him change his mind."

He spurred on his horse till he was riding at Gunther's side.

"Gunther, turn back," he pleaded. "It's madness to say that the gold is yours—if gold it is—and it would be shameful for a king to rob a traveller through his kingdom. I beg you to let him go."

But Gunther, the gold-lust upon him, was deaf to all that he said.

Meantime, the two travellers, bearing away from the Rhine, came to the mountainous wooded region known as the Vosges. As they pushed deeper into the wilderness, they came on a lonely ravine that offered them protection, a natural stronghold among the rocks approachable in only one direction, by a narrow way. There was lush green grass at the bottom.

Walter said as soon as he saw it: "Let's rest here for a while. We'll be safe from attack, and there is good grazing for Lion."

Now the need for sleep came suddenly on him. He said to Hildegund: "I have kept watch for you these many nights past—now you must keep watch for me. If you see horsemen, wake me." Too tired for anything more, he took off his armour, stretched himself out on the ground, and fell asleep almost instantly.

Moving quietly so as not to wake him, Hildegund unloaded Lion and turned him loose to graze, then stood guard for many hours, singing softly under her breath to keep herself awake.

Her eyesight was keen, and she saw the cloud of dust that accompanied the Burgundians while they were still some way off. She woke Walter and helped him arm, holding his spear for him while he strapped on his sword, the famous blade Mimming, made by Wayland Smith in ancient times, an heirloom of his clan that had gone with him into exile.

As the troop drew nearer, Hildegund saw their spears and was seized with panic: she thought it was the Huns. She said: "I beg you, Walter, to cut my throat rather than let me fall into their hands again."

But Walter told her to take heart. "For those are not Huns but Burgundians—look, there is Hagen, our friend. They must be after the gold, but there's not one of them I need be afraid of, except Hagen himself, who knows how I fight—and *he* will not come against me. But in any event, no Nibelung is going home to boast to his wife of stealing *our* treasure."

Now Gunther sent Gamelo, the governor of Metz, down the narrow ravine to demand the gold in his name. Walter refused to surrender it, instead offering to pay a tithe for right of way across his country. This was not enough.

Again Gamelo was sent to claim the gold, and again Walter refused to give it up, at the same time raising his offer. Still it was not enough. Gunther wanted the whole, for the gold worked in his mind like some dull poison, deadening every sense.

Hagen said: "Accept his offer. He'll never give up the gold, and we're not men enough to take it. Gunther, make no mistake—if there's a fight, we'll get the worst of it."

"There are twelve of *us*," Gunther said. "But there," he added sourly, "I can see you're turning out to be a coward, like your father."

Hagen slowly went white. "As good as spit in my face," he thought bitterly. "If you want the gold," he said, "why don't you fight for it yourself, man to man in single combat? *I* am unwilling to add disloyalty to dishonour."

He wheeled his horse abruptly and rode it up the side of the ravine, its hooves slithering in the shale and small boulders. He dismounted half way up, and sat down on a rocky outcrop, placed his sword across his knees, and waited to see what would happen.

Gunther sent Gamelo for the third time to claim the gold, and for the third time Walter refused him. "If you want it, take it," he said. "I will never give it up freely."

From where he sat on his horse's back, Gamelo hurled his spear to enforce Gunther's claim: it was the last act of his life. But still

Gunther persisted. Scaramund, Werinhard, Ekivrid—one by one he sent them down into that narrow place, and one by one they fell, like barley before the reaper. Hadaward next—and the Burgundians who were left began to marvel at Walter's tirelessness. Only Hagen was not amazed—Hagen, who had fought so often beside him. But now came the turn of Batavrid, Hagen's sister's-son, and Hagen, who had sat brooding and silent while his companions met their deaths, rose to his feet and cried out in an anguish that was terrible to hear: "Boy, how shall I tell your mother?"

Walter heard his cry from the hillside as it came echoing down the ravine, and waved the boy back. "For your uncle's sake, turn back and don't make me fight you!" he shouted. But the lad came steadily on, too green in judgment, perhaps, to know how to swallow his pride, and so like the rest he perished.

Hagen scarcely cared what followed, though Gunther sent them all down—Gerwit, Randolf, Helmot, Trogus, Tanastus—one by one down to certain destruction. And now here was Gunther climbing up the hill, commanding, exhorting, cajoling, and finally, abject at last, beseeching him to take up the combat, "if only to get your revenge".

"Your gold-lust will be my ruin," Hagen said. "I will not put vengeance for my nephew above the oaths I swore so long ago to Walter, but because you are, God help us, the king, you have first claim on my loyalty. I will do what you want—but not here.

"Let us ride off and hide in the coverts. If Walter thinks we have gone, he'll come out into the open and we can take him from behind. It's the only way we shall kill him."

Gunther flung an arm round his neck and kissed him. Then they rounded up some of the strays that had lost their masters and rode off together to look for a place in which to lay an ambush.

Walter now asked himself what it was best to do, set out at once or remain in his fastness. He thought with foreboding of the kiss given Hagen by the king, and decided to stay where he was until morning.

At sunrise he surveyed his grim harvest. He had killed many men in his time, but none whose deaths gave him less satisfaction. He had to despoil them just the same. But as he stripped them of their armour according to custom, he closed their staring eyes: that much he could do for them.

He had been too restless to sleep and during the night had gathered in six more of the riderless horses. He roped four together in a line, to carry the armour, and saddled the other two to ride. Lion carried the boxes as usual.

Now he woke Hildegund, and they rode cautiously out of the ravine and into the open, Walter taking the lead, his sharp eyes scanning the country all around for signs of danger, listening for the click of hoof on rock or the half-muffled jingle of harness.

As everything seemed quiet, he sent Hildegund ahead with the string of laden horses, while he brought up the rear with Lion. "If they come, they'll come from behind us."

They did not have long to wait. Hildegund kept looking back over her shoulder, and they had scarcely gone a mile when she saw two horsemen riding fast down the hillside behind them. She had no doubt who it was: Gunther and Hagen, come for Walter's life.

"They're here," she said. "Let's leave the gold and escape. They're both fresh and you are tired."

Walter shook his head. "Yesterday's killings would be a senseless waste if we were to run away now. Here, catch hold of Lion's reins and lead him into that knot of trees with the other horses. I'll take my stand on this slope."

Gunther was exultant, certain that very soon now the gold would be his, and already beginning to crow. As he drew near, he shouted: "So you're out of your lair at last! Let's see if you fight so well out in the open."

Walter did not reply, but turned to Hagen. "Hagen, wait!" he said. "You owe me an explanation. I *had* hoped that, if you found out I was in your country, you'd take me back to your King and he'd offer me hospitality. I never expected *this*. In God's name, come to your senses!"

Hagen only looked grim. He answered curtly: "It was you who broke faith with me, by killing my sister's-son. I want vengeance."

Was he speaking the truth? Walter did not think so. But no time to ponder that, for now Hagen was swinging himself off his horse,

Walter and Hildegund

and Gunther the same. Walter dismounted quickly and slapped his horse on the rump to send it out of the way. Then he took up his stance on the slope, feet apart and lightly balanced, weighing his spear in his hand.

If Gunther and Hagen felt any shame at setting two on one, they did not show it. They came in very fast, with spears and then swords. First one, then the other, attacked him, but he fended them off with his spear so they could not make contact. They changed their tactics then, and began to rush him together, trying to tire him out: the moment he weakened they would have him. But he would not wait for that. He must act while he had the strength, and stake everything on one throw in one powerful, final effort.

Taking Hagen as his target, he hurled his spear with such force that it ran clear through his shield and mailcoat, pinning them into the flesh of his side. Whilst Hagen was busy trying to detach himself, Walter drew his sword and leapt at Gunther, forced his shield aside, and with a great scything stroke swept his right leg clean off at the thigh.

Gunther slowly heeled over, but before Walter could finish him off, Hagen was back in action and interposed his helmeted head between his lord and the blow. The impetus of the stroke was too great for Walter to check it, and Mimming crashed heavily down on Hagen's bronze helm, striking sparks from the ridge-guard, but the rain-patterned blade itself was shattered into pieces.

It was more to him than a weapon. He knew its lineage like his own name. It was his history, his identity, the badge of his kingship, the sign that marked him as Walter, son of Albhere, and in battle it had seemed to channel into him the courage of all those of his line who had wielded it before him. It was his constant friend, on whom his life depended, a living presence, called by name.

And now like Hagen it had failed him.

Only the hilt was left. In a passion of fury, grief, despair, regret, he cast it from him. And while his right hand was still stretched out, in this unguarded moment, Hagen struck it off at the wrist.

One of the lessons Attila had taught them was how to override pain until there was time for it. Walter had learnt it well. No flinching, no hesitation; not a muscle moved in his face. But thrusting the bleeding stump swiftly into the strap of his shield, he freed his left hand to draw a sword he wore on the right, short, one-edged, meant for in-fighting. He had to get inside Hagen's guard in order to use it, had to move quickly. And before Hagen could respond, he had taken a thrust to the head that had gouged out his right eye.

Now the fight was finished. Would they ever fight again? Not Gunther, certainly. And the others were too maimed to go on for the moment. They threw down their weapons and sat down beside him, as he lay there on the ground vainly trying to staunch his gouting blood with a handful of grass.

Walter shouted for Hildegund, and she came running out of the grove with wine to revive them. She was appalled by what she saw. But she had witnessed worse mutilations.

When she had stopped the bleeding, and dressed their wounds with herbs bound with linen torn from her smock, she poured out a cup of wine, and for the first time hesitated. The cup was the only one they had brought with them. Whom should she serve first?

"Give it to Hagen," said Walter. "And next you may give it to me. But serve Gunther last, although he has lost most blood. He has no right to drink before warriors, for he has squandered other men's lives and only risked his own when the odds were in his favour. He's not fit to be called a king."

And Gunther thought about that and said nothing.

Walter and Hagen soon fell to talking of old times as they sat resting, and their bitterness and rage began to ebb away from them. Eventually Walter said: "I don't want to make this a feuding matter. Will you set my killing your sister's-son against your broken oath, your eye against my hand, so that we can be quits?"

"Gladly," Hagen replied. "Gunther is my lord and I'm bound to uphold him, but never in my life shall I have less stomach for it."

He clasped Walter's one good hand, and they renewed their vows of friendship.

And now they lifted Gunther on to his horse, and Hagen led him back to the city. The first thing Gunther did when he got there, before he would let them put him to bed, was to send out an escort for Walter and Hildegund; and they had not long set out on the last stage of their journey before the Burgundians overtook them, and saw them safely home across the border into Aquitaine.

The wedding took place when the forest was in full leaf, and the meadows bright with flowers. Gunther and Hagen came, and the three men were fully reconciled. In the same spirit, Walter sent word of the wedding to Attila, inviting him to attend, but as he expected, got no answer.

The ferocious lord of the Huns had laughed shortly at the message. By now his fury had given way to a bitter amusement at Walter's audacity.

"I bred him," he said to the Queen, "so who am I to complain of his behaviour? I would have done the same. But I will not go to his wedding."

retold by JENNIFER WESTWOOD

The Curse of Andvari's Ring

While it was still the custom of Odin to wander through Midgard in disguise, he came one day in company with Hoenir and Loki to a beautiful river which ran swiftly through a deep valley.

As they followed it up towards its source they found a big waterfall in a deep and solitary glen; and on a rock beside the fall they saw an otter blinking its eyes happily as it prepared to eat a salmon which it had caught.

Loki at once picked up a stone and flung it at the otter with such good aim that a moment later it lay dead upon the dead salmon.

"Ah-ha!" cried Loki. "Two at a blow! Trust me to get both an otter and a salmon with one stone!"

He picked up his double catch, and the three Æsir went on again until they came to a house set in the midst of rich farm-lands and walled about strongly as if it were the home of some great lord.

The three travellers came up to the gateway, and finding it open, went in to the great hall where sat a dark man with flashing eyes alone on a seat beside the fire.

"Greetings, strangers!" he cried. "Tell me who you are and why you come hither to the hall of Hreidmarr the master of magic?"

"We are poor pilgrims journeying through the world," answered Odin, doffing his broad-brimmed hat politely as he leant on his staff and surveyed Hreidmarr with his one eye, "and seeing your strong house set amidst such fruitful fields of corn, we turned aside to visit you."

"Poor though we may be," added Loki quickly, "we are strong and clever in our own ways. Look here at this otter and salmon which I laid low with the cast of a single stone!"

The Curse of Andvari's Ring

When he saw what Loki carried in his hands Hreidmarr rose to his feet and shouted:

"Come hither, my sons Fafnir and Reginn! Come and bind these evil men who have slain your brother Otter!"

Then, while he held them powerless by his magic, two strong youths came into the hall and bound them securely with iron chains.

"And now," said Hreidmarr grimly as he sat gloating over his three captives, "it remains only to decide how you shall die."

"For what reason would you kill us?" asked slow Hoenir, hoping to win out of danger by the smooth power of argument.

"You must know," answered Hreidmarr, "that I am a master of black magic such as is known among the trolls and swart elves. And my three sons share my art, but in addition have the power of changing their shapes at will. My eldest son Otter chose to pass his time in the shape of an otter so that he might catch the fish in which he delighted as they sprang down the waterfall not far from here which is called Andvari's Force. The otter which you slew is this very son of mine, and justice demands a life for a life."

"But justice allows also of wergild," Hoenir replied stolidly, "that is a payment for a slaying if it be done by chance. My companion here flung a stone at what seemed but a common beast of the riverside. Come now, decide on the wergild that shall pay for the death of your son."

Then Hreidmarr consulted with Fafnir and Reginn, and at last he said:

"Strangers, we will take wergild, and it shall be this: enough good red gold to fill the skin of the otter which was my son, and to cover it so that not a hair may remain showing. Two of you shall stay here in chains, while the third goes forth to fetch the golden payment."

The three Æsir consulted apart, and the end of it was that cunning Loki was sent out to find the golden ransom. "Go to the black elves and to the dwarfs," Odin instructed him. "Use all your arts, for we are in the hands of wizards who must not know who we are. Therefore I cannot send to Asgard for help."

"Depend upon me," answered Loki with a cunning smile. "I

know where the gold is to be got—though it will indeed require all my arts to win it for our use."

So, while Odin and Hoenir remained in chains, and Fafnir and Reginn skinned the dead otter to measure out the wergild, Loki set forth in search of treasure.

He went straight back to Andvari's Force, from which the otter had taken the shining salmon, and sat himself down beside the rushing waters.

Loki could see through the roaring arch of green and silver, and presently he perceived Andvari the Dwarf in the likeness of a pike hiding in the mouth of his cave which was behind the waterfall; and there was a glimmer of gold in the darkness of the cave behind him.

"How can I catch him?" thought Loki. "I could never take him with my hands, and he is far too wise to be caught by any hook however cunningly I might bait it . . ."

Then Loki thought of Ran, the cruel wife of Ægir, the giant who ruled the Sea, who caught shipwrecked sailors in her net and drew them down to the bottom of the ocean. Ran was not friendly to the Æsir, but she recognised the evil giant blood in Loki, and willingly lent him her net.

"But do not let the Æsir see it," she warned him, "nor yet the men who dwell in Midgard. For a day may come when you will wish to escape, and only a net such as mine could snare you."

Loki took Ran's net and returned to Andvari's Force. There he cast it into the water and drew it up so smartly that the great pike was entangled in its meshes and lay gasping on the bank.

Loki grasped him in his hands and held him until Andvari returned to his own dwarfish shape and asked sulkily what he wanted.

When Loki told him, Andvari to save his life was forced to give up all his treasure. He carried it up out of the cave behind the arch of falling waters and stacked it on the bank—and it was a very great pile indeed, such a treasure of rich gold as had never before been seen in Midgard.

When at last it was all there, Andvari the dwarf turned sulkily away. But as he did so he put out his hand and swept quickly under it one little golden ring.

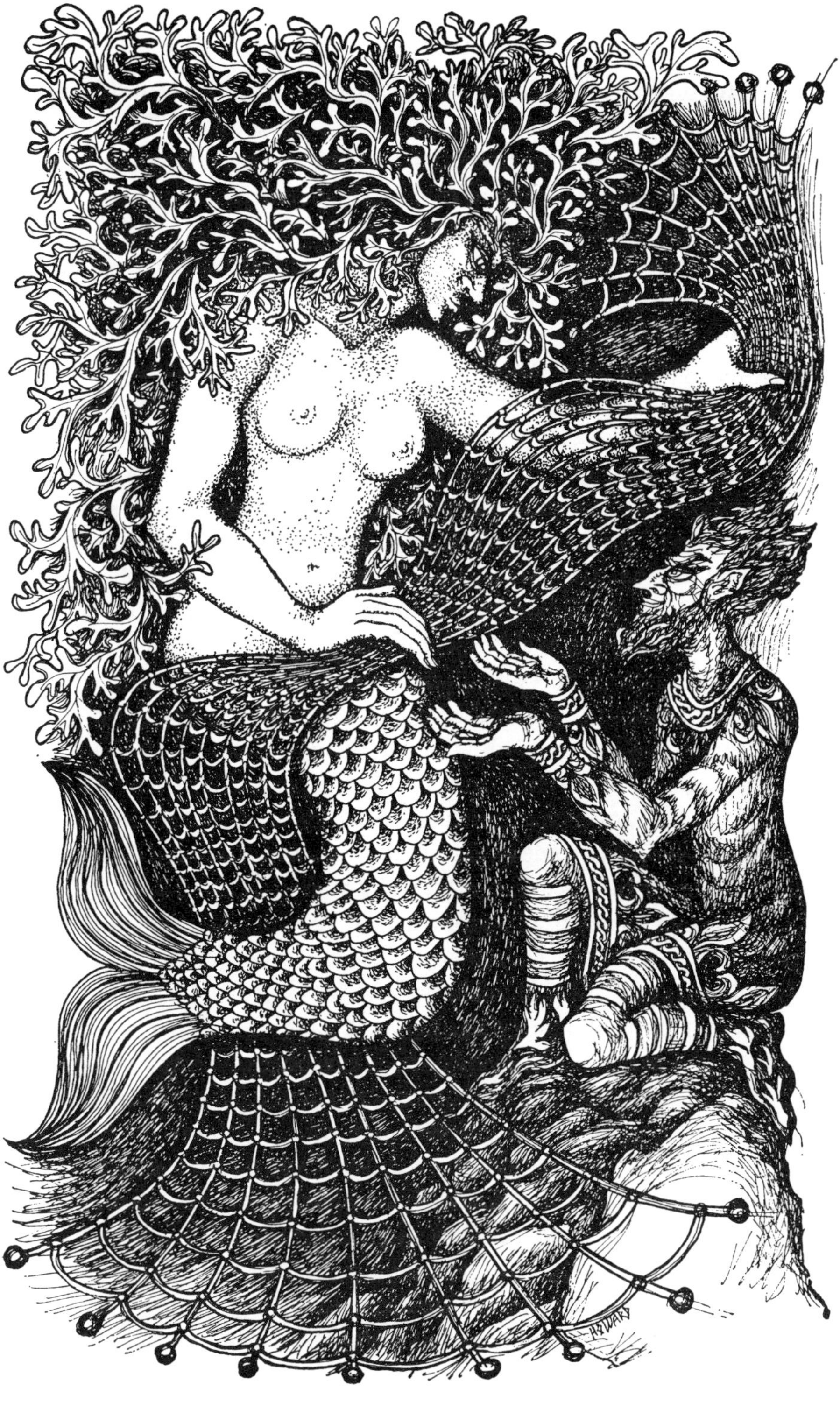

Watchful Loki saw this, however, and sternly bade him fling it back on to the pile.

"Let me keep just this ring," begged Andvari. "If I have it, I can make more gold: but the charm will not work for any who is not of the dwarf race."

"Not one scrap shall you keep," said Loki viciously, and he snatched back the ring and held it firmly in his own hand.

"Then," answered the dwarf, "take with it my curse. And know that the curse goes with the ring and brings ruin and sorrow upon all who wear it until both ring and gold come back into the deep waters."

So saying Andvari turned himself into a pike once more and dived to the bottom of the river.

But Loki collected the gold and carried it back to Hreidmarr's dwelling where Odin and Hoenir were waiting anxiously for him.

When they saw the gold, Hreidmarr filled the otter skin full of it and set it up on end. Then they piled gold round it until the skin was completely hidden—and the gold was all used up.

As the gold was being stacked, Odin noticed Andvari's Ring and it seemed so fair to him that he took it out of the pile and slipped it on his own finger. When the gold was all heaped up, he exclaimed:

"Now, Hreidmarr, our wergild is paid. See, the skin of the otter is altogether hidden under the gold."

Hreidmarr examined the heap carefully.

"Not so!" he exclaimed. "One hair on the snout is still showing. Cover that also, or the wergild is not paid and your lives are forfeit."

With a sigh Odin took the ring from his finger and covered the last hair with it; and so the wergild was paid and they were set at liberty.

When they were free, and Odin held his spear once more and there was no longer any danger, Loki turned to Hreidmarr and said:

"With the ring of Andvari goes Andvari's Curse: evil and sorrow upon all who wear it!"

Then the three Æsir returned to Asgard. But they left behind them the curse of Andvari's Ring which had already begun to work on Hreidmarr and his two sons.

"You must give us some part of the wergild," Fafnir and Reginn

The Curse of Andvari's Ring

told their father. "Otter was our brother as well as your son."

"Not one gold ring shall either of you have," answered Hreidmarr, and he locked up the treasure in his strongest room.

Then Fafnir and Reginn made a plot together, and the end of it was that Reginn murdered their father Hreidmarr for the sake of Andvari's gold.

"And now," said Reginn when the evil deed was done, "let us share the treasure between us in equal portions."

"Not one gold ring shall you have," answered Fafnir. "Little do you deserve it indeed, seeing that you slew our father for its sake. Now go hence speedily, or I will slay you also! A life for a life is the law: and your life is forfeit for the murder of Hreidmarr."

So Fafnir drove Reginn away, and he himself set Hreidmarr's Helmet of Terror on his head and carried all the treasure which had been Andvari's hoard to Gnita Heath far from the haunts of men and hid it in a cave. Then he took upon himself the form of a terrible dragon and lay down upon the gold and gloated over it after the custom of dragons.

But Reginn, vowing vengeance in his heart, went to the court of Hialprek, King of the Danes, and became his smith. There he received into his charge the young hero Sigurd the Volsung, the son of Sigmund to whom once on a time Odin had given a magic sword....

retold by ROGER LANCELYN GREEN

Sigurd was the greatest of the Germanic heroes. The dwarf-smith Reginn refashioned for him the miraculous sword Gram that had belonged to Sigurd's father, Sigmund, and taunted him into trying his strength against the dragon Fafnir (Reginn's brother). Sigurd killed Fafnir and won the gold hoard, including the cursed ring; but when he tasted a drop of the dragon's blood, he understood the speech of all the birds and was warned that Reginn intended to kill him and so win back the treasure for himself. The story of Sigurd the Volsung is taken up again in the words of William Morris (p. 121).

Beowulf Fights the Dragon

The action of Beowulf, *the only full-length heroic poem that survives from Anglo-Saxon England, takes place in Denmark and Sweden— an indication of the common ancestry of the tribes that settled throughout North-west Europe. Beowulf is a hero who embodies bravery and loyalty and strives for fame. In his youth, he crosses the sea to Denmark and rids King Hrothgar and his court of two appalling monsters, Grendel and his mother. Beowulf becomes King of the Geats (a tribe in South Sweden) and rules in peace for fifty years until his people are attacked by a dragon. Old as he is, Beowulf resolves to fight it alone.*

> Then the bold warrior, stern-faced beneath his helmet,
> stood up with his shield; sure of his own strength,
> he walked in his corslet towards the cliff;
> the way of the coward is not thus!
> Then that man endowed with noble qualities,
> he who had braved countless battles, weathered
> the thunder when warrior troops clashed together,
> saw a stone arch set in the cliff
> through which a stream spurted; steam rose
> from the boiling water; he could not stay long
> in the hollow near the hoard for fear
> of being scorched by the dragon's flames.
> Then, such was his fury, the leader of the Geats
> threw out his chest and gave a great roar,
> the brave man bellowed; his voice, renowned
> in battle, hammered the grey rock's anvil.

Beowulf Fights the Dragon

The guardian of the hoard knew the voice for human;
violent hatred stirred within him. Now no time
remained to entreat for peace. At once
the monster's breath, burning battle vapour,
issued from the barrow; the earth itself snarled.
The lord of the Geats, standing under the cliff,
raised his shield against the fearsome stranger;
then that sinuous creature spoiled
for the fight. The brave and warlike king
had already drawn his keen-edged sword,
(it was an ancient heirloom); a terror of each other
lurked in the hearts of the two antagonists.
While the winged creature coiled himself up,
the friend and lord of men stood unflinching
by his shield; Beowulf waited ready armed.

   Then, fiery and twisted, the dragon swiftly
shrithed towards its fate. The shield protected
the life and body of the famous prince
for far less time than he had looked for.
It was the first occasion in all his life
that fate did not decree triumph for him
in battle. The lord of the Geats raised
his arm, and struck the mottled monster
with his vast ancestral sword; but the bright blade's
edge was blunted by the bone, bit
less keenly than the desperate king required.
The defender of the barrow bristled with anger
at the blow, spouted murderous fire, so that flames
leaped through the air. The gold-friend of the Geats
did not boast of famous victories; his proven sword,
the blade bared in battle, had failed him
as it ought not to have done. That great Ecgtheow's
greater son had to journey on from this world
was no pleasant matter; much against his will,
he was obliged to make his dwelling
elsewhere—sooner or later every man must leave
this transitory life. It was not long

before the fearsome ones closed again.
The guardian of the hoard was filled with fresh hope,
his breast was heaving; he who had ruled a nation
suffered agony, surrounded by flame.
And Beowulf's companions, sons of nobles—
so far from protecting him in a troop together,
unflinching in the fight—shrank back into the forest
scared for their own lives. One man alone
obeyed his conscience. The claims of kinship
can never be ignored by a right-minded man.

   His name was Wiglaf, a noble warrior,
Weohstan's son, kinsman of Ælfhere,
a leader of the Swedes; he saw that his lord,
helmeted, was tormented by the intense heat.
Then he recalled the honours Beowulf had bestowed
on him—the wealthy citadel of the Wægmundings,
the rights to land his father owned before him.
He could not hold back then; he grasped the round,
yellow shield; he drew his ancient sword,
reputed to be the legacy of Eanmund,
Ohthere's son. . . .
                This was the first time
the young warrior had weathered the battle storm,
standing at the shoulder of his lord.
His courage did not melt, nor did his kinsman's sword
fail him in the fight. The dragon found that out
when they met in mortal combat.

   Wiglaf spoke, constantly reminding
his companions of their duty—he was mournful.
"I think of that evening we emptied the mead-cup
in the feasting-hall, partook and pledged our lord,
who presented us with rings, that we would repay him
for his gifts of armour, helmets and hard swords,
if ever the need, need such as this, arose.
For this very reason he asked us
to join with him in this journey, deemed us
worthy of renown, and gave me these treasures;

he looked on us as loyal warriors,
brave in battle; even so, our lord,
guardian of the Geats, intended to perform
this feat alone, because of all men
he had achieved the greatest exploits,
daring deeds. Now the day has come
when our lord needs support, the might
of strong men; let us hurry forward
and help our leader as long as fire remains,
fearsome, searing flames. God knows
I would rather that fire embraced my body
beside the charred body of my gold-giver;
it seems wrong to me that we should shoulder
our shields, carry them home afterwards,
unless we can first kill the venomous foe,
guard the prince of the Geats. I know
in my heart his feats of old were such
that he should not now be the only Geat to suffer
and fall in combat; in common we shall share
sword, helmet, corslet, the trappings of war."

Then that man fought his way through the fumes,
went helmeted to help his lord. He shouted out:
"Brave Beowulf, may success attend you—
for in the days when you were young, you swore
that so long as you lived you would never allow
your fame to decay; now, O resolute king,
renowned for your exploits, you must guard your life
with all your skill. I shall assist you."

At this the seething dragon attacked a second time;
shimmering with fire the venomous visitor fell on his foes,
the men he loathed. With waves of flame, he burnt
the shield right up to its boss; Wiglaf's
corslet afforded him no protection whatsoever.
But the young warrior still fought bravely, sheltered
behind his kinsman's shield after his own
was consumed by flames. Still the battle-king
set his mind on deeds of glory; with prodigious strength

he struck a blow so violent that his sword stuck
in the dragon's skull. But Nægling snapped!
Beowulf's old grey-hued sword
failed him in the fight. Fate did not ordain
that the iron edge should assist him
in that struggle; Beowulf's hand was too strong.
Indeed I have been told that he overtaxed
each and every weapon, hardened by blood, that he bore
into battle; his own great strength betrayed him.

   Then the dangerous dragon, scourge of the Geats,
was intent a third time upon attack; he rushed
at the renowned man when he saw an opening:
fiery, battle-grim, he gripped the hero's neck
between his sharp teeth; Beowulf was bathed
in blood; it spurted out in streams.
Then, I have heard, the loyal thane
alongside the Geatish king displayed great courage,
strength and daring, as was his nature.
To assist his kinsman, that man in mail
aimed not for the head but lunged at the belly
of their vile enemy (in so doing his hand
was badly burnt); his sword, gleaming and adorned,
sank in up to the hilt and at once the flames
began to abate. The king still had control then
over his senses; he drew the deadly knife,
keen-edged in battle, that he wore on his corslet;
then the lord of the Geats dispatched the dragon.
Thus they had killed their enemy—their courage
enabled them—the brave kinsmen together
had destroyed him. Such should a man,
a thane, be in time of necessity!
                                That was the last
of all the king's achievements, his last
exploit in the world. Then the wound
the earth-dragon had inflicted with his teeth
began to burn and swell; very soon he
was suffering intolerable pain as the poison

boiled within him. Then the wise leader
tottered forward and slumped on a seat
by the barrow; he gazed at the work of giants,
saw how the ancient earthwork contained
stone arches supported by columns.
Then, with his own hands, the best of thanes
refreshed the renowned prince with water,
washed his friend and lord, blood-stained
and battle-weary, and unfastened his helmet.
   Beowulf began to speak, he defied
his mortal injury; he was well aware
that his life's course, with all its delights,
had come to an end; his days on earth
were exhausted, death drew very close:
"It would have made me happy, at this time,
to pass on war-gear to my son, had I
been granted an heir to succeed me,
sprung of my seed. I have ruled the Geats
for fifty winters; no king of any
neighbouring tribe has dared to attack me
with swords, or sought to cow and subdue me.
But in my own home I have awaited
my destiny, cared well for my dependants,
and I have not sought trouble, or sworn
any oaths unjustly. Because of all these things
I can rejoice, drained now by death-wounds;
for the Ruler of Men will have no cause to blame me
after I have died on the count that I deprived
other kinsmen of their lives. Now hurry,
dear Wiglaf; rummage the hoard
under the grey rock, for the dragon sleeps,
riddled with wounds, robbed of his treasure.
Be as quick as you can so that I may see
the age-old store of gold, and examine
all the priceless, shimmering stones; once I
have set eyes on such a store, it will be
more easy for me to die, to abandon

the life and land that have so long been mine."
    Then, I have been told, as soon as he heard
the words of his lord, wounded in battle,
Wiglaf hastened into the earth-cavern,
still wearing his corslet, his woven coat of mail.
After the fierce warrior, flushed with victory,
had walked past a daïs, he came upon
the hoard—a hillock of precious stones,
and gold treasure glowing on the ground;
he saw wondrous wall-hangings; the lair
of the serpent, the aged twilight-flier;
and the stoups and vessels of a people
long dead, now lacking a polisher,
deprived of adornments. There were many old,
rusty helmets, and many an armlet
cunningly wrought. A treasure hoard,
gold in the ground, will survive its owner
easily, whosoever hides it!
And he saw also hanging high
over the hoard a standard fashioned with gold strands,
a miracle of handiwork; a light shone from it,
by which he was able to distinguish the earth
and look at the adornments. There was no sign
of the serpent, the sword had savaged and slain him.
Then I heard that Wiglaf rifled the hoard
in the barrow, the antique work of giants—
he chose and carried off as many cups and salvers
as he could; and he also took the standard,
the incomparable banner; Beowulf's sword,
iron-edged, had injured
the guardian of the hoard, he who had held it
through the ages and fought to defend it
with flames—terrifying, blistering,
ravening at midnight—until he was slain.
Wiglaf hurried on his errand, eager to return,
spurred on by the treasures; in his heart he was troubled
whether he would find the prince of the Geats,

so grievously wounded, still alive
in the place where he had left him.
Then at last he came, carrying the treasures,
to the renowned king; his lord's life-blood
was ebbing; once more he splashed him
with water, until Beowulf revived a little,
began to frame his thoughts.
                      Gazing at the gold,
the warrior, the sorrowing king, said:
"With these words I thank
the King of Glory, the Eternal Lord,
the Ruler, for all the treasures here before me,
that in my lifetime I have been able
to gain them for the Geats.
And now that I have bartered my old life
for this treasure hoard, you must serve
and inspire our people. I will not long be with you.
Command the battle-warriors, after the funeral fire,
to build a fine barrow overlooking the sea;
let it tower high on Whaleness
as a reminder to my people.
And let it be known as *Beowulf's barrow*
to all seafarers, to men who steer their ships
from far over the swell and the saltspray."

   Then the prince, bold of mind, detached
his golden collar and gave it to Wiglaf,
the young spear-warrior, and also his helmet
adorned with gold, his ring and his corslet,
and enjoined him to use them well;
"You are the last survivor of our family,
the Wægmundings; fate has swept
all my kinsmen, those courageous warriors,
to their doom. I must follow them."

   Those were the warrior's last words
before he succumbed to the raging flames
on the pyre; his soul migrated from his breast
to meet the judgement of righteous men.

Then the brave warrior, Weohstan's son,
directed that orders be given to many men
(to all who owned houses, elders of the people)
to fetch wood from far to place beneath
their prince on the funeral pyre:
"Now flames,
the blazing fire, must devour the lord of warriors
who often endured the iron-tipped arrow-shower,
when the dark cloud loosed by bow strings
broke above the shield-wall, quivering;
when the eager shaft, with its feather garb,
discharged its duty to the barb."

    I have heard that Weohstan's wise son
summoned from Beowulf's band his seven
best thanes, and went with those warriors
into the evil grotto; the man leading
the way grasped a brand. Then those retainers
were not hesitant about rifling the hoard
as soon as they set eyes on any part of it,
lying unguarded, gradually rusting,
in that rock cavern; no man was conscience-stricken
about carrying out those priceless treasures
as quickly as he could. Also, they pushed the dragon,
the serpent over the precipice; they let the waves take him,
the dark waters embrace the warden of the hoard.
Then the wagon was laden with twisted gold,
with treasures of every kind, and the king,
the old battle-warrior, was borne to Whaleness.

    Then, on the headland, the Geats prepared a mighty pyre
for Beowulf, hung round with helmets and shields
and shining mail, in accordance with his wishes;
and then the mourning warriors laid
their dear lord, the famous prince, upon it.

    And there on Whaleness, the heroes kindled
the most mighty of pyres; the dark wood-smoke
soared over the fire, the roaring flames
mingled with weeping—the winds' tumult subsided—

until the body became ash, consumed even
to its core. The heart's cup overflowed;
they mourned their loss, the death of their lord.
And, likewise, a maiden of the Geats,
with her tresses swept up, intoned
a dirge for Beowulf time after time,
declared she lived in dread of days to come
dark with carnage and keening, terror of the enemy,
humiliation and captivity.
                        Heaven swallowed the smoke.
  Then the Geats built a barrow on the headland—
it was high and broad, visible from far
to all seafarers; in ten days they built the beacon
for that courageous man; and they constructed
as noble an enclosure as wise men
could devise, to enshrine the ashes.
They buried rings and brooches in the barrow,
all those adornments that brave men
had brought out from the hoard after Beowulf died.
They bequeathed the gleaming gold, treasure of men,
to the earth, and there it still remains
as useless to men as it was before.
  Then twelve brave warriors, sons of heroes,
rode round the barrow, sorrowing;
they mourned their king, chanted
an elegy, spoke about that great man:
they exalted his heroic life, lauded
his daring deeds; it is fitting for a man,
when his lord and friend must leave this life,
to mouth words in his praise
and to cherish his memory.
Thus the Geats, his hearth-companions,
grieved over the death of their lord;
they said that of all kings on earth
he was the kindest, the most gentle,
the most just to his people, the most eager for fame.

               translated by KEVIN CROSSLEY-HOLLAND

Wayland Smith

Wayland was one of three brothers, alike enough to them in some respects, in others not at all. All three were broad and handsome men, but beside the other two Wayland appeared clumsy, his shoulders almost too broad for the rest of his body, while he moved as clumsily as a bear too, tripping over things, knocking them down; except only when he was at work—and then his clumsiness like a bear's was also elegance; then each of his movements meshed in with the next, each of his muscles co-ordinated, the whole of him was focused to one end, like a sword towards the man it is killing. That end was perfection. For whereas his brothers were mainly warriors and hunters, destroyers of other men and beasts, Wayland was mainly a smith, a maker, the best in his country. There was nothing he could not make; swords and helmets for heroes, shields inlaid and ornamented—brilliant, impenetrable coats of war; but also more peaceable things, drinking cups and plates, arm-rings and collars, even finely-wrought decorations for a woman's breast, over the working of which he bent closely, using the smallest and most delicate of tools, his brown eyes turned green in the light of his furnace.

Now Wayland and his brothers fell in love, but not with ordinary women. They took to wife three swan maidens, hiding their feathered cloaks so that they could not turn back to swans and fly away again. The name of Wayland's wife was Hervor, he loved her utterly, and she in her way loved him—knowing not only how to give him what he wanted, but also how to show him what she wanted and to take it from him gladly—knowing when to talk to him and when to be silent. Wayland even let her come to his smithy while he was working; the furnace glowed equally then on her smooth white skin and on the metal he was working. When he brought his hammer down on the anvil he knew she heard it too, the ring of iron on iron, the even notes of his making. And when he had finished and he held it up to her, whatever it was, the object of war or of peace, she need look at him only without a word and he would know if she liked it.

What she would not do, however, though he wanted it, was wear the jewels that he made. He forged necklaces for her and brooches for her breast and rings for her ears and for her fingers. But she would only ever take one thing from him, perhaps the most beautiful of all, a simple gold arm-ring, engraved with an intricate pattern. And even this she left behind her when she went away from him. For they went away, all three of them, the three swan maidens, one autumn morning early. Hervor had warned the smith often enough. "Always believe I love you," she had said. "No matter what, I love you. Hold me in your heart when I am gone." But he had thought himself safe, all the brothers did, knowing the cloaks safely hidden, knowing they were truly loved. As soon as they discovered their loss, Wayland's two brothers put on their travelling cloaks, took up their hunting bows, buckled on their swords. They swore they would not rest until they had found their wives and set off grimly into the deep green forest. But Wayland remained in his smithy. "I am a maker," he said to himself, "I am not a traveller. I will travel in my making only, Hervor will come to me when she chooses to, when she needs to come to me." And he took up her gold arm-ring and he threaded it on a rope made of flax with seven hundred others and hung it upon the wall where Hervor would see it if she came to find it.

And then he began to work again. The fire in his smithy never died. The ring of hammer on anvil continued day and night. Such things he made, more finely wrought than ever, each one perfect for its purpose, whether of war or peace; whether sword or battle-axe, helmet or battle-shirt, arm-ring or neck-ring, wine-bowl, ale-cup or goblet, ornament for breast or neck or finger. Just as Wayland controlled the might of fire and steel, the huge muscles shifting across his back as he swung the great hammer, so too his eyes and fingers continued to make perfect harmony over work small and cunning, intricate and fine. The fame of his making spread far beyond his hall.

He grew still more bearlike over the years, his back more bent, his shoulders broader. His wiry black hair fell down his back now and had turned just a little grey. Outside his smithy he moved as clumsily as ever, but he did not often leave it or his hall now, with their bright fires burning and the dark shadows stirring in the corners, except to go hunting for his food, pursuing bear and elk through the living forest that surrounded him.

But there was another country quite close by; a cold grey land of rock and ice and darkness where no trees grew or flowers, where no birds sang in the early morning. The king of this land was called King Nidud, and hearing of Wayland's skill he sent armed men over the mountains to find him. Wayland was out hunting at the time, his hall and smithy empty but for all the things he'd made, on which the firelight leapt and glinted. The warriors looked round them in amazement, but in the end took only one thing away with them, the most beautiful thing of all, the ring Wayland had threaded on a thread with seven hundred others, the red-gold ring that was Hervor's, engraved with a pattern like a maze.

When Wayland returned that night he brought branches of pine to throw upon his fires. He brought the carcase of a bear intending to eat all he wanted that night, then smoke the meat that was left for the hungry weeks to come. He skinned the bear and jointed it, he set a leg to roast upon the fire. Then as usual he took from the wall the seven hundred rings, red-gold and white-gold, and lay down beside the fire to count them. He saw immediately that Hervor's ring had gone. Immediately he was overcome with joy. She has been here, he thought. She has taken her ring; soon, she will come back to me.

That night almost for the first time he could not work. He ate such meat he could. He sat by the fire feeding it with pine branches. The next day the same. And at last after darkness had come he heard footsteps outside his door. Then he flung it open widely. But he did not find Hervor standing there, he found a line of warriors, the moonlight glinting on their battle-shirts, on the metal bosses of their round shields, on the chains which they held ready to bind him. They seized him before he had had time to draw his sword. Then they carried him off to their cold grey land, through the forest and over the mountain, until they brought him at last to the hall of King Nidud himself; to where the king sat at meat with his wife and his two small sons whom he was rearing to be warriors, and his beautiful daughter, Bodvild.

King Nidud smiled to see Wayland. He smiled still more to see Wayland's sword still hanging from his belt. He ordered it to be brought to him. He held it in his hand and tested its weight. He ran his fingers along its finely-tempered blade. He gazed at the patterns that were worked upon the hilt, at the inlay of gold set in hardened steel. Then he took it and buckled it at his side. All the time Wayland was watching him, chained between two warriors, quite motionless. Only his eyes moved, his eyes that were brown except sometimes when he was at his forge, but which were green now with fury. They moved from King Nidud's satisfied and smiling face, towards King Nidud's cold, unsmiling queen; from her to the king's sons, the fledgling warriors; and from them at last to his beautiful daughter, Bodvild, the king's most favourite; on whose arm shone the red-gold ring that was Hervor's. Chained as he was then his fury broke; he leapt forward, his movement as concentrated, as precise as it would be if he was working; his strength so huge, two warriors could scarcely hold him, a third and then a fourth had to come to their rescue, and still Wayland struggled, growling like a bear.

"That one," observed King Nidud's queen who had begun to smile at last. "That one is dangerous. If you intend keeping it my lord, you should see it is well-tamed."

"And how should you advise I tame him?" The king was still fingering Wayland's stolen sword.

"It is like a bear, it moves like a bear, clumsy and elegant together. See how its eyes move; see how it shows its teeth. I suggest you lame it like a bear; I would cut the leather sinews of its knees."

Wayland, though panting, stood motionless once more; he was watching her.

"Its eyes are glittering like a serpent's now," observed Nidud's queen. "I tell you this one is dangerous."

But she did not seem afraid of him. King Nidud also smiled, so did his two sons, their eyes shining with excitement to see such things in their father's hall. Only Bodvild looked at Wayland with sorrow and compassion, though touching meanwhile Hervor's golden ring. She gazed at her father beseechingly. King Nidud said,

"So shall it be. He is mine now. Cut the sinews with his own sword, then take him away. He shall work for me now and for no one else. The sun never shines on my land, let me be dazzled instead by the gleam of Wayland's gold."

So they lamed the smith cruelly, as you would clip the pinions of a wild bird and so impede its flight. Afterwards he could only hobble awkwardly. Then they took him to an island off the cold grey land, and made him a smithy there and commanded him to work. But first he had to build King Nidud's treasure house which he made a labyrinth of such intricacy that only he himself and the king would know the secret of it. This the king ordered. "The treasure shall lie at its heart," he said; "no one, except me shall look on it." He sent slaves to work with Wayland Smith by day, small, dark, silent men from the mountains. It took them a year to dig the multiplicity of passages, to build up so many walls, which Wayland then set with designs in metal, showing the battle deeds of King Nidud's forefathers. When it was finished all the slaves were killed to prevent them betraying the secrets of the labyrinth, and Wayland was left quite alone on his island, with no means of escaping it, or so King Nidud thought; who did not know that the maze was not the only thing Wayland had designed and built that year; did not know how each night Wayland had hobbled to the sea-shore and gathered the feathers and bones of dead sea-birds there, how little by little he had worked out the secret of their flight, and so constructed him a pair of wings, setting the sea-birds' feathers on a frame made of their bones. But these wings he had hid in a chest in his smithy. The time for using them had not yet come.

"Hervor, my wife," he said, speaking to her inside his head as he often did these days, "Hervor my white swan. The day will come that I am revenged and you will have a bird too for a husband."

He rarely slept now. The fire in his smithy burned brightly always. His only visitor was King Nidud, Wayland's own sword still hanging at his side. But now he too wore a helmet made by Wayland, and a battle-shirt also of his working. Back in his hall hung a sharp battle-axe and a fine war-collar. On his table stood wine-bowls and ale-cups and chased golden goblets. His sons wore collars made by Wayland. On his wife's breast lay many of his jewels. Only Bodvild would take nothing more, wore nothing but Hervor's ring upon her small white arm and thought of Wayland constantly.

This was the worst time of Wayland's life, who nevertheless, in fear sometimes and in longing always, did not cease to work; though his mind remained with his lost wife, his lost freedom, his lost strength and pride. The flames of his furnace seemed cruel as the fires of hell. And outside his smithy it was dark and bleak and cold and the wind howled and snow fell on snow, all the year long. No trees grew, no flowers; no birds sang in the morning. The only life was Wayland's. The only thing that grew was the gold beneath Wayland's hammer, the beauty that he made with it. There were chests full of the things he had made stacked in the corners of the smithy, waiting to be taken to the treasure chamber in the maze; but only King Nidud ever saw the treasures there. And as for Wayland he could scarcely remember what love and warmth felt like. He could scarcely remember Hervor's face. Despair would have eaten him entirely, if he had not kept it at bay with his thoughts of revenge on King Nidud and his wife and his sons and his daughter, Bodvild.

Now it happened that as the two little boys grew up they became increasingly curious about their father's prisoner. They wanted to see more of the things that Wayland made. They wanted to get closer to the lamed bear themselves, if only to bait him. It is our right, they told themselves. Soon we too will be warriors, soon we too will have the right to wear helmet and battle-shirt, to carry swords and battle-axes. We should be allowed to choose some for ourselves. It is our right, they said.

So they took a boat and they rowed across the sea to Wayland's island. They left the boat hidden behind a rock a little out from the shore and started to walk through the sea towards the beach. Wayland came out of his smithy and saw them coming. "Children," he thought, not recognising them at first. And at first the sight of them, of the bright-faced fair-haired boys, moved him deeply, he had not seen children for many years. One of the boys was so small the water came nearly to his shoulders, and seeing this Wayland thought to himself, I was tall enough once to walk through water nine yards deep, and lame as he was he strode into the sea and took the boy upon his shoulders and carried him dry to shore. The other boy followed them. But he was watching Wayland closely and in a little while began to imitate his awkward walk; the boy on the smith's shoulders began laughing to see it. And Wayland heard the laughter and the cruelty there was in it, and gradually the burden became almost too great for him to bear. He set the boy down thankfully and looked at the brothers, but he was frowning and suspicious now.

"Who are you? What do you want of me?" he asked.

"We are the sons of your master King Nidud. We have seen some of the things you have made. We have heard you make others yet more incredible—swords sharp enough to cut off a dragon's head, steel coats strong enough to withstand a dragon's teeth. We have come to choose the armour we will wear when we are older. We have come to choose some of your weapons for ourselves."

Wayland took them to his smithy and opened a chest or two. But he did not like the way they nudged each other with sly and greedy looks, the way they whispered together and sniggered the moment his back was turned. He began to see his revenge against their father, King Nidud. The two boys were pointing to yet another corner now.

"Show us what you have in there," they said. "Show us jewels, show us gold collars and arm-rings. We are the sons of a king, such things will be for us."

Wayland told them the keys to this chest were lost. "Tonight at at my furnace I will forge some more," he said, "Come back tomorrow. Come secretly. Tell no one where you mean to go, say only you will be hunting in the forest or on the mountain. And we will spend a day together. I will show you all the secrets of my making."

So the two brothers departed, still nudging each other and giggling, still imitating the way that Wayland walked. And the next day having pretended to set out towards the mountains, they came running instead to the sea shore and took their boat and rowed once

Wayland Smith

more towards Wayland's island. The smith waited for them upon the beach, but this time he let the younger boy walk through the water, did not carry him in upon his shoulders.

In his smithy a chest stood ready in a dark corner. Wayland opened it with a bright new key. The light from the furnace barely reached this far, the two boys had to bend closely to see what they would see, their heads close together, their eyes shining at the sight of the riches they had intended plundering. They were too engrossed to hear Wayland come behind them. He felled each of them with an easy blow. They lay without a sound, and at once he took an axe and cut off both their heads.

He buried the bodies in another corner beneath a pile of soot-blackened bellows. And when he had wiped up all the blood he carried the two heads to his workbench beside the fire. There he took out the eyes and extracted all the teeth and laid them carefully aside. Then he scraped the hair from the skulls, and the flesh and skin and he let the brains run out from inside them, until he was left with clean and empty bone; and then, smelting silver, he mounted these skulls most beautifully, engraving the bright metal with pictures of what he had just done, how he had killed the two boys and cut off both their heads.

"These goblets are my gift to King Nidud," he said.

When he had finished he took the two pairs of eyes, one green pair and one brown, the colours of his own, and he polished them to shining jewels and set them too in silver. "A necklace for King Nidud's queen," Wayland told himself and laid them beside the skulls. Then he took all the teeth and polished them also, formed patterns with them and made two brooches, such beautiful brooches that working them he almost forgot they were the result of such destruction. "But to make one thing you must always destroy another," he told himself, angrily. "These brooches are for the breast of King Nidud's daughter."

Now Bodvild had not set eyes on Wayland since that first day he became her father's captive. She had thought of him often with curiosity and pity. She became more and more determined to see him. And at last she broke her golden arm-ring engraved with lines interwoven like a maze, and she too crossed the water to Wayland's island, carrying the pieces with her, and she handed them to him without a word, and looked at him longingly. He stroked them with his fingers, as silent as she was. He thought of Hervor his wife. I have never made anything more beautiful than this, he told himself.

Bodvild said nervously at last, "No one could mend this but you. I love it like myself—will you do it for me?"

Wayland still did not speak to her. He went into his smithy and Bodvild followed him, looking round her curiously to see his tools hung neatly upon the wall, his anvil beside the furnace, the furnace itself not only heat but light, giving each implement a shadow the same size as itself. Bodvild saw her own shadow on the wall, and she saw Wayland's too, his mighty shoulders, his head bent over his work bench. From time to time he looked at her. She was only the second woman who had ever watched him work; on whose face the light of his furnace had glowed, in whose ears had sounded the ring of his hammer on the anvil. And when he had finished he handed the arm-ring to her, and she too did not speak, simply smiled at him, and he knew as he had once known that a woman loved what he did for its own sake and for his, and not simply for the metal from which it had been made.

He could hardly bear to see it. "Your mother," he said, speaking very slowly, "your mother will envy you now still more; that your father should have given you this ring."

"My mother may take everything I have but this. You made it and it is beautiful."

Bodvild sat down on a bearskin beside the fire. Wayland brought her ale in a silver cup. He too sat down and he looked at her, trying not to remember his lost wife, and he too drank ale with Bodvild. But when her cup was empty he filled it up again; and again she emptied it and again he filled it. And the warmth of the fire and the ale entered both of them. His eyes turned green when he looked at her and she was not afraid of him though she thought she ought to be. But she did not want to be afraid of him. And when he looked at her he did not know if it was hate that he felt or love. In the end anyway he did what he had to, what they both wanted, for whatever reason; drowsy and warm Bodvild knew Wayland there on the bearskin beside his furnace, and for the first time in her life she had

Wayland Smith

a husband, and for the second time in his life, so briefly, Wayland himself had a wife.

But he awoke in the cold dawn, angry and mocking her.

"Think of what your father will say to this."

"I do not care what my father says. And how do you think he should ever know?"

"He will know. He will have the bitter knowledge of it and I shall be revenged on both of you." And Bodvild went away weeping because Wayland had forgotten her now, because of his cruelty where there had been some gentleness before. Wayland watching her go felt pity stir in him. But she did not look back; he did not call her.

In King Nidud's hall the queen was weeping for her two lost sons. They had searched for them everywhere, through the forests and across the mountains, but no one had seen them. She thought of Wayland's magic powers, and she too at last sought out the man whose laming she had suggested to the king. She entered his smithy, stood watching as he worked. But he laid his hammer down as soon as he saw that she had come.

"I have lost my two sons, my two warrior boys."

"I can tell you where to find them. You must swear one thing first."

"I will swear anything."

"Then swear on ship and sword and stallion; swear on shield and coat of steel; swear you'll not harm the one who has been my wife; and swear you will not harm our son though she rears him in King Nidud's hall."

King Nidud's wife was still proud, still angry; but worn weak by weeping she did not hesitate, put her hand on the anvil and swore as she was asked.

"*Now* tell me. Where are my sons?"

Wayland took from one of his chests the two skull goblets, mounted in silver; the four eyes, two brown jewels and two green, that he had made into a necklace; the small teeth that were now an ivory brooch for Bodvild, and he laid them down before King Nidud's wife. She looked at them astonished, not knowing what she saw.

"But where are my sons? What have you done with them?"

The smith pointed to a corner, shadowed and dark, to a pile of old bellows and other implements. "Dig there," he said, "under the soot-blackened bellows from my forge. If you look carefully you will see the marks of blood. If you dig further you will find small bones, the bones of boys, your sons. These goblets are their skulls set in silver for your husband; these eyes are theirs made into a necklace for you, these brooches I made from their teeth as breast ornaments for your daughter, Bodvild."

"And that is not all," he said. "Tell your husband this: his gift is death. I have proved now it is also mine. But besides that I have brought to this land what he cannot bring, what he has tried to prevent ever coming here. I have brought life. Life stirs in the belly of your daughter Bodvild, and that too King Nidud cannot now undo."

All the while Wayland had been strapping on to him the wings he had made of bird bones and feathers from the sea-shore. And then, his work done, he rose into the air upon them, leaving behind his smithy, the cold stone of the island, leaving behind all the beautiful things he had made and the maze that was the treasure house for the man who had imprisoned him; whose secret intricacies now lay openly below him. Like the swan maiden Hervor, his wife, he flew high in the air and was free at last, of the gold and silver, the hammer and the anvil, free of his lameness, free of his slavery. Below him the queen was raging and weeping. Below him King Nidud came running to the shore, ordering his tallest horsemen to chase after Wayland on their tallest horses. Rank upon rank of them appeared, but none were tall enough. Wayland had risen far above their heads. King Nidud ordered out his archers, the most far-shooting, far-seeing of his whole war-band. They drew their bows, they released their arrows, higher and higher, they darted, curving as they fell—for Wayland flew far above arrows, above archers, above horsemen, far above King Nidud, his wife and his dead sons; far above Bodvild and the child in her belly.

She wept for him bitterly. She called him in her heart. But when her father reproached her, reviling Wayland too for what he had done to her, she said simply, "I was willing." Nothing more.

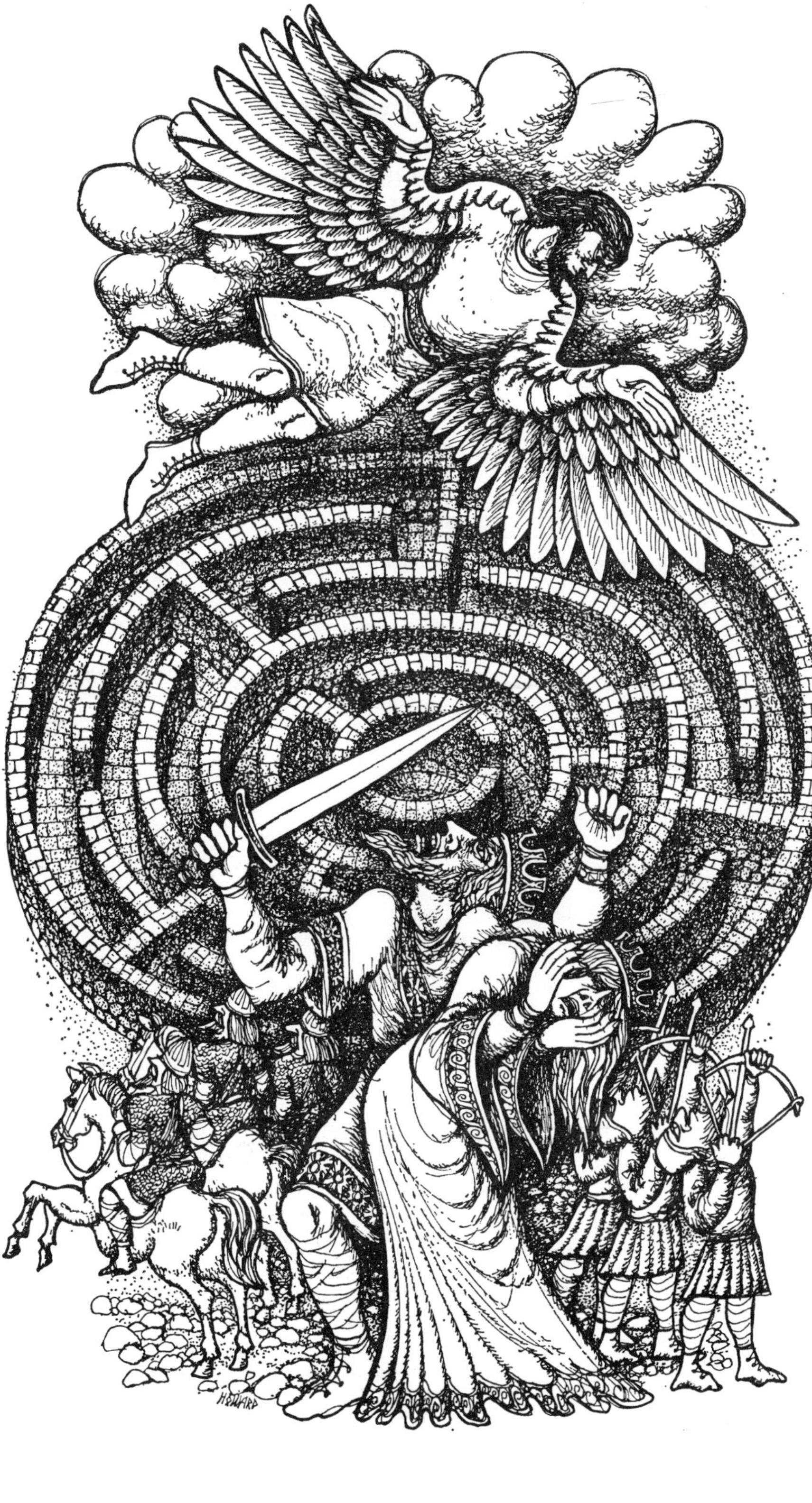

How bitter King Nidud was, how furiously angry. But with all his powers he could not put the eyes back in the skull sockets and the skulls back on the bodies and the flesh back on the bones, any more than he could destroy the life that was growing in his daughter's belly.

"I have sworn she shall not be harmed, nor the son that grows inside her," his queen told him coldly; as much death in her voice now as there was death in King Nidud's heart.

Wayland flew far away from that icy, lightless land where no birds sang in the early morning, back to his own smithy, his own hall in the deep green of the forest. He remained lame for ever. He remained a smith for ever; but maybe one day Hervor came to him, maybe one day the light from the furnace fell upon her face and the ring of the anvil sounded in her ears; maybe for a little while again she stayed with him.

retold by PENELOPE FARMER

How Sigurd Awoke Brynhild upon Hindfell

This episode from the Volsunga Saga *follows immediately after Sigurd has slain the dragon Fafnir on Gnita Heath, called "Glittering Heath" by William Morris. "The Wrath" is another name for Sigurd's sword, Gram; and "Fafnir's bane" is the cursed treasure hoard he has won from the dragon. Until she fell from grace, Brynhild was one of the Valkyries or "Choosers of the Slain" (Morris calls her a "Victory-Wafter"), beautiful young spirit women who gave victory or defeat as Odin dictated and brought the Einheriar or heroes back to Valhalla to await the last great battle at Ragnarok.*

As this triumphant section ends, Sigurd gives Andvari's ring to Brynhild, innocent of the curse upon it. The Volsunga Saga *goes on to record Sigurd's and Brynhild's association with the Niblungs and to chart the tragic course of their lives.*

By long roads rideth Sigurd amidst that world of stone,
And somewhat south he turneth; for he would not be alone,
But longs for the dwellings of man-folk, and the kingly people's speech,
And the days of the glee and the joyance, where men laugh each to each.
But still the desert endureth, and afar must Greyfell fare
From the wrack of the Glittering Heath, and Fafnir's golden lair.
Long Sigurd rideth the waste, when, lo, on a morning of day
From out of the tangled crag-walls, amidst the cloud-land grey
Comes up a mighty mountain, and it is as though there burns
A torch amidst of its cloud-wreath; so thither Sigurd turns,

For he deems indeed from its topmost to look on the best of the earth;
And Greyfell neigheth beneath him, and his heart is full of mirth.

So he rideth higher and higher, and the light grows great and strange,
And forth from the clouds it flickers, till at noon they gather and change,
And settle thick on the mountain, and hide its head from sight;
But the winds in a while are awakened, and day bettereth ere the night,
And, lifted a measureless mass o'er the desert crag-walls high,
Cloudless the mountain riseth against the sunset sky,
The sea of the sun grown golden, as it ebbs from the day's desire;
And the light that afar was a torch is grown a river of fire,
And the mountain is black above it, and below is it dark and dun;
And there is the head of Hindfell as an island in the sun.

Night falls, but yet rides Sigurd, and hath no thought of rest,
For he longs to climb that rock-world and behold the earth at its best;
But now mid the maze of the foot-hills he seeth the light no more,
And the stars are lovely and gleaming on the lightless heavenly floor.
So up and up he wendeth till the night is wearing thin;
And he rideth a rift of the mountain, and all is dark therein,
Till the stars are dimmed by dawning and the wakening world is cold;
Then afar in the upper rock-wall a breach doth he behold,
And a flood of light poured inward the doubtful dawning blinds:
So swift he rideth thither and the mouth of the breach he finds,
And sitteth awhile on Greyfell on the marvellous thing to gaze:
For lo, the side of Hindfell enwrapped by the fervent blaze,
And nought 'twixt earth and heaven save a world of flickering flame,
And a hurrying shifting tangle, where the dark rents went and came.

Great groweth the heart of Sigurd with uttermost desire,
And he crieth kind to Greyfell, and they hasten up, and nigher,
Till he draweth rein in the dawning on the face of Hindfell's steep:

How Sigurd Awoke Brynhild upon Hindfell

But who shall heed the dawning where the tongues of that wildfire leap?
For they weave a wavering wall, that driveth over the heaven
The wind that is born within it; nor ever aside is it driven
By the mightiest wind of the waste, and the rain-flood amidst it is nought;
And no wayfarer's door and no window the hand of its builder hath wrought.
But thereon is the Volsung smiling as its breath uplifteth his hair,
And his eyes shine bright with its image, and his mail gleams white and fair,
And his war-helm pictures the heavens and the waning stars behind:
But his neck is Greyfell stretching to snuff at the flame-wall blind,
And his cloudy flank upheaveth, and tinkleth the knitted mail,
And the gold of the uttermost waters is waxen wan and pale.

Now Sigurd turns in his saddle, and the hilt of the Wrath he shifts,
And draws a girth the tighter; then the gathered reins he lifts,
And crieth aloud to Greyfell, and rides at the wildfire's heart;
But the white wall wavers before him and the flame-flood rusheth apart,
And high o'er his head it riseth, and wide and wild is its roar
As it beareth the mighty tidings to the very heavenly floor:
But he rideth through its roaring as the warrior rides the rye,
When it bows with the wind of the summer and the hid spears draw anigh;
The white flame licks his raiment and sweeps through Greyfell's mane,
And bathes both hands of Sigurd and the hilts of Fafnir's bane,
And winds about his war-helm and mingles with his hair,
But nought his raiment dusketh or dims his glittering gear;
Then it fails and fades and darkens till all seems left behind,
And dawn and the blaze is swallowed in mid-mirk stark and blind.

But forth a little further and a little further on
And all is calm about him, and he sees the scorched earth wan
Beneath a glimmering twilight, and he turns his conquering eyes,
And a ring of pale slaked ashes on the side of Hindfell lies;

And the world of the waste is beyond it; and all is hushed and grey,
And the new-risen moon is a-paleing, and the stars grow faint with day.
Then Sigurd looked before him and a Shield-burg there he saw,
A wall of the tiles of Odin wrought clear without a flaw,
The gold by the silver gleaming, and the ruddy by the white;
And the blazonings of their glory were done upon them bright,
As of dear things wrought for the war-lords new come to Odin's hall.
Piled high aloft to the heavens uprose that battle-wall,
And far o'er the topmost shield-rim for a banner of fame there hung
A glorious golden buckler; and against the staff it rung
As the earliest wind of dawning uprose on Hindfell's face
And the light from the yellowing east beamed soft on the shielded place.

But the Wrath cried out in answer as Sigurd leapt adown
To the wasted soil of the desert by that rampart of renown;
He looked but little beneath it, and the dwelling of God it seemed,
As against its gleaming silence the eager Sigurd gleamed:
He draweth not sword from scabbard, as the wall he wendeth around,
And it is but the wind and Sigurd that wakeneth any sound:
But, lo, to the gate he cometh, and the doors are open wide,
And no warder the way withstandeth, and no earls by the threshold abide;
So he stands awhile and marvels; then the baleful light of the Wrath
Gleams bare in his ready hand as he wendeth the inward path:
For he doubteth some guile of the gods, or perchance some dwarf-king's snare,
Or a mock of the giant people that shall fade in the morning air:
But he getteth him in and gazeth; and a wall doth he behold,
And the ruddy set by the white, and the silver by the gold;
But within the garth that it girdeth no work of man is set,
But the utmost head of Hindfell ariseth higher yet;
And below in the very midmost is a giant-fashioned mound,
Piled high as the rims of the Shield-burg above the level ground;
And there, on that mound of the giants, o'er the wilderness forlorn,
A pale grey image lieth, and gleameth in the morn.

How Sigurd Awoke Brynhild upon Hindfell

So there was Sigurd alone; and he went from the shielded door,
And aloft in the desert of wonder the Light of the Branstock he bore;
And he set his face to the earth-mound, and beheld the image wan,
And the dawn was growing about it; and, lo, the shape of a man
Set forth to the eyeless desert on the tower-top of the world,
High over the cloud-wrought castle whence the windy bolts are hurled.

Now he comes to the mound and climbs it, and will see if the man be dead;
Some king of the days forgotten laid there with crownèd head,
Or the frame of a god, it may be, that in heaven hath changed his life,
Or some glorious heart belovèd, God-rapt from the earthly strife:
Now over the body he standeth, and seeth it shapen fair,
And clad from head to foot-sole in pale grey-glittering gear,
In a hauberk wrought as straitly as though to the flesh it were grown:
But a great helm hideth the head and is girt with a glittering crown.

So thereby he stoopeth and kneeleth, for he deems it were good indeed
If the breath of life abide there and the speech to help at need;
And as sweet as the summer wind from a garden under the sun
Cometh forth on the topmost Hindfell the breath of that sleeping-one.
Then he saith he will look on the face, if it bear him love or hate,
Or the bonds for his life's constraining, or the sundering doom of fate.
So he draweth the helm from the head, and, lo, the brow snow-white,
And the smooth unfurrowed cheeks, and the wise lips breathing light;
And the face of a woman it is, and the fairest that ever was born,
Shown forth to the empty heavens and the desert world forlorn:
But he looketh, and loveth her sore, and he longeth her spirit to move,
And awaken her heart to the world, that she may behold him and love.
And he toucheth her breast and her hands, and he loveth her passing sore;

And he saith: "Awake! I am Sigurd"; but she moveth never the more.

Then he looked on his bare bright blade, and he said: "Thou—what wilt thou do?
For indeed as I came by the war-garth thy voice of desire I knew."
Bright burnt the pale blue edges for the sunrise drew anear,
And the rims of the Shield-burg glittered, and the east was exceeding clear:
So the eager edges he setteth to the dwarf-wrought battle-coat
Where the hammered ring-knit collar constraineth the woman's throat;
But the sharp Wrath biteth and rendeth, and before it fail the rings,
And, lo, the gleam of the linen, and the light of golden things:
Then he driveth the blue steel onward, and through the skirt, and out,
Till nought but the rippling linen is wrapping her about;
Then he deems her breath comes quicker and her breast begins to heave,
So he turns about the War-Flame and rends down either sleeve,
Till her arms lie white in her raiment, and a river of sun-bright hair
Flows free o'er bosom and shoulder and floods the desert bare.

Then a flush cometh over her visage and a sigh up-heaveth her breast,
And her eyelids quiver and open, and she wakeneth into rest;
Wide-eyed on the dawning she gazeth, too glad to change or smile,
And but little moveth her body, nor speaketh she yet for a while;
And yet kneels Sigurd moveless her wakening speech to heed,
While soft the waves of the daylight o'er the starless heavens speed,
And the gleaming rims of the Shield-burg yet bright and brighter grow,
And the thin moon hangeth her horns dead-white in the golden glow.
Then she turned and gazed on Sigurd, and her eyes met the Volsung's eyes.
And mighty and measureless now did the tide of his love arise,
For their longing had met and mingled, and he knew of her heart that she loved,

How Sigurd Awoke Brynhild upon Hindfell   61

As she spake unto nothing but him and her lips with the speech-flood moved:

"O, what is the thing so mighty that my weary sleep hath torn,
And rent the fallow bondage, and the wan woe over-worn?"

He said: "The hand of Sigurd and the Sword of Sigmund's son,
And the heart that the Volsungs fashioned this deed for thee have done."

But she said: "Where then is Odin that laid me here alow?
Long lasteth the grief of the world, and man-folk's tangled woe!"

"He dwelleth above," said Sigurd, "but I on the earth abide,
And I came from the Glittering Heath the waves of thy fire to ride."

But therewith the sun rose upward and lightened all the earth,
And the light flashed up to the heavens from the rims of the glorious girth;
But they twain arose together, and with both her palms outspread,
And bathed in the light returning, she cried aloud and said:

"All hail O Day and thy Sons, and thy kin of the coloured things!
Hail, following Night, and thy Daughter that leadeth thy wavering wings!
Look down with unangry eyes on us today alive,
And give us the hearts victorious, and the gain for which we strive!
All hail, ye Lords of God-home, and ye Queens of the House of Gold!
Hail thou dear Earth that bearest, and thou Wealth of field and fold!
Give us, your noble children, the glory of wisdom and speech,
And the hearts and the hands of healing, and the mouths and hands that teach!"
Then they turned and were knit together; and oft and o'er again
They craved, and kissed rejoicing, and their hearts were full and fain.

Then Sigurd looketh upon her, and the words from his heart arise:
"Thou art the fairest of earth, and the wisest of the wise;
O who art thou that lovest? I am Sigurd, e'en as I told;
I have slain the foe of the gods, and gotten the Ancient Gold;

And great were the gain of thy love, and the gift of mine earthly days,
If we twain should never sunder as we wend on the changing ways.
O who art thou that lovest, thou fairest of all things born?
And what meaneth thy sleep and thy slumber in the wilderness forlorn?"

She said: "I am she that loveth: I was born of the earthly folk,
But of old Allfather took me from the kings and their wedding yoke:
And he called me the Victory-Wafter, and I went and came as he would,
And I chose the slain for his war-host, and the days were glorious and good,
Till the thoughts of my heart overcame me, and the pride of my wisdom and speech,
And I scorned the earth-folk's Framer and the Lord of the world I must teach:
For the death-doomed I caught from the sword, and the fated life I slew,
And I deemed that my deeds were goodly, and that long I should do and undo.
But Allfather came against me and the god in his wrath arose;
And he cried: 'Thou hast thought in thy folly that the gods have friends and foes,
That they wake, and the world wends onward, that they sleep, and the world slips back,
That they laugh, and the world's weal waxeth, that they frown and fashion the wrack:
Thou hast cast up the curse against me; it shall fall aback on thine head;
Go back to the sons of repentance, with the children of sorrow wed!
For the gods are great unholpen, and their grief is seldom seen,
And the wrong that they will and must be is soon as it hath not been.'

"Yet I thought: 'Shall I wed in the world, shall I gather grief on the earth?
Then the fearless heart shall I wed, and bring the best to birth,
And fashion such tales for the telling, that Earth shall be holpen at least,

How Sigurd Awoke Brynhild upon Hindfell

If the gods think scorn of its fairness, as they sit at the changeless feast.'

"Then somewhat smiled Allfather; and he spake: 'So let it be!
The doom thereof abideth; the doom of me and thee.
Yet long shall the time pass over ere thy waking-day be born:
Fare forth, and forget and be weary 'neath the Sting of the Sleepful Thorn!'

"So I came to the head of Hindfell and the ruddy shields and white,
And the wall of the wildfire wavering around the isle of night;
And there the Sleep-thorn pierced me, and the slumber on me fell,
And the night of nameless sorrows that hath no tale to tell.
Now I am she that loveth; and the day is nigh at hand
When I, who have ridden the sea-realm and the regions of the land,
And dwelt in the measureless mountains and the forge of stormy days,
Shall dwell in the house of my fathers and the land of the people's praise;
And there shall hand meet hand, and heart by heart shall beat,
And the lying-down shall be joyous, and the morn's uprising sweet.
Lo now, I look on thine heart and behold of thine inmost will,
That thou of the days wouldst hearken that our portion shall fulfil;
But O, be wise of man-folk, and the hope of thine heart refrain!
As oft in the battle's beginning ye vex the steed with the rein,
Lest at last in its latter ending, when the sword hath hushed the horn,
His limbs should be weary and fail, and his might be over-worn.
O be wise, lest thy love constrain me, and my vision wax o'er-clear,
And thou ask of the thing that thou shouldst not, and the thing that thou wouldst not hear.

"Know thou, most mighty of men, that the Norns shall order all,
And yet without thine helping shall no whit of their will befall;
Be wise! 'tis a marvel of words, and a mock for the fool and the blind;
But I saw it writ in the heavens, and its fashioning there did I find:
And the night of the Norns and their slumber, and the tide when the world runs back,

And the way of the sun is tangled, it is wrought of the dastard's lack.
But the day when the fair earth blossoms, and the sun is bright above,
Of the daring deeds is it fashioned and the eager hearts of love.

"Be wise, and cherish thine hope in the freshness of the days,
And scatter its seed from thine hand in the field of the people's praise;
Then fair shall it fall in the furrow, and some the earth shall speed,
And the sons of men shall marvel at the blossom of the deed:
But some the earth shall speed not; nay rather, the wind of the heaven
Shall waft it away from thy longing—and a gift to the gods hast thou given,
And a tree for the roof and the wall in the house of the hope that shall be,
Thou it seemeth our very sorrow, and the grief of thee and me.

"Strive not with the fools of man-folk: for belike thou shalt overcome;
And what then is the gain of thine hunting when thou bearest the quarry home?
Or else shall the fool overcome thee, and what deed thereof shall grow?
Nay, strive with the wise man rather, and increase thy woe and his woe;
Yet thereof a gain hast thou gotten; and the half of thine heart hast thou won
If thou mayst prevail against him, and his deeds are the deeds thou hast done:
Yea, and if thou fall before him, in him shalt thou live again,
And thy deeds in his hand shall blossom, and his heart of thine heart shall be fain.

"When thou hearest the fool rejoicing, and he saith, 'It is over and past,
And the wrong was better than right, and hate turns into love at the last,
And we strove for nothing at all, and the gods are fallen asleep;

How Sigurd Awoke Brynhild upon Hindfell

For so good is the world a growing that the evil good shall reap:'
Then loosen thy sword in the scabbard and settle the helm on thine head,
For men betrayed are mighty, and great are the wrongfully dead.

"Wilt thou do the deed and repent it? thou hadst better never been born:
Wilt thou do the deed and exalt it? then thy fame shall be outworn:
Thou shalt do the deed and abide it, and sit on thy throne on high,
And look on today and tomorrow as those that never die.

"Love thou the gods—and withstand them, lest thy fame should fail in the end,
And thou be but their thrall and their bondsman, who wert born for their very friend:
For few things from the gods are hidden, and the hearts of men they know,
And how that none rejoiceth to quail and crouch alow.

"I have spoken the words, belovèd, to thy matchless glory and worth;
But thy heart to my heart hath been speaking, though my tongue hath set it forth:
For I am she that loveth, and I know what thou wouldst teach
From the heart of thine unlearned wisdom, and I needs must speak thy speech."

Then words were weary and silent, but oft and o'er again
They craved and kissed rejoicing, and their hearts were full and fain.

Then spake the Son of Sigmund: "Fairest, and most of worth,
Hast thou seen the ways of man-folk and the regions of the earth?
Then speak yet more of wisdom; for most meet meseems it is
That my soul to thy soul be shapen, and that I should know thy bliss."

So she took his right hand meekly, nor any word would say,
Not e'en of love or praising, his longing to delay;
And they sat on the side of Hindfell, and their fain eyes looked and loved,

As she told of the hidden matters whereby the world is moved:
And she told of the framing of all things, and the houses of the heaven;
And she told of the star-worlds' courses, and how the winds be driven;
And she told of the Norns and their names, and the fate that abideth the earth;
And she told of the ways of king-folk in their anger and their mirth;
And she spake of the love of women, and told of the flame that burns,
And the fall of mighty houses, and the friend that falters and turns,
And the lurking blinded vengeance, and the wrong that amendeth wrong,
And the hand that repenteth its stroke, and the grief that endureth for long;
And how man shall bear and forbear, and be master of all that is;
And how man shall measure it all, the wrath, and the grief, and the bliss.

"I saw the body of Wisdom, and of shifting guise was she wrought,
And I stretched out my hands to hold her, and a mote of the dust they caught;
And I prayed her to come for my teaching, and she came in the midnight dream—
And I woke and might not remember, nor betwixt her tangle deem:
She spake, and how might I hearken; I heard, and how might I know;
I knew, and how might I fashion, or her hidden glory show?
All things I have told thee of Wisdom are but fleeting images
Of her hosts that abide in the Heavens, and her light that Allfather sees:
Yet wise is the sower that sows, and wise is the reaper that reaps,
And wise is the smith in his smiting, and wise is the warder that keeps:
And wise shalt thou be to deliver, and I shall be wise to desire;
—And lo, the tale that is told, and the sword and the wakening fire!
Lo now, I am she that loveth, and hark how Greyfell neighs,
And Fafnir's Bed is gleaming, and green go the downward ways,

How Sigurd Awoke Brynhild upon Hindfell

The road to the children of men and the deeds that thou shalt do
In the joy of thy life-days' morning, when thine hope is fashioned anew.
Come now, O Bane of the Serpent, for now is the high-noon come,
And the sun hangeth over Hindfell and looks on the earth-folk's home;
But the soul is so great within thee, and so glorious are thine eyes,
And me so love constraineth, and mine heart that was called the wise,
That we twain may see men's dwellings and the house where we shall dwell,
And the place of our life's beginning, where the tale shall be to tell."

So they climb the burg of Hindfell, and hand in hand they fare,
Till all about and above them is nought but the sunlit air,
And there close they cling together rejoicing in their mirth;
For far away beneath them lie the kingdoms of the earth,
And the garths of men-folk's dwellings and the streams that water them,
And the rich and plenteous acres, and the silver ocean's hem,
And the woodland wastes and the mountains, and all that holdeth all;
The house and the ship and the island, the loom and the mine and the stall,
The beds of bane and healing, the crafts that slay and save,
The temple of God and the Doom-ring, the cradle and the grave.

Then spake the Victory-Wafter: "O King of the Earthly Age,
As a god thou beholdest the treasure and the joy of thine heritage,
And where on the wings of his hope is the spirit of Sigurd borne?
Yet I bid thee hover awhile as a lark alow on the corn;
Yet I bid thee look on the land 'twixt the wood and the silver sea
In the bight of the swirling river, and the house that cherished me!
There dwelleth mine earthly sister and the king that she hath wed;
There morn by morn aforetime I woke on the golden bed;
There eve by eve I tarried mid the speech and the lays of kings;
There noon by noon I wandered and plucked the blossoming things;
The little land of Lymdale by the swirling river's side,
Where Brynhild once was I called in the days ere my father died;

The little land of Lymdale 'twixt the woodland and the sea,
Where on thee mine eyes shall brighten and thine eyes shall beam on me."

"I shall seek thee there," said Sigurd, "when the day-spring is begun,
Ere we wend the world together in the season of the sun."

"I shall bide thee there," said Brynhild, "till the fullness of the days,
And the time for the glory appointed, and the springing-tide of praise."

From his hand then draweth Sigurd Andvari's ancient Gold;
There is nought but the sky above them as the ring together they hold,
The shapen ancient token, that hath no change nor end,
No change, and no beginning, no flaw for God to mend:
Then Sigurd cries: "O Brynhild, now hearken while I swear,
That the sun shall die in the heavens and the day no more be fair,
If I seek not love in Lymdale and the house that fostered thee,
And the land where thou awakedst 'twixt the woodland and the sea!"

And she cried: "O Sigurd, Sigurd, now hearken while I swear
That the day shall die for ever and the sun to blackness wear,
Ere I forget thee, Sigurd, as I lie 'twixt wood and sea
In the little land of Lymdale and the house that fostered me!"

Then he set the ring on her finger and once, if ne'er again,
They kissed and clung together, and their hearts were full and fain.

So the day grew old about them and the joy of their desire,
And eve and the sunset came, and faint grew the sunset fire,
And the shadowless death of the day was sweet in the golden tide;
But the stars shone forth on the world, and the twilight changed and died;
And sure if the first of man-folk had been born to that starry night,
And had heard no tale of the sunrise, he had never longed for the light:
But Earth longed amidst her slumber, as 'neath the night she lay,
And fresh and all abundant abode the deeds of Day.

retold by WILLIAM MORRIS

SAGAS

The Burning of Bergthorsknoll

Njal's Saga was written by an unknown author in about 1280 and is considered the greatest of the Icelandic prose sagas. The action, which takes place about 300 years before the saga was written, spans about fifty years and describes the relationships and blood feuds in which Njal Thorgeirsson and his family become enmeshed. The tragic climax, involving Njal, his family and retainers, is reprinted here. (Before the saga ends, Kari takes full and bloody vengeance for the burning of Bergthorsknoll.)

Flosi was saying to his men, "We shall now ride to Bergthorsknoll, to reach there by nightfall."

When they arrived, they rode into a hollow in the knoll, where they tethered their horses and waited late into the night.

"Now we shall walk slowly up to the house," said Flosi, "keeping close together, and see what they do."

Njal was standing outside with his sons and Kari and all the servants ranged in front of the house. They were nearly thirty in all.

Flosi halted and said, "We shall note carefully what action they take, for I suspect that we shall never get the better of them if they stay out of doors."

"This would turn out a sorry trip if we did not dare to make an attack on them," said Grani.

"We shall certainly attack them," said Flosi, "even though they remain outside. But we would have to pay a heavy price, and not many would live to tell the tale, whichever side wins."

Njal said to his men, "How many do you think they are?"

"They are a tightly-knit force," said Skarp-Hedin, "and strong in numbers, too; but they suspect that they will have a hard task to overcome us, and that is why they have halted."

"I do not think so," said Njal. "I want everyone to go inside, for they found it hard to overcome Gunnar of Hlidarend, even though he was only one against many. This house is just as strongly built as his was, and they will never be able to overcome us."

"That is the wrong way to look at it," said Skarp-Hedin. "The men who attacked Gunnar were chieftains of such character that they would have preferred to turn back rather than burn him in his house. But these people will not hesitate to use fire if they cannot overcome us in any other way, for they will resort to any means to destroy us. They will assume, and quite rightly, that it will cost them their lives if we escape. And I for one am reluctant to be suffocated like a fox in its den."

Njal said, "Now you are going to override my advice and show me disrespect, my sons—and not for the first time. But when you were younger you did not do so, and things went better for you then."

"Let us do as our father wishes," said Helgi. "That will be best for all of us."

"I am not so sure of that," said Skarp-Hedin, "for he is a doomed man now. But still I do not mind pleasing my father by burning in the house with him, for I am not afraid of dying."

To Kari he said, "Let us all keep close together, brother-in-law, so that we do not get separated."

"That is what I had intended," said Kari, "but if fate wills it otherwise, then it shall be so and nothing can be done about it."

"Then you avenge us," said Skarp-Hedin. "And we shall avenge you if we survive."

Kari agreed. Then they all went inside and stood guard at the doors.

Flosi said, "Now they are doomed, for they have gone indoors. We shall advance on the house at once and form up in strength round the doors to make sure that not one of them escapes, neither Kari nor the Njalssons; for otherwise it will cost us our lives."

Flosi and his men came up to the house and surrounded the whole building, in case there might be a secret door somewhere.

The Burning of Bergthorsknoll

Flosi himself and his own men went up to the front of the house. Hroald Ozurarson rushed at Skarp-Hedin and lunged at him with a spear; Skarp-Hedin hacked the spear-shaft in two and sprang at him, swinging his axe. The axe fell on Hroald's shield and dashed it against him; the upper horn of the axe caught him full in the face, and he fell back dead at once.

Kari said, "There is no escaping you, Skarp-Hedin; you are the bravest of us all."

"I don't know about that," said Skarp-Hedin, and he was seen to draw back his lips in a grin.

Kari and Grim and Helgi lunged often with their spears and wounded many men, and Flosi and the attackers were kept at bay.

Flosi said, "We have suffered heavy losses amongst our men, several wounded and one dead, the one we would least have wanted to lose. It is obvious that we cannot defeat them with weapons; and there are many here who are showing less fight than they said they would. Now we must resort to another plan. There are only two courses open to us, neither of them good: we must either abandon the attack, which would cost us our own lives, or we must set fire to the house and burn them to death, which is a grave responsibility before God, since we are Christian men ourselves. But that is what we must do."

Then they kindled a fire and made a great blaze in front of the doors.

Skarp-Hedin said, "So you're making a fire now, lads! Are you thinking of doing some cooking?"

"Yes," said Grani, "and you won't need it any hotter for roasting."

"So this is your way," said Skarp-Hedin, "of repaying me for avenging your father, the only way you know; you value more highly the obligation that has less claim on you."

The women threw whey on the flames and doused the fire.

Kol Thorsteinsson said to Flosi, "I have an idea. I have noticed that there is a loft above the cross-beams of the main room. That is where we should start a fire, and we can use the heap of chickweed behind the house as kindling."

They brought the chickweed up and set fire to it, and before those inside knew what was happening, the ceiling of the room was ablaze from end to end. Flosi's men also lit huge fires in front of all the doors. At this, the womenfolk began to panic.

Njal said to them, "Be of good heart and speak no words of fear, for this is just a passing storm and it will be long before another like it comes. Put your faith in the mercy of God, for He will not let us burn both in this world and the next."

Such were the words of comfort he brought them, and others more rousing than these.

Now the whole house began to blaze. Njal went to the door and said, "Is Flosi near enough to hear my words?"

Flosi said that he could hear him.

Njal said, "Would you consider making an agreement with my sons, or letting anyone leave the house?"

"I will make no terms with your sons," replied Flosi. "We shall settle matters now, once and for all, and we are not leaving until every one of them is dead. But I shall allow the women and children and servants to come out."

Njal went back inside the house and said to his household, "All those with permission to go out must do so now. Leave the house now, Thorhalla Asgrim's-daughter, and take with you all those who are allowed to go."

Thorhalla said, "This is not the parting from Helgi I had ever expected; but I shall urge my father and my brothers to avenge the killings that are committed here."

"You will do well," said Njal, "for you are a good woman."

She went out, taking many people with her.

Astrid of Djupriverbank said to Helgi, "Come out with me. I will drape you in a woman's cloak and put a head-scarf over you."

Helgi protested at first, but finally yielded to their entreaties. Astrid wrapped a scarf round his head, and Thorhild laid the cloak over his shoulders. Then he walked out between them, along with his sisters Thorgerd and Helga and several other people.

When Helgi came outside, Flosi said, "That's a very tall and broad-shouldered woman—seize her." When Helgi heard this, he threw off the cloak; he was carrying a sword under his arm, and now he struck out at one of the men, slicing off the bottom of the

The Burning of Bergthorsknoll

shield and severing his leg. Then Flosi came up and struck at Helgi's neck, cutting off his head with one blow.

Flosi went up to the door and called Njal and Bergthora over to speak to him; when they came, he said, "I want to offer you leave to come out, for you do not deserve to burn."

"I have no wish to go outside," said Njal, "for I am an old man now and ill-equipped to avenge my sons; and I do not want to live in shame."

Flosi said to Bergthora, "You come out, Bergthora, for under no circumstances do I want you to burn."

Bergthora replied, "I was given to Njal in marriage when young, and I have promised him that we would share the same fate."

Then they both went back inside.

"What shall we do now?" asked Bergthora.

"Let us go to our bed," said Njal, "and lie down."

Then Bergthora said to little Thord, Kari's son, "You are to be taken out. You are not to burn."

The boy replied, "But that's not what you promised, grandmother. You said that we would never be parted; and so it shall be, for I would much prefer to die beside you both."

She carried the boy to the bed. Njal said to his steward, "Take note where we lay ourselves down and how we dispose ourselves, for I shall not move from here however much the smoke or flames distress me. Then you can know where to look for our remains."

The steward said he would.

An ox had recently been slaughtered, and the hide was lying nearby. Njal told the steward to spread the hide over them, and he promised to do so.

Njal and Bergthora lay down on the bed and put the boy between them. Then they crossed themselves and the boy, and commended their souls to God. These were the last words they were heard to speak. The steward took the hide and spread it over them, and then left the house. Ketil of Mork seized his arm and dragged him clear, and questioned him closely about his father-in-law Njal; the steward told him everything that had happened.

Ketil said, "Great sorrow has been allotted us, that we should all share such terrible ill luck."

Skarp-Hedin had seen his father go to lie down and the preparations he had made.

"Father is going early to bed," he said. "And that is only natural, for he is an old man."

Skarp-Hedin and Kari and Grim snatched up the blazing brands as soon as they fell and hurled them at those outside. After a while the attackers threw spears at them, which they caught in flight and hurled back. Flosi told his men to stop—"for we shall always come off worse in every exchange of blows with them. You would be wiser to wait until the fire conquers them."

They did as he said.

Now the main beams fell down from the roof.

Skarp-Hedin said, "My father must be dead now, and not a groan or a cough has been heard from him."

They went over to the far end of the room. One end of the crossbeam had fallen there, and it was almost burned through in the middle. Kari said to Skarp-Hedin, "Use that beam to jump out, and I shall give you a hand and come right behind you. That way we can both escape, for the smoke is all drifting in this direction."

"You go first," said Skarp-Hedin, "and I shall follow you at once."

"That is not wise," said Kari, "for I can go out some other way if this does not succeed."

"No," said Skarp-Hedin, "you go out first, and I shall be right on your heels."

Kari said, "It is every man's instinct to try to save his own life, and I shall do so now. But this parting will mean that we shall never see each other again. Once I jump out of the flames, I shall not feel inclined to run back into the fire to you; and then each of us must go his own way."

"I shall laugh, brother-in-law, if you escape," said Skarp-Hedin, "for you will avenge us all."

Kari took hold of a blazing brand and ran up the sloping crossbeam; he hurled the brand down from the wall at those who were in his way outside, and they scattered. Kari's clothes and hair were on fire by now, as he threw himself down off the wall and dodged away in the thick of the smoke.

Someone said, "Was that a man jumping down from the roof?"

"Far from it," said someone else. "It was Skarp-Hedin throwing another brand at us."

After that, no one suspected anything.

Kari ran until he reached a small stream; he threw himself into it and extinguished his blazing clothes. From there he ran under cover of the smoke until he reached a hollow, where he rested. It has ever since been called Kari's Hollow.

Meanwhile, Skarp-Hedin had jumped on to the cross-beam directly behind Kari, but when he reached that part of the beam which was most severely burned, it broke beneath him. Skarp-Hedin managed to land on his feet and made a second attempt at once, by taking a run at the wall. But the roof-beam came down on him and he toppled back once more.

"It is clear now what is to be," said Skarp-Hedin, and made his way along the side wall.

Gunnar Lambason jumped up on to the wall and saw Skarp-Hedin. "Are you crying now, Skarp-Hedin?" he asked.

"No," said Skarp-Hedin, "but it is true that my eyes are smarting. Am I right in thinking that you are laughing?"

"I certainly am," said Gunnar, "and for the first time since you killed Thrain."

"Then here is something to remind you of it," said Skarp-Hedin.

He took from his purse the jaw-tooth he had hacked out of Thrain, and hurled it straight at Gunnar's eye; the eye was gouged from its socket on to the cheek and Gunnar toppled off the wall.

Skarp-Hedin went over to his brother Grim. They joined hands and stamped on the fire. But when they reached the middle of the room, Grim fell dead. Skarp-Hedin went to the gable-end of the house; then, with a great crash, the whole roof fell in. Skarp-Hedin was pinned between roof and gable, and could not move an inch.

Flosi and his men stayed by the blaze until broad daylight. Then a man came riding towards them. Flosi asked him his name, and he replied that he was Geirmund, a kinsman of the Sigfussons.

"You have taken drastic action here," said Geirmund.

"People will call it a drastic action, and an evil one too," said Flosi. "But nothing can be done about it now."

Geirmund asked, "How many people of note have perished here?"

Flosi said, "Among the dead here are Njal and Bergthora, their sons Helgi, Grim, and Skarp-Hedin, Kari Solmundarson and his son Thord, and Thord Freedman. We are not sure about those others who are less well known to us."

"You have listed amongst the dead a man who to my certain knowledge has escaped," said Geirmund, "for I talked to him only this morning."

"Who is that?" asked Flosi.

"Kari Solmundarson," said Geirmund. "My neighbour Bard and I met him with his hair burnt off and his clothes badly charred, and Bard lent him a horse."

"Had he any weapons with him?" asked Flosi.

"He was carrying the sword 'Life-Taker'," said Geirmund, "and one of its edges was blue and discoloured. We said that the metal must have softened, but Kari replied that he would soon harden it again in the blood of the Sigfussons and the other Burners."

"What did he tell you of Skarp-Hedin and Grim?" asked Flosi.

"He said that they were both alive when he left them," replied Geirmund, "but that they must be dead by now."

"What you have told us," said Flosi, "gives us little hope of being left in peace; for the man who has escaped is the one who comes nearest to being the equal of Gunnar of Hlidarend in everything. You had better realise, you Sigfussons and all the rest of our men, that this Burning will have such consequences that many of us will lie lifeless and others will forfeit all their wealth.

"I suspect that none of you Sigfussons will now dare to stay on at your farms, and I certainly cannot blame you for that. So I invite you all to stay with me in the east, and let us all stand or fall together." They thanked him.

Then Modolf Ketilsson said:

> *One pillar of Njal's house*
> *Was not destroyed in the fire*
> *That devoured all the others,*
> *The fire the bold Sigfussons lit.*
> *Now at last, Njal,*
> *Brave Hoskuld's death is avenged;*
> *Fire swept through the building,*
> *Bright flames blossomed in the house.*

"We must find other things to boast about than burning Njal to death," said Flosi, "for there is no achievement in that."

Flosi climbed on to the gable wall with Glum Hildisson and several others.

"Is Skarp-Hedin dead yet, do you think?" asked Glum.

The others said that he must have been dead for some time.

The fire still burned fitfully, flaring up and sinking again. Then they heard this verse being uttered somewhere down amongst the flames:

> *The woman will find it hard*
> *To stop the cloudburst of her tears*
> *At this outcome*
> *Of the warrior's last battle....*

Grani Gunnarsson said, "Was Skarp-Hedin alive or dead when he spoke that verse?"

"I shall not make any guesses about that," replied Flosi.

translated by MAGNUS MAGNUSSON and HERMANN PÁLSSON

Gestumblindi's Riddles

There was a great man in Reithgotaland called Gestumblindi, who was not on good terms with King Heithrek.

In the King's retinue there were seven men whose duty it was to decide all the disputes that arose in that country.

King Heithrek worshipped Frey, and he used to give Frey the biggest boar he could find. They regarded it as so sacred that in all important cases they used to take the oath on its bristles. It was the custom to sacrifice this boar at the "sacrifice of the herd". On Yule Eve the "boar of the herd" was led into the hall before the King. Then men laid their hands on his bristles and made solemn vows. King Heithrek himself made a vow that however deeply a man should have wronged him, if he came into his power he should not be deprived of the chance of receiving a trial by the King's judges; but he should get off scot free if he could propound riddles which the King could not answer. But when people tried to ask the King riddles, not one was put to him which he could not solve.

The King sent a message to Gestumblindi bidding him come to him on an appointed day; otherwise the King said that he would send to fetch him. Neither alternative pleased Gestumblindi, because he knew himself to be no match for the King in a contest of words; neither did he think he had much to hope from a trial before the judges, for his offences were many. On the other hand, he knew that if the King had to send men to bring him it would cost him his life. Then he proceeded to sacrifice to Odin and to ask his help, promising him great offerings.

One evening a stranger visited Gestumblindi, and said that he also was called Gestumblindi. They were so much alike that neither

Gestumblindi's Riddles

could be distinguished from the other. They exchanged clothes, and the landowner went into hiding, and everyone thought the stranger was the landowner himself.

This man went to vist the King and greeted him. The King looked at him and was silent.

Gestumblindi said: "I am come, Sire, to make my peace with you."

"Will you stand trial by the judges?" asked the King.

"Are there no other means of escape?" asked Gestumblindi.

"If," replied the King, "you can ask me riddles which I cannot answer, you shall go free."

"I am not likely to be able to do that," replied Gestumblindi; "yet the alternative is severe."

"Do you prefer the trial?" asked the King.

"Nay," said he, "I would rather ask riddles."

"That is quite in order," said the King, "and much depends on the issue. If you can get the better of me you shall marry my daughter and none shall gainsay you. Yet I don't imagine you are very clever, and it has never yet happened that I have been unable to solve the riddles that have been put to me."

Then a chair was placed for Gestumblindi, and the people began to listen eagerly to the words of wisdom.

Gestumblindi began as follows:

I would that I had that which I had yesterday. Guess O King, what that was:—Exhauster of men, retarder of words, yet originator of speech. King Heithrek, read me this riddle!

Heithrek replied:

Your riddle is a good one, Gestumblindi. I have guessed it.— Give him some ale. That is what confounds many people's reason. Some are made garrulous by it, but some become confused in their speech.

Gestumblindi said:

I went from home, I made my way from home, I looked upon a road of roads. A road was beneath me, a road above and a road on every side. King Heithrek, read me this riddle!

Heithrek replied:

Your riddle is a good one, Gestumblindi. I have guessed it. You went over a bridge, and the course of the river was beneath it, and birds were flying over your head and on either side of you; that was their road; you saw a salmon in the river, and that was his road.

Gestumblindi said:

What was the drink that I had yesterday? It was neither wine nor water, mead nor ale, nor any kind of food; and yet I went away with my thirst quenched. King Heithrek, read me this riddle!

Heithrek replied:

Your riddle is a good one, Gestumblindi. I have guessed it. You lay in the shade and cooled your lips in dew. But if you are the Gestumblindi I took you for, you are a more intelligent man than I expected; for I had heard that your conversation showed no brains, yet now you are setting to work cleverly.

Gestumblindi said:

I expect that I shall soon come to grief; yet I should like you to listen a while longer.

Then he continued:

Who is that clanging one who traverses hard paths which he has trod before? He kisses very rapidly, has two mouths and walks on gold alone. King Heithrek, read me this riddle!

Heithrek replied:

Your riddle is a good one, Gestumblindi. I have guessed it. That is the goldsmith's hammer, with which gold is forged.

Gestumblindi said:

What is that huge one that passes over the earth, swallowing lakes and pools? He fears the wind, but he fears not man, and carries on hostilities against the sun. King Heithrek, read me this riddle!

Heithrek replied:

Your riddle is a good one, Gestumblindi. I have guessed it. That

Gestumblindi's Riddles

is fog. One cannot see the sea because of it. Yet as soon as the wind blows, the fog lifts; but men can do nothing to it. Fog kills the sunshine. You have a cunning way of asking riddles and conundrums, whoever you are.

Gestumblindi said:

What is that huge one that controls many things and of which half faces towards Hell? It saves people's lives and grapples with the earth, if it has a trusty friend. King Heithrek, read me this riddle!

Heithrek replied:

Your riddle is a good one, Gestumblindi. I have guessed it. That is an anchor with its thick strong cable. It controls many a ship, and grips the earth with one of its flukes which is pointing towards Hell. It is a means of safety to many people. Greatly do I marvel at your readiness of speech and wisdom.

Gestumblindi said:

What is the marvel which I have seen outside Delling's doorway? —White fliers smiting the rock, and black fliers burying themselves in sand! King Heithrek, read me this riddle!

Heithrek replied:

Your riddle is a good one, Gestumblindi. I have guessed it. But now your riddles are growing trivial. That is hail and rain; for hail beats upon the street; whereas rain-drops fall into the sand and sink into the earth.

Gestumblindi said:

What is the marvel which I have seen outside Delling's doorway? I saw a black hog wallowing in mud, yet no bristles were standing up on his back. King Heithrek, read me this riddle!

Heithrek replied:

Your riddle is a good one, Gestumblindi. I have guessed it. That is a dung-beetle. But we have talked too long when dung-beetles come to exercise the wits of great men.

Gestumblindi said:

"It is best to put off misfortune"; and though there are some who overlook this truth, many will want to go on trying. I myself too see now that I shall have to look out for every possible way of escape. What is the marvel that I have seen outside Delling's doorway? This creature has ten tongues, twenty eyes, forty feet, and walks with difficulty. King Heithrek, read me this riddle!

Heithrek replied:

Your riddle is a good one, Gestumblindi. I have guessed it. That was a sow with nine little pigs.

Then the King had the sow killed and they found they had killed with her nine little pigs, as Gestumblindi had said.
Then the King said:

I am beginning to suspect that I have to deal with a cleverer man than myself in this business; but I don't know who you can be.

Gestumblindi said:

I am such as you can see; and I am very anxious to save my life and be quit of this task.

You must go on asking riddles, replied the King, till you have exhausted your stock, or else till I fail to solve them.

Gestumblindi said:

What is the marvel which I have seen outside Delling's doorway? It flies high, with a whistling sound like the whirring of an eagle. Hard it is to clutch, O King. King Heithrek, read me this riddle!

Heithrek replied:

Your riddle is a good one, Gestumblindi. I have guessed it. That is an arrow, said the King.

Gestumblindi said:

What is the marvel which I have seen outside Delling's doorway? It has eight feet and four eyes, and carries its knees higher than its body. King Heithrek, read me this riddle!

Heithrek replied:

I notice firstly that you have a long hood; and secondly that you look downwards more than most people, since you observe every creature of the earth.—That is a spider.

Gestumblindi said:

What is the marvel which I have seen outside Delling's doorway?

Gestumblindi's Riddles

It shines upon men in every land; and yet wolves are always struggling for it. King Heithrek, read me this riddle!

Heithrek replied:

Your riddle is a good one, Gestumblindi. I have guessed it. It is the sun. It gives light to every land and shines down on all men. But the wolves are called Skoll and Hati. Those are the wolves who accompany the sun, one in front and one behind.

Gestumblindi said:

Who are the girls who fight without weapons around their lord? The dark red ones always protect him, and the fair ones seek to destroy him. King Heithrek, read me this riddle!

Heithrek replied:

Your riddle is a good one, Gestumblindi. I have guessed it. That is a game of chess. The pieces smite one another without weapons around the king, and the red assist him.

Gestumblindi said:

Who are the merry-maids who glide over the land for the father's pleasure? They bear a white shield in winter and a black one in summer. King Heithrek, read me this riddle!

Heithrek replied:

Your riddle is a good one, Gestumblindi. I have guessed it. Those are ptarmigan.

Gestumblindi said:

Who are the damsels who go sorrowing for their father's pleasure? These white-hooded ladies have shining hair, and are very wide awake in a gale. King Heithrek, read me this riddle!

Heithrek replied:

Your riddle is a good one, Gestumblindi. I have guessed it. Those are the billows, which are called Ægir's maidens.

Gestumblindi said:

Who are the brides who go about the reefs and trail along the firths? These white-hooded ladies have a hard bed and do not play much when the weather is calm. King Heithrek, read me this riddle.

Heithrek replied:

Your riddle is a good one, Gestumblindi. I have guessed it. Those again are Ægir's maidens; but your pleading has now become so weak that you will have to stand trial by the judges.

Gestumblindi said:

I am loath to do so; and yet I fear that it will very soon come to that. I saw a barrow-dweller pass by, a corpse sitting on a corpse, the blind riding on the blind towards the ocean-path. Lifeless was the steed. King Heithrek, read me this riddle!

Heithrek replied:

Your riddle is a good one, Gestumblindi. I have guessed it. It is that you came to a river; and an ice-floe was floating along the stream, and on it a dead horse way lying, and on the horse was a dead snake; and thus the blind was carrying the blind when they were all three together.

Gestumblindi said:

What is that beast which protects the Danes? Its back is bloody but it shields men, encounters spears and saves men's lives. Man fits his hand to its body. King Heithrek, read me this riddle!

Heithrek replied:

Your riddle is a good one, Gestumblindi. I have guessed it. That is a shield. It protects many people and often has a bloody back.

Gestumblindi said:

Four walking, four hanging, two pointing the way, two warding off the dogs, one, generally dirty, dangling behind! King Heithrek, read me this riddle!

Heithrek replied:

Your riddle is a good one, Gestumblindi. I have guessed it. That is a cow. She has four feet and four udders, two horns and two eyes, and the tail dangles behind.

Gestumblindi said:

Who is that solitary one who sleeps in the grey ash, and is made from stone only? This greedy one has neither father nor mother. There will he spend his life. King Heithrek, read me this riddle.

Heithrek replied:

Your riddle is a good one, Gestumblindi. I have guessed it. That is a spark struck by a flint and hidden in the hearth.

Gestumblindi said:

In summer time at sunset I saw the King's body-guard awake and very joyful. The nobles were drinking their ale in silence, but the ale-butts stood screaming. King Heithrek, read me this riddle!

Heithrek replied:

Your riddle is a good one, Gestumblindi. I have guessed it. That is a sow with her litter. When the little pigs are feeding, she squeals and they are silent.—But I can't imagine who you are who can compose such things so deftly out of such unpromising materials!

The King then silently made a sign that the door of the hall was to be closed.

Gestumblindi said:

I saw maidens like dust. Rocks were their beds. They were black and swarthy in the sunshine, but the darker it grew, the fairer they appeared. King Heithrek, read me this riddle!

Heithrek replied:

Your riddle is a good one, Gestumblindi. I have guessed it. They are pale embers on the hearth.

Gestumblindi said:

Who are those two who have ten feet, three eyes and one tail? King Heithrek, read me this riddle!

Heithrek replied:

You are hard up when you have to turn back to things of long ago to bring forward against me. That is Odin riding his horse Sleipnir. It had eight feet and Odin two, and they had three eyes —Sleipnir two and Odin one.

Gestumblindi said:

Tell me lastly, Heithrek, if you are wiser than any other prince, what did Odin whisper in Balder's ear, before he was placed upon the pyre?

The King replied:

I am sure it was something scandalous and cowardly and thoroughly contemptible. You are the only person who knows the words which you spoke, you evil and wretched creature.

Then the King drew Tyrfing, and struck at Gestumblindi; but he changed himself into a falcon and flew out through the window of the hall. And the sword struck the tail of the falcon; and that is why it has had a short tail ever since, according to heathen superstition. But Odin had now become wroth with the King for striking at him; and that night he was slain.

translated by NORA KERSHAW

Thorstein Staff-Struck

There was a man living in Sunnudal by the name of Thorarin, an old man of ailing sight. He had been a stark red viking in his youth, and was no easy person to deal with now that he was old. He had an only son, whose name was Thorstein, a big man, strong and calm tempered, who worked so hard on his father's farm that the labour of three other men would not have stood them in better stead. Thorarin was on the poor side rather, yet he owned a fine assortment of weapons. They owned stud-horses too, this father and son, and selling horses was their main source of wealth, for never a one of them fell short in heart or performance.

There was a man called Thord, a housecarle of Bjarni of Hof, who had charge of Bjarni's riding-horses, for he had the name of one who really knew horses. Thord was a very overbearing sort of person; he also made many aware that he was a great man's servant, yet he was none the better man for that, and became no better liked. There were other men too staying at Bjarni's, one named Thorhall and the other Thorvald, great mouthers-over of everything they heard in the district. Thorstein and Thord arranged a horse-fight for the young stallions, and when they drove them at one another Thord's horse showed the less heart for biting. Once he saw his horse getting the worst of it, Thord struck Thorstein's horse a great blow over the nose, but Thorstein saw this and struck Thord's horse a far greater blow in return, whereupon Thord's horse took to its heels, and everyone raised a loud hullabaloo of derision. With that Thord struck at Thorstein with his horse-staff and caught him on the eyebrow, so that the skin hung down over the eye. Thorstein tore a strip from his shirt and tied up his forehead, acting as though nothing in particular had happened. He asked them to keep this from his father, and there the matter ended for the time being. But Thorvald and Thorhall made it a subject of ill-natured jest and nicknamed him Thorstein Staff-struck.

That winter, a short while before Yule, the women rose for their work at Sunnudal. At the same time Thorstein rose; he carried in hay, and afterwards lay down on a bench. The next thing, in came old Thorarin his father, and asked who was lying there. Thorstein said it was he.

"Why are you afoot so early, son?" asked old Thorarin.

"There are few, I fancy, to leave any of the work to that I am responsible for here," replied Thorstein.

"There is nothing wrong with your head-bones, son?" asked old Thorarin.

"Not that I know of," said Thorstein.

"Have you nothing to tell me, son, of the horse-fighting that was held last summer? Were you not knocked dizzy as a dog there, kinsman?"

"I saw no gain in honour," Thorstein told him, "by reckoning it a blow rather than an accident."

"I would never have thought," said Thorarin, "that I could have a coward for a son."

"Speak only those words now, father," Thorstein advised him, "which you will not consider overmuch in the days to come."

"I will not speak about it as much as my heart would have me," Thorarin agreed.

At these words Thorstein rose to his feet, took his weapons, and left the house. He walked on till he came to the stables where Thord looked after Bjarni's horses, and where he happened then to be. He met Thord face to face and had this to say to him: "I want to know, friend Thord, whether it was by accident that I got a blow from you last summer at the horse-fight, or did it come about intentionally—in which case are you willing to pay reparation for it?"

"If you have two cheeks," retorted Thord, "then stick your tongue into each in turn, and, if you like, call it accident in one and intention in the other. And that is all the reparation you are going to get from me."

"Then rest assured," said Thorstein, "it may well be I shall not come claiming payment a second time."

Then Thorstein ran at Thord and dealt him his death-blow, after which he walked to the house at Hof and met a woman outside and said to her, "Tell Bjarni that an ox has gored his groom Thord, and that he will be waiting for him there till he comes, alongside the stables."

"Get off home, man," said she. "I will report this when I think fit."

So now Thorstein went off home and the woman went about her work. Bjarni rose during the morning, and when he was seated to his food he asked where was Thord, and men answered that he must have gone off to the horses. "All the same," said Bjarni, "I think he would have come home by now if he was all right." Then the woman whom Thorstein had met started on her piece. "True it is what they often say of us women, how there is little sense to draw on where we she-creatures are concerned. Thorstein Staff-struck came here only this morning to report that an ox had so gored Thord that he was past helping himself; but I lacked the heart to wake you at the time, and it has slipped my mind ever since."

Bjarni got up from table. He went to the stables where he found Thord dead, and later he was buried. Bjarni now set on foot a lawsuit and had Thorstein outlawed for the killing. But Thorstein went on living at home in Sunnudal and working for his father, and Bjarni let things lie just the same.

That autumn there were men sitting by the singeing-fires at Hof, while Bjarni lay out of doors by the kitchen wall and listened from there to their conversation. And now the brothers Thorhall and Thorvald began to hold forth. "We did not expect when first we came to live with Killer-Bjarni that we would be singeing lambs' heads here, while Thorstein, his forest outlaw, should singe the heads of wethers. It would be no bad thing to have been more sparing of his kinsmen in Bodvarsdal,* and his outlaw not sit as high

---

* There had been a bitter feud between the kinsmen Bjarni and Thorkel, who was supported by Thorstein's father, Thorarin. Although it was inconclusive, four men were killed on either side; the result of this was that Thorstein—filling the gap—became a man of greater influence at Sunnudal than would otherwise have been the case. The story of this feud comprises part of the saga of *The Vapnfjord Men*.

as he now in Sunnudal. But, 'E'en doers are done for once wounds befall them', and we have no idea when he proposes to wipe this stain from his honour."

Some man or other answered: "Such words are better swallowed than spoken, and it sounds as though trolls must have plucked at your tongues. For our part, we believe that he has no mind to take the food out of the mouth of Thorstein's blind father or those other poor creatures who live at Sunnudal. And I shall be very surprised if you are singeing lambs' heads here much oftener, or gloating over what happened in Bodvarsdal."

Men now went to their meal and afterwards to sleep, and Bjarni gave no indication of knowing what had been talked about. In the morning he routed out Thorhall and Thorvald, bidding them ride to Sunnudal and bring him Thorstein's head, divorced from his trunk, by breakfast-time, "For you appear to me the likeliest to remove this stain from my honour, considering I have not the courage for it myself." They now felt they had opened their mouths too wide for sure, but made off even so until they came to Sunnudal. Thorstein was standing in the doorway, whetting a short-sword, and when they came up he asked them what they were up to.

They said they had the job of looking for stray horses.

Then they had only a short way to look, Thorstein told them—"Here they are, by the home-fence."

"It is not certain," they said, "that we shall find them, unless you show us the way more clearly."

So Thorstein came outside, and when they had come down into the home-field Thorvald hoisted up his axe and ran at him, but Thorstein gave him such a shove with his arm that he fell headlong forward, and Thorstein drove the short-sword through him. Then Thorhall would have attacked him, but he too went the same road as Thorvald. Thorstein then bound them both on horseback, fixed the reins on the horses' necks, got the whole outfit headed in the right direction, and the horses made their way home to Hof.

There were housecarles out of doors at Hof, and they went inside and told Bjarni that Thorvald and his brother had returned home, adding that they had not run their errand to no purpose. Bjarni went outside and saw how things had turned out. In the main he

Thorstein Staff-Struck

had no comment to make, but had them buried, and everything now stayed quiet till Yule was past.

Then one evening when she and Bjarni had gone to bed, his wife Rannveig began to hold forth. "What do you imagine is now the most talked-about thing in the district?" she asked.

"I have no idea," said Bjarni. "There are plenty whose chatter strikes me as not worth bothering about."

"Well, the most frequent subject of gossip is this," she told him. "Men just cannot imagine what Thorstein Staff-struck must do for you to decide you need take vengeance on him. He has now killed three of your housecarles, and it seems to your followers that there is no hope of support where you are concerned if this is left unavenged. You do all the wrong things and leave the right undone."

"It comes to this, here again," replied Bjarni, "just as the proverb has it: 'None takes warning from his fellow's warming.' So I will see that you get what you are asking for. And yet Thorstein has killed few without good reason."

They gave over talking and slept the night through. In the morning Rannveig woke up as Bjarni was taking down his shield. She asked him what he was proposing to do.

"Thorstein and I," he replied, "must now settle a point of honour in Sunnudal."

"How many men are you taking with you?" she asked.

"I shall not lead an army against him," said Bjarni. "I am going alone."

"Don't do it," she begged. "Don't expose yourself all alone to the weapons of that fiend!"

"Aye," said Bjarni, "and are you now not carrying on like a true woman, crying one minute over the very thing you provoked the minute before? For a long while now I have suffered only too often the jeers both of you and of others, and it is useless to try and stop me now that I am settled to go."

Bjarni now made his way to Sunnudal, where Thorstein was standing in the doorway. They exchanged a few words.

"You must come and fight with me today, Thorstein," said Bjarni, "in single combat on this same mound which stands here in the home-field."

"It is quite hopeless for me to fight with you," maintained Thorstein, "but I will get abroad by the first ship that sails, for I know the manliness of your nature, how you will get all the work I see to done for my father, if I must be off and leave him."

"It is useless to cry off," warned Bjarni.

"Then let me go in and see my father first," said Thorstein.

"Do that," said Bjarni.

Thorstein went into the house and told his father that Bjarni had come there and challenged him to single combat. Old Thorarin answered him thus: "Any one, if he contends with a man higher in rank than himself, and lives in the same district with him, and does him some dishonour too, can expect to find that he will not wear out many shirts. Nor can I make outcry for you, for you seem to me richly to have deserved it. Now take your weapons and defend yourself like a man, for I have known the day when I would not have bowed my back to such as Bjarni, great champion though he is. And I would rather lose you than have a coward for a son."

Out again went Thorstein, and he and Bjarni went off to the mound, where they began fighting in deadly earnest, and cut away most of each other's shield. And when they had been fighting for a very long time, Bjarni said to Thorstein, "Now I grow thirsty, for I am less used to the work than you."

"Then go to the brook," said Thorstein, "and drink."

Bjarni did so, laying his sword down beside him. Thorstein picked it up, looked at it, and said: "You will not have had this sword in Bodvarsdal."

Bjarni made no reply. They went back up on to the mound and fought for a while again, and Bjarni found his opponent skilled with his weapons and altogether tougher than he had expected. "A lot goes wrong for me today," he complained. "Now my shoe-string is loose."

"Tie it up then," said Thorstein.

Bjarni bent down, but Thorstein went indoors to fetch out two shields and a sword; he went back to Bjarni on the mound, saying to him, "Here is a shield and sword which my father sends you. The sword will not prove blunter in the stroke than the one you have owned so far. Besides, I have no heart to stand defenceless under your blows any longer. Indeed, I would gladly give over this game, for I fear that your good fortune will show better results than my ill luck. And if I could have the say here—well, in the last resort, every man loves his life."

"It is useless to beg off," said Bjarni. "We must fight on."

"I'll not be the one to strike first," said Thorstein.

Then Bjarni cut away Thorstein's entire shield, whereupon Thorstein cut away Bjarni's too.

"A great stroke that!" cried Bjarni.

"You struck one no less," replied Thorstein.

"That same weapon you have had all day so far is biting better for you now," said Bjarni.

"I would spare myself disaster, if I might," Thorstein told him. "For I fight with you in fear and trembling. I should like to commit the whole thing to your verdict."

It was now Bjarni's turn to strike, and they were both quite defenceless. Said Bjarni: "It would be a bad bargain to choose a foul deed in place of good hap. I shall count myself fully repaid for my three housecarles by you alone, if only you will be true to me."

"I have had opportunity enough today to betray you, if my weak fortune was to prove stronger than your good luck. No, I will not betray you."

"I see," said Bjarni, "that you are past question a man. Will you now give me leave to go inside to your father, to tell him just what I like?"

"Go how you will, for all I care," warned Thorstein. "But watch your step!"

Bjarni then went inside to the bed-closet where old Thorarin was lying. Thorarin asked who came there, and Bjarni told him it was he.

"What news have you to tell me, Bjarni mine?"

"The slaying of Thorstein your son."

"Did he show fight?" asked Thorarin.

"In my opinion, no man was ever brisker in battle than your son Thorstein."

"It is not surprising then," said the old man, "that you were hard to handle in Bodvarsdal, if you have now got the better of my son."

"I want to invite you to Hof," said Bjarni, "where you shall sit in the second high-seat for as long as you live, and I will be to you in place of a son."

"My state," said the old man, "is like any other man's whose say goes for nothing—and a fool dotes on a promise. And such are the promises of you chieftains, when you wish to comfort a man after any such mishap, that nothing is too good for us for a month, but then our worth is fixed at that of other paupers, and with that our sorrows drop but slowly out of mind. And yet anyone who shakes hands on a deal with a man like you can rest well satisfied with his lot, whatever the verdict given. So I will take your offer after all. Now come over here to where I am in bed—you will have to come close, for the old fellow is all a-tremble in his legs for age and sickness, and never believe that my son's death has not pierced my old heart!"

Bjarni now went up to the bed and took old Thorarin by the hand, and found him fumbling for a big knife which he wanted to stick into Bjarni. "Why, you old stinkard!" cried Bjarni. "Any settlement between us now must be hitched to your deserts. Your son Thorstein is alive and shall come home with me to Hof, but you shall be provided with thralls to do your work, and shall lack for nothing for the rest of your days."

Thorstein went home with Bjarni to Hof and followed him till his death-day, and was reckoned pretty well any man's match for valour and prowess. Bjarni fully maintained his reputation, and was the more beloved and magnanimous the older he grew. He was the most undaunted of men, and became a firm believer in Christ in the last years of his life. He went abroad and made a pilgrimage south, and on that journey he died. He rests in a town called Sutri, a short way this side of Rome. Bjarni was a man blest in his offspring. His son was Skegg-Broddi, a man widely known to story and in his day unrivalled.

And that is the end of what there is to tell about Thorstein Staff-struck.

translated by GWYN JONES

The Hauntings at Frodriver

In the year 1000, the Christian religion was introduced into Iceland by her apostles Gizur the White, and Hialto. The same year is assigned as the date of a very curious legend. A ship from Iceland chanced to winter in a haven near Helgafels. Among the passengers was a woman named Thorgunna, a native of the Hebrides, who was reported by the sailors to possess garments and household furniture of a fashion far surpassing those used in Iceland. Thurida, sister of the pontiff Snorro, and wife of Thorodd, a woman of a vain and covetous disposition, attracted by these reports, made a visit to the stranger, but could not prevail upon her to display her treasures. Persisting, however, in her enquiries, she pressed Thorgunna to take up her abode at the house of Thorodd. The Hebridean reluctantly assented, but added, that as she could labour at every usual kind of domestic industry, she trusted in that manner to discharge the obligation she might lie under to the family, without giving any part of her property, in recompense of her lodging. As Thurida continued to urge her request, Thorgunna accompanied her to Froda, the house of Thorodd, where the seamen deposited a huge chest and cabinet, containing the property of her new guest, which Thurida viewed with curious and covetous eyes. So soon as they had pointed out to Thorgunna the place assigned for her bed, she opened the chest, and took forth such an embroidered bed coverlid, and such a splendid and complete set of tapestry hangings, and bed furniture of English linen, interwoven with silk, as had never been seen in Iceland. "Sell to me," said the covetous matron, "this fair bed furniture."—"Believe me," answered Thorgunna, "I will not lie upon straw in order to feed thy pomp and vanity;" an

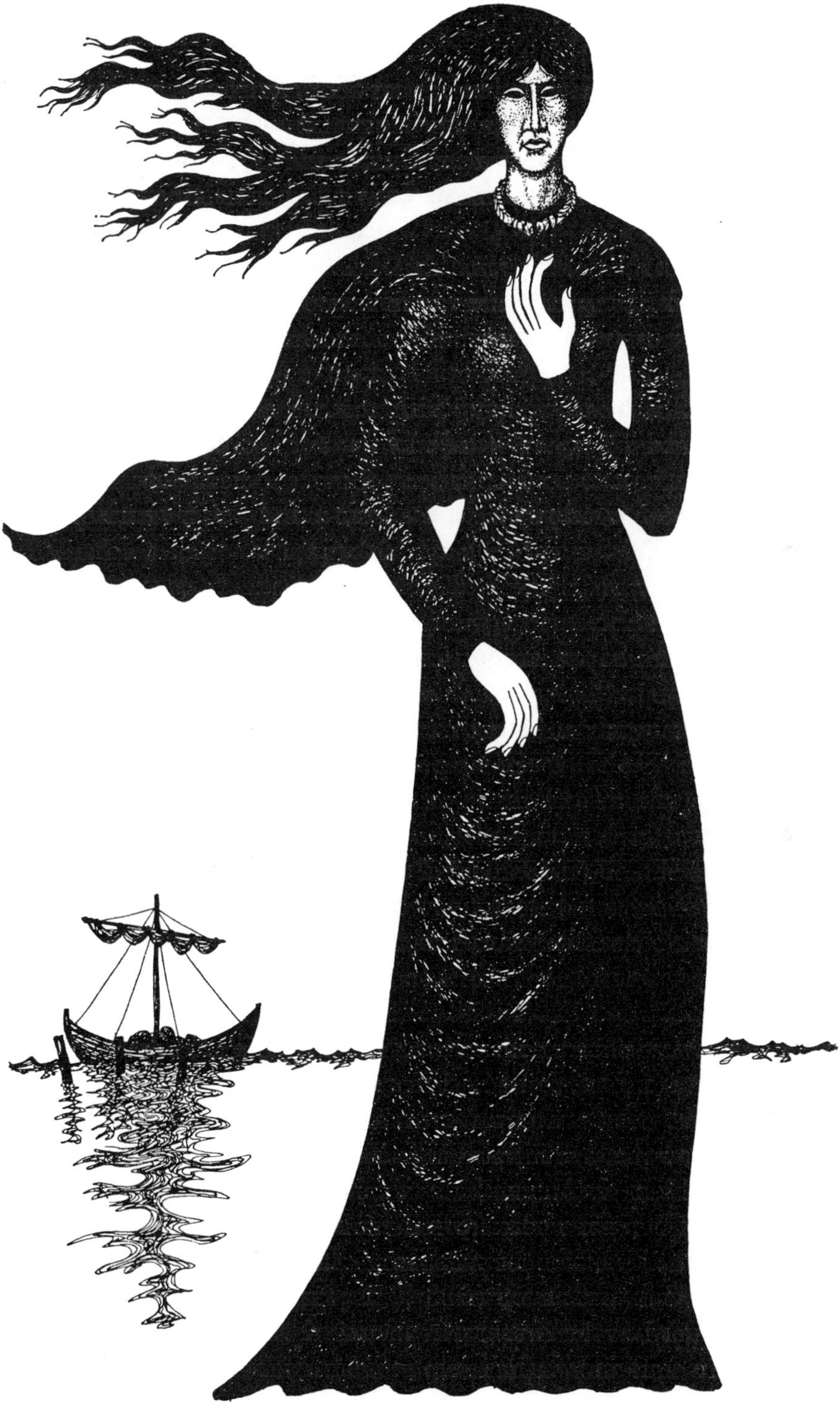

answer which so greatly displeased Thurida, that she never again repeated her request. Thorgunna, to whose character subsequent events added something of a mystical solemnity, is described as being a woman of a tall and stately appearance, of a dark complexion, and having a profusion of black hair. She was advanced in age; assiduous in the labours of the field and of the loom; a faithful attendant upon divine worship; grave, silent, and solemn in domestic society. She had little intercourse with the household of Thorodd, and shewed particular dislike to two of its inmates. These were Thorer, who, having lost a leg in the skirmish between Thorbiorn and Thorarin the Black, was called Thorer-Widlegr (wooden-leg), from the substitute he had adopted; and his wife, Thorgrima, called Galldrakinna (wicked sorceress) from her supposed skill in enchantments. Kiartan, the son of Thurida, a boy of excellent promise, was the only person of the household to whom Thorgunna shewed much affection; and she was much vexed at times when the childish petulance of the boy made an indifferent return to her kindness.

After this mysterious stranger had dwelt at Froda for some time, and while she was labouring in the hay-field with other members of the family, a sudden cloud from the northern mountain led Thorodd to anticipate a heavy shower. He instantly commanded the hay-workers to pile up in ricks the quantity which each had been engaged in turning to the wind. It was afterwards remembered that Thorgunna did not pile up her portion, but left it spread on the field. The cloud approached with great celerity, and sunk so heavily around the farm, that it was scarce possible to see beyond the limits of the field. A heavy shower next descended, and so soon as the clouds broke away, and the sun shone forth, it was observed that it had rained blood. That which fell upon the ricks of the other labourers soon dried up, but what Thorgunna had wrought upon remained wet with gore. The unfortunate Hebridean, appalled at the omen, betook herself to her bed, and was seized with a mortal illness. On the approach of death she summoned Thorodd, her landlord, and entrusted to him the disposition of her property and effects. "Let my body," said she, "be transported to Skalholt, for my mind presages that in that place shall be founded the most distinguished church in this island. Let my golden ring be given to the priests who shall celebrate my obsequies, and do thou indemnify thyself for the funeral charges out of my remaining effects. To thy wife I bequeath my purple mantle, in order that, by this sacrifice to her avarice, I may secure the right of disposing of the rest of my effects at my own pleasure. But for my bed, with its covering, hangings, and furniture, I entreat they may be all consigned to the flames. I do not desire this, because I envy any one the possession of these things after my death, but because I wish those evils to be avoided which I plainly foresee will happen if my will be altered in the slightest particular." Thorodd promised faithfully to execute this extraordinary testament in the most pointed manner. Accordingly, so soon as Thorgunna was dead, her faithful executor prepared a pile for burning her splendid bed. Thurida entered, and learned with anger and astonishment the purpose of these preparations. To the remonstrances of her husband she answered, that the menaces of future danger were only caused by Thorgunna's selfish envy, who did not wish any one should enjoy her treasures after the decease. Then, finding Thorodd inaccessible to argument, she had recourse to caresses and blandishments, and at length extorted permission to separate, from the rest of the bed-furniture, the tapestried curtains and coverlid; the rest was consigned to the flames, in obedience to the will of the testator. The body of Thorgunna being wrapt in new linen, and placed in a coffin, was next to be transported through the precipices and morasses of Iceland to the distant district she had assigned for her place of sepulture. A remarkable incident occurred on the way. The transporters of the body arrived at evening late, weary, and drenched with rain, in a house called Nether-Ness, where the niggard hospitality of the proprietor only afforded them house-room, without any supply of food or fuel. But so soon as they entered, an unwonted noise was heard in the kitchen of the mansion, and the figure of a woman, soon recognised to be the deceased Thorgunna, was seen busily employed in preparing victuals. Their inhospitable landlord being made acquainted with this frightful circumstance, readily agreed to supply every refreshment which was necessary, on which the vision instantly disappeared. The apparition having become public, they had no reason to ask twice for hospitality, as they proceeded on their journey, and arrived safely at Skalholt, where Thorgunna, with all due ceremonies of religion, was deposited quietly in the grave. But the consequences of the breach of her testament were felt severely at Froda.

The author, for the better understanding of the prodigies which happened, describes the manner of living at Froda; a simple and patriarchal structure, built according to the fashion used by the wealthy among the Icelanders. The apartment was very large, and a part boarded off contained the beds of the family. On either side was a sort of store-room, one of which contained meal, the other dried fish. Every evening large fires were lighted in this apartment, for dressing the victuals; and the domestics of the family usually sat around them for a considerable time, until supper was prepared. On the night when the conductors of Thorgunna's funeral returned to Froda, there appeared, visible to all who were present, a meteor, or spectral appearance, resembling a half-moon, which glided around the boarded walls of the mansion in an opposite direction to the course of the sun, and continued to perform its revolutions until the domestics retired to rest. This apparition was renewed every night during a whole week, and was pronounced by Thorer with the wooden leg, to presage pestilence or mortality. Shortly after a herdsman shewed signs of mental alienation, and gave various indications of having sustained the persecution of evil demons. This man was found dead in his bed one morning, and then commenced a scene of ghost-seeing unheard of in the annals of superstition. The first victim was Thorer, who had presaged the calamity. Going out of doors one evening, he was grappled by the spectre of the deceased shepherd as he attempted to re-enter the house. His wooden leg stood him in poor stead in such an encounter; he was hurled to the earth, and so fearfully beaten, that he died in consequence of the bruises. Thorer was no sooner dead, than his ghost associated itself to that of the herdsman and joined him in pursuing and assaulting the inhabitants of Froda. Meantime an infectious disorder spread fast among them, and several of the bondsmen died one after the other. Strange portents were seen within doors, the meal was displaced and mingled, and the dried fish flung about in a most alarming manner, without any visible agent. At length, while the servants were forming their evening circle round the fire, a spectre, resembling the head of a seal-fish, was seen to emerge out of the pavement of the room, bending its round black eyes full on the tapestried bed-curtains of Thorgunna. Some of the domestics ventured to strike at this figure, but, far from giving way, it rather erected itself further from the floor, until Kiartan, who seemed to have a natural predominance over these supernatural prodigies, seizing a huge forge-hammer, struck the seal repeatedly on the head, and compelled it to disappear, forcing it down into the floor, as if he had driven a stake into the earth. This prodigy was found to intimate a new calamity. Thorodd, the master of the family, had some time before set forth on a voyage to bring home a cargo of dried fish; but, in crossing the river Enna, the skiff was lost, and he perished with the servants who attended him. A solemn funeral feast was held at Froda, in memory of the deceased, when, to the astonishment of the guests, the apparition of Thorodd and his followers seemed to enter the apartment dropping with water. Yet this vision excited less horror than might have been expected; for the Icelanders, though nominally Christians, retained, among other pagan superstitions, a belief that the spectres of such drowned persons as had been favourably received by the goddess Ran, were wont to shew themselves at their funeral feast. They saw, therefore, with some composure, Thorodd, and his dripping attendants, plant themselves by the fire, from which all mortal guests retreated to make room for them. It was supposed this apparition would not be renewed after the conclusion of the festival. But so far were their hopes disappointed, that, so soon as the mourning guests had departed, the fires being lighted, Thorodd and his comrades marched in on one side, drenched as before with water; on the other entered Thorer, heading all those who had died in the pestilence, and who appeared covered with dust. Both parties seized the seats by the fire, while the half-frozen and terrified domestics spent the night without either light or warmth. The same phenomenon took place the next night, though the fires had been lighted in a separate house, and at length Kiartan was obliged to compound matters with the spectres by kindling a large fire for them in the principal apartment, and one for the family and domestics in a separate hut. This prodigy continued during the whole feast of Jol; other portents also happened to appal this devoted family, the contagious disease again broke forth, and when any one fell a sacrifice to it, his spectre was sure to join the troop of persecutors, who had now almost full possession of the mansion of Froda. Thorgrima Galldrakinna, wife of Thorer, was one of these victims, and, in short, of thirty servants belonging to the household, eighteen died, and five fled for fear of the apparitions, so that only seven remained in the service of Kiartan.

Kiartan had now recourse to the advice of his maternal uncle Snorro, in consequence of whose counsel, what will perhaps appear surprising to the reader, judicial measures were instituted against the spectres. A Christian priest was, however, associated with Thordo Kausa, son of Snorro, and with Kiartan, to superintend and sanctify the proceedings. The inhabitants were regularly summoned to attend upon the inquest, as in a cause between man and man, and the assembly was constituted before the gate of the mansion, just as the spectres had assumed their wonted station by the fire. Kiartan boldly ventured to approach them, and snatching a brand from the fire, he commanded the tapestry belonging to Thorgunna to be carried out of doors, set fire to it, and reduced it to ashes with all the other ornaments of her bed, which had been so inconsiderately preserved at the request of Thurida. A tribunal being then constituted with the usual legal solemnities, a charge was preferred by Kiartan against Thorer with the wooden leg, by Thordo Kausa against Thorodd, and by others chosen as accusers against the individual spectres present, accusing them of molesting the mansion, and introducing death and disease among its inhabitants. All the solemn rites of judicial procedure were observed on this singular occasion; evidence was adduced, charges given, and the cause formally decided. It does not appear that the ghosts put themselves on their defence, so that sentence of ejectment was pronounced against them individually in due and legal form. When Thorer heard the judgment, he arose, and saying, "I have sate while it was lawful for me to do so," left the apartment by the door opposite to that at which the judicial assembly were constituted.

The Hauntings at Frodriver

Each of the spectres, as they heard their individual sentence, left the place, saying something which indicated their unwillingness to depart, until Thorodd himself was solemnly appointed to depart. "We have here no longer," said he, "a peaceful dwelling, therefore will we remove." Kiartan then entered the hall with his followers, and the priest with holy water, and celebration of a solemn mass, completed the conquest over the goblins, which had been commenced by the power and authority of the Icelandic law.

translated by SIR WALTER SCOTT

The Expedition of Thorfin Karlsefni

Late in the tenth century, the Norwegian Eric the Red, banished first from Norway and then from Iceland for lawless killings, discovered Greenland and founded a colony at Brattahlid. He had in his care there a woman called Gudrid whom Eric's son, Leif, had rescued from shipwreck and who had been twice widowed. Leif sailed on west from Greenland and set foot on land (first sighted fifteen years before by Bjarni Herjolfsson) that he called Vinland or "Wineland" because of the grapes growing there. This discovery quickly led to further explorations. Thorfin Karlsefni, hero of this extract from the thirteenth-century Eric the Red's Saga *was Leif Ericsson's brother-in-law; he was the first man to try to colonise Vinland—an ambition reluctantly called off when it became clear that the "savages" (in fact, American Indians) would give them no peace.*

The location of the places mentioned in the saga has been much argued: Helluland is probably south Baffin Island and Markland south-eastern Labrador; Vinland itself probably extended from north Newfoundland, perhaps as far south as New England. A Norse settlement dating from c. 1000 has been unearthed in Newfoundland.

Ireland, mentioned at the end of the extract, was part of the kingdom of Norway at this time; and a 'teredo' is a ship-worm, a mollusc that bores into and destroys submerged timbers.

Thord Horsehead had a son called Thorfin Karlsefni, who lived in the north at Reynisness in Skagafjord, as it now is called. Besides being of a good stock Karlsefni was a wealthy man. His mother's name was Thorunn. He was in the cruising trade, and had a good reputation as a sailor.

One summer Karlsefni made ready his ship for a voyage to Greenland. Snorri Thorbrandson from Alptafjord joined him, and they had forty men with them. A man named Bjarni Grimolfson from Breidafjord, and another called Thorhall Gamlison from Eastfjord both made ready their ship the same summer as Karlsefni to go to Greenland; they had forty men on board. They put to sea with these two ships, when they were ready. We are not told how long they were at sea; suffice it to say that both these ships arrived at Ericsfjord in the autumn. Eric and other settlers rode to the ships, where they began to trade freely: the skippers told Gudrid to help herself from their wares, but Eric was not behindhand in generosity, for he invited the crews of both ships to his home at Brattahlid for the winter. The traders accepted this offer and went with Eric. Thereupon their stuff was removed to the house at Brattahlid, where there was no lack of good large out-buildings in which to store their goods, and the merchants had a good time with Eric during the winter.

But as it drew towards Christmas Eric began to be less cheerful than usual. One day Karlsefni came to speak to Eric, and said: "Is anything the matter, Eric? It seems to me that you are rather more silent than you used to be; you are treating us with the greatest generosity, and we owe it to you to repay you so far as lies in our power, so tell us what is troubling you." "You have been good and courteous guests," replied Eric, "my mind is not troubled by any lack of response on your part, it is rather that I am afraid it will be said when you go elsewhere that you never passed a worse Christmas than when you stayed with Eric the Red at Brattahlid in Greenland." "That shall not be so," replied Karlsefni, "we have on our ships malt and meal and corn, and you are welcome to take of it what you will, and make as fine a feast as your ideas of hospitality suggest." Eric accepted this offer, and a Christmas feast was prepared, which was so splendid that people thought they had hardly ever seen so magnificent a feast in a poor country.

And after Christmas Karlsefni asked Eric for Gudrid's hand, since it appeared to him to be a matter under Eric's control, and moreover he thought her a beautiful and accomplished woman. Eric answered, saying that he would certainly entertain his suit, but that she was a good match; that it was likely that she would be fulfilling her destiny if she was married to him, and that he had heard good of Karlsefni. So then the proposal was conveyed to her, and she left it to Eric to decide for her. And now it was not long before this proposal was accepted, and the festivities began again, and their wedding was celebrated. There was a very merry time at Brattahlid in the winter with much playing at draughts and story-telling, and a great deal to make their stay pleasant.

At this time there was much discussion at Brattahlid during the winter about a search for Wineland the Good, and it was said that it would be a profitable country to visit; Karlsefni and Snorri resolved to search for Wineland, and the project was much talked about, so it came about that Karlsefni and Snorri made ready their ship to go and look for the country in the summer. The man named Bjarni, and Thorhall, who have already been mentioned, joined the expedition with their ship, and the crew which had accompanied them. There was a man named Thorvard, who was connected by marriage with Eric the Red. He also went with them, and Thorhall who was called the Hunter, he had been long engaged with Eric as hunter in the summer, and had many things in his charge. Thorhall was big and strong and dark, and like a giant: he was rather old, of a temper hard to manage, taciturn and of few words as a rule, cunning but abusive, and he was always urging Eric to the worse course. He had had little dealings with the faith since it came to Greenland. Thorhall was rather unpopular, yet for a long time Eric had been in the habit of consulting him. He was on the ship with Thorvard's men, for he had a wide experience of wild countries. They had the ship which Thorbjörn had brought out there, and they joined themselves to Karlsefni's party for the expedition, and the majority of the men were Greenlanders. The total force on board their ships was 160 men. After this they sailed away to the Western Settlement and the Bear Isles. They sailed away from the Bear Isles with a northerly wind. They were at sea two days. Then they found land, and rowing ashore in boats they examined the country, and found there a quantity of flat stones, which were so

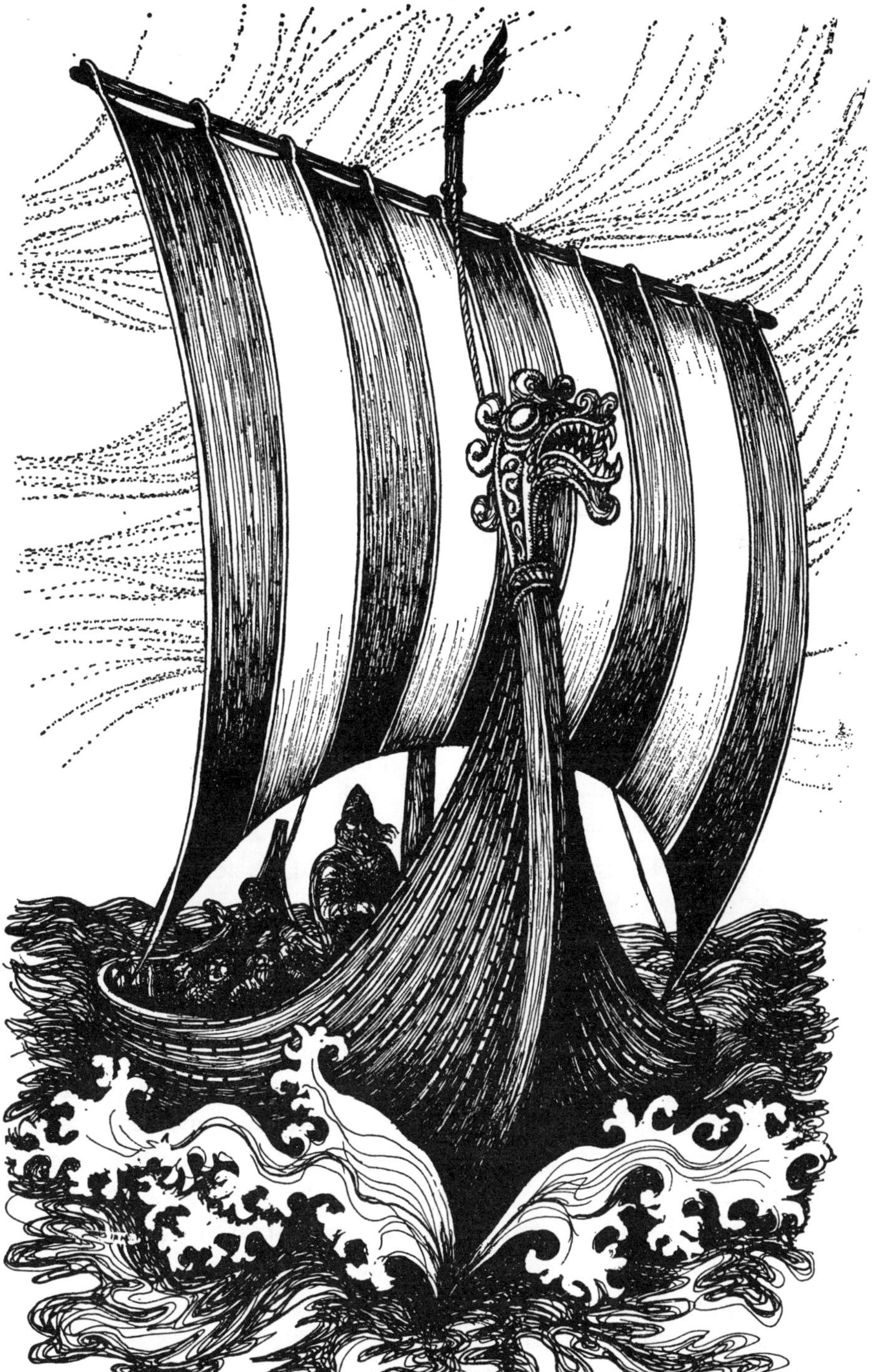
HOWARD

large that two men could easily have lain sole to sole on them: there were many arctic foxes there. They gave the place a name, calling it Helluland. Then they sailed for two days with north wind, and changed their course from south to south-east, and then there was a land before them on which was much wood and many beasts. An island lay there off shore to the south-east, on which they found a bear, and they called it Bjarney (Bear Island), but the land where the wood was they called Markland (woodland).

Then when two days were passed they sighted land, up to which they sailed. There was a cape where they arrived. They beat along the coast, and left the land to starboard: it was a desolate place, and there were long beaches and sands there. They rowed ashore, and found there on the cape the keel of a ship, so they called the place Keelness: they gave the beaches also a name, calling them Furdustrands (the Wonder Beaches) because the sail past them was long. Next the country became indented with bays, into one of which they steered the ships.

Now when Leif was with king Olaf Tryggvason and he commissioned him to preach Christianity in Greenland, the king gave him two Scots, a man called Hake and a woman Hekja. The king told Leif to make use of these people if he had need of speed, for they were swifter than deer: these people Leif and Eric provided to accompany Karlsefni. Now when they had coasted past Furdustrands they set the Scots ashore, telling them to run southward along the land to explore the resources of the country and come back before three days were past. They were dressed in what they called a "kjafal", which was made with a hood above, and open at the sides without sleeves: it was fastened between the legs, where a button and a loop held it together: otherwise they were naked. They cast anchor and lay there in the meanwhile. And when three days were past they came running down from the land, and one of them had in his hand a grape-cluster while the other had a wild ear of wheat. They told Karlsefni that they thought that they had found that the resources of the country were good. They received them into their ship, and went their ways, till the country was indented by a fjord. They took the ships into the fjord. There was an island outside, about which there were strong currents, so they called it

The Expedition of Thorfin Karlsefni

Straumsey (Tide or Current Island). There were so many birds on the island that a man's feet could hardly come down between the eggs. They held along the fjord, and called the place Straumsfjord, and there they carried up their goods from the ships and prepared to stay: they had with them all sorts of cattle, and they explored the resources of the country there. There were mountains there, and the view was beautiful. They did nothing but explore the country. There was plenty of grass there. They were there for the winter, and the winter was severe, but they had done nothing to provide for it, and victuals grew scarce, and hunting and fishing deteriorated. Then they went out to the island, in the hope that this place might yield something in the way of fishing or jetsam. But there was little food to be obtained on it, though their cattle throve there well. After this they cried to God to send them something to eat, and their prayer was not answered as soon as they desired. Thorhall disappeared and men went in search of him: that lasted three successive days. On the fourth day Karlsefni and Bjarni found Thorhall on a crag; he was gazing into the air with staring eyes, open mouth, and dilated nostrils, and scratching and pinching himself and reciting something. They asked him why he had come there. He said it was no business of theirs, told them not to be surprised at it, and said that he had lived long enough to make it unnecessary for them to trouble about him. They told him to come home with them, and he did so. Soon afterwards there came a whale, and they went to it and cut it up, but no one knew what sort of whale it was. Karlsefni had a great knowledge of whales, but still he did not recognise this one. The cooks boiled this whale, and they ate it, but were all ill from it: then Thorhall came up and said: "Was not the Red-Beard more useful than your Christ? This is my reward for chanting of Thor my patron; seldom has he failed me." But when they heard this none of them would avail themselves of the food, and they threw it down off the rocks and committed their cause to God's mercy: the state of the weather then improved and permitted them to row out, and from that time there was no lack of provision during the spring. They went into Straumsfjord, and got supplies from both places, hunting on the mainland, and eggs and fishing from the sea.

Now they consulted about their expedition, and were divided. Thorhall the Hunter wished to go north by Furdustrands and past Keelness, and so look for Wineland, but Karlsefni wished to coast south and off the east coast, considering that the region which lay more to the south was the larger, and it seemed to him the best plan to explore both ways. So then Thorhall made ready out by the islands, and there were no more than nine men for his venture, the rest of the party going with Karlsefni. And one day as Thorhall was carrying water to his ship he drank it, and recited this verse:

> *They flattered my confiding ear*
> *With tales of drink abounding here:*
> *My tale upon the thirsty land!*
> *A warrior, trained to bear a brand,*
> *A pail instead I have to bring,*
> *And bow my back beside the spring:*
> *For ne'er a single draught of wine*
> *Has passed these parching lips of mine.*

After this they set out, and Karlsefni accompanied them by the islands.

Before they hoisted their sail Thorhall recited a verse:

> *Now let the vessel plough the main*
> *To Greenland and our friends again:*
> *Away, and leave this strenuous host*
> *Who praise this God-forsaken coast*
> *To linger in a desert land,*
> *And boil their whales in Furdustrand.*

Afterwards they parted, and they sailed north past Furdustrands and Keelness, and wished to bear westward; but they were met by a storm and cast ashore in Ireland, where they were much ill-treated and enslaved. There Thorhall died, according to the reports of traders.

Karlsefni coasted south with Snorri and Bjarni and the rest of their party. They sailed a long time, till they came to a river which flowed down from the land and through a lake into the sea: there were great shoals of gravel there in front of the estuary and they

The Expedition of Thorfin Karlsefni

could not enter the river except at high tide. Karlsefni and his party sailed into the estuary, and called the place Hop.

They found there wild fields of wheat wherever the ground was low, but vines wherever they explored the hills. Every brook was full of fish. They made pits where the land met high-water mark, and when the tide ebbed there were halibut in the pits. There was a great quantity of animals of all sorts in the woods. They were there a fortnight, enjoying themselves, without noticing anything further: they had their cattle with them.

And one morning early, as they looked about them, they saw nine skin canoes, on which staves were waved with a noise just like threshing, and they were waved with the sun. Then Karlsefni said, "What is the meaning of this?" Snorri answered him, "Perhaps this is a sign of peace, so let us take a white shield and lift it in answer," and they did so. Then these men rowed to meet them, and, astonished at what they saw, they landed. They were swarthy men and ugly, with unkempt hair on their heads. They had large eyes and broad cheeks. They stayed there some time, showing surprise. Then they rowed away south past the cape.

Karlsefni and his men had made their camp above the lake, and some of the huts were near the mainland while others were near the lake. So they remained there that winter; no snow fell, and their cattle remained in the open, finding their own pasture. But at the beginning of spring they saw one morning early a fleet of skin canoes rowing from the south past the cape, so many that the sea was black with them, and on each boat there were staves waved. Karlsefni and his men raised their shields, and they began to trade: the people wanted particularly to buy red cloth, in exchange for which they offered skins and grey furs. They wished also to buy swords and spears, but Karlsefni and Snorri forbade this. The savages got for a dark skin a span's length of red cloth, which they bound round their heads. Thus things continued for awhile, but when the cloth began to give out they cut it into pieces so small that they were not more than a finger's breadth. The savages gave as much for it as before, or more.

It happened that a bull belonging to Karlsefni's party ran out of the wood, and bellowed loudly: this terrified the savages, and they ran out to their canoes, and rowed south along the coast, and there was nothing more seen of them for three consecutive weeks. But when that time had elapsed they saw a great number of the boats of the savages coming from the south like a rushing torrent, and this time all the staves were waved widdershins, and all the savages yelled loudly. Upon this Karlsefni's men took a red shield and raised it in answer. The savages ran from their boats and thereupon they met and fought; there was a heavy rain of missiles; the savages had war-slings too. Karlsefni and Snorri observed that the savages raised up on a pole a very large globe, closely resembling a sheep's paunch and dark in colour, and it flew from the pole up on land over the party, and made a terrible noise where it came down. Upon this a great fear came on Karlsefni and his party, so that they wished for nothing but to get away up stream, for they thought that the savages were setting upon them from all sides, nor did they halt till they came to some rocks where they made a determined resistance.

Freydis came out, and seeing Karlsefni's men retreating she cried out, "Why are such fine fellows as you running away from these unworthy men, whom I thought you could have butchered like cattle? Now if I had a weapon it seems to me that I should fight better than any of you." They paid no attention to what she said. Freydis wished to follow them, but was rather slow because she was not well; yet she went after them into the wood, pursued by the savages. She found before her a dead man, Thorbrand Snorreson, with a flat stone standing in his head: his sword lay beside him. This she took up, and prepared to defend herself with it. Then the savages set upon her, but she drew out her breast from beneath her clothes and beat the sword upon it: with that the savages were afraid, and running back to their ships they withdrew. Karlsefni's men came up to her and praised her courage. Two men of Karlsefni's force fell, but four of the savages, although the former were outnumbered. So then they went back to their huts, and bound their wounds, and considered what that force could have been which set upon them from the land side; it now appeared to them that the attacking party consisted solely of those who came from the ships, and that the others must have been a delusion.

Moreover the savages found a dead man with an axe lying beside

The Expedition of Thorfin Karlsefni

him. One of them took up the axe and cut at a tree, and then each of the others did so, and they thought it a treasure and that it cut well. Afterwards one of them cut at a stone, and the axe broke, whereupon he thought that it was useless, since it did not stand against the stone, and threw it down.

It now appeared to Karlsefni's party that though this country had good resources yet they would live in a perpetual state of warfare and alarm on account of the aborigines. So they prepared to depart, intending to return to their own country. They coasted northward, and found five savages in skins sleeping by the sea; these had with them receptacles in which was beast's marrow mixed with blood. They concluded that these men must have been sent from the country: they killed them. Later on they discovered a promontory and a quantity of beasts: the promontory had the appearance of a cake of dung, because the beasts lay there in the winter. Now they came to Straumsfjord, where there was plenty of every kind.

Some men say that Bjarni and Freydis stayed there with a hundred men and went no further, while Karlsefni and Snorri went south with forty men, staying no longer at Hop than a scant two months, and returning the same summer.

Karlsefni went with one ship to look for Thorhall the Hunter, while the main body remained behind, and they travelled north past Keelness, and then bore along to the west of it, leaving the land on their port side. Then there was nothing but desolate woods, with hardly any open places. And when they had sailed a long time, a river came down from the land from the east to the west: they entered the mouth of the river and lay by its southern bank. It happened one morning that Karlsefni and his men saw before them on an open place a speck, which glittered before them, and they shouted at it; it moved, and it was a uniped, which darted down to the bank of the river by which they lay. Thorvald, son of Eric the Red, was sitting by the rudder, and the uniped shot an arrow into his entrails. Thorvald drew out the arrow, crying, "There is fat about my belly, we have reached a good country, though we are hardly allowed to enjoy it." Thorvald died of this wound soon afterwards. Then the uniped rushed away, and back northward. Karlsefni and his men pursued him, and saw him from time to time.

The last they saw of him was that he ran towards a certain creek. Then Karlsefni and his men turned back. Thereupon a man sang this little ditty:

> *Hear, Karlsefni, while I sing*
> *Of a true but wondrous thing,*
> *How thy crew all vainly sped,*
> *Following a uniped:*
> *Strange it was to see him bound*
> *Swiftly o'er the broken ground.*

Then they went away, and back north, and imagined that they saw Uniped Land. They would not then risk their people further.

They considered that those mountains which were at Hop and those which they now found were all one, and were therefore close opposite one another, and that the distance from Straumsfjord was the same in both directions. They were at Straumsfjord the third winter.

At this time the men were much divided into parties, which happened because of the women, the unmarried men claiming the wives of those who were married, which gave rise to the greatest disorder. There Karlsefni's son, Snorri, was born the first autumn, and he was three winters old when they left.

On sailing from Wineland they got a south wind, and came to Markland, where they found five savages, one of whom was bearded. There were two women and two children: Karlsefni's men caught the boys, but the others escaped, disappearing into the ground. But they kept the two boys with them and taught them speech, and they were christened. They called their mother Vætilldi and their father Uvægi. They said that the savages' country was governed by kings, one of whom was called Avalldamon and the other Valldidida. They said that there were no houses there: people lived in dens or caves. They reported that another country lay on the other side, opposite to their own, where people lived who wore white clothes, and uttered loud cries, and carried poles, and went with flags. It is thought that this was Hvitramannaland, or Ireland the Great. So then they came to Greenland, and stayed with Eric the Red for the winter.

Then Bjarni Grimolfson was carried into the sea of Ireland, and came into a sea infested by the teredo, and the first thing they noticed was that the ship beneath them was worm-eaten. So they discussed what plan should be adopted. They had a boat which was coated with seal-tar. It is said that the teredo does not eat wood which is coated with seal-tar. The majority declared in favour of the proposal to man the boat with such men as she would accommodate. But when this was tested the boat would not accommodate more than half the crew. Bjarni then said that the manning of the boat should be by lot, and not by rank. But every man who was there wished to go in the boat, and she could not take them all. For this reason they agreed to the course of drawing lots for the manning of the boat from the ship. So the result of the drawing was that Bjarni drew a seat in the boat, and about half the crew with him. So those who had been chosen by the lots went from the ship into the boat. When they had got into the boat, a young Icelander, who had been one of Bjarni's companions, said, "Do you mean, Bjarni, to desert me here?" Bjarni replied, "So it has turned out." "This is not what you promised me", said he, "when I left my father's house in Iceland to go with you." "But still", said Bjarni, "I do not see any other course in this predicament: but answer me, what course do you advise?" "The course I see," said he, "is that we change places, and you come here while I go there." Bjarni answered, "Be it so. For I see that you cling greedily to life, and think it a hard thing to die." Thereupon they changed places. This man went down into the boat, while Bjarni got on board the ship, and men say that Bjarni was lost there in the teredo sea, with those men who were on board with him. But the boat and those on board of her went their ways, till they came to land, at Dublin in Ireland, where they afterwards told this story.

translated by G. M. GATHORNE-HARDY

Authun and the Bear

There was a man by the name of Authun, a Westfirther by origin, and rather poorly off. He went abroad from the Westfirths with the help of a good farmer, Thorstein, and of skipper Thorir, who had received hospitality from Thorstein over the winter. Authun had been staying there too, and working for Thorir, and received this for his reward, a passage abroad with the skipper to look after him. Before going on board ship Authun set aside the bulk of his money for his mother, and it was reckoned enough to keep her for three years. They now sailed out and away. They had an easy passage and Authun spent the winter with skipper Thorir, who owned a farm in Mœr, in Norway. The following summer they sailed for Greenland, and spent the winter there.

The story tells how Authun bought a bear there, an absolute treasure, and gave every penny he had for it. The following summer they returned to Norway and had an excellent passage. Authun took his bear with him, and was proposing to go south to Denmark, find king Svein, and make him a present of the beast. So when he reached the south of Norway, where the Norwegian king was then in residence, he left the ship, taking his bear with him, and rented himself a lodging.

King Harald was soon told how a bear, an absolute treasure, had come ashore, and that his owner was an Icelander. The king sent for him immediately, and when Authun came into the king's presence he greeted him with due courtesy. The king received his greeting affably, and then: "You have a bear," he said, "an absolute treasure?"

Well, yes, he agreed, he had a beast of a kind.

"Are you willing to sell him to us," asked the king, "for the same price you gave for him?"

"I don't want to, sire," he replied.

"Then would you like me to give you twice the price?" asked the king. "And indeed that would be fairer, since you paid out all you had for him."

"I don't want to, sire."

"You want to give him to me then?" said the king.

"No, sire," he replied.

"Then what do you want to do with him?"

"Go to Denmark," replied Authun, "and give him to king Svein."

"Is it possible," asked king Harald, "that you are such a silly man that you have not heard how a state of war exists between our two countries? Or do you think yourself so blest with luck that you can make your way there with this precious thing when others, for all that they have compelling business there, cannot manage it unscathed?"

"Sire," said Authun, "it is for you to command, yet I cannot willingly agree to anything except what I have already decided."

"Then why should you not go your road," said the king to that, "even as you wish? But come and see me when you return, and tell me how king Svein rewards you for the bear. It may be that you are a man of happy fortune."

"I promise to do so," said Authun.

He now proceeded south along the coast, and east to Vik, and from there to Denmark, and by this time had spent his last penny and was forced to beg food, both for himself and for the bear. He went to see king Svein's steward, a man named Aki, and asked him for some victuals, both for himself and for the bear. "For I am proposing," he said, "to make a present of him to king Svein." Aki said he would sell him food if that was what he was after, but Authun confessed that he had no money to pay for it. "And yet," he said, "I should like my business to be so forwarded that I can produce my bear before the king." "I will give you food and lodging then, whatever you need, until you see the king, but in return I require a half share in this creature. You might look at it this way: the bear will only die on your hands, for you need considerable

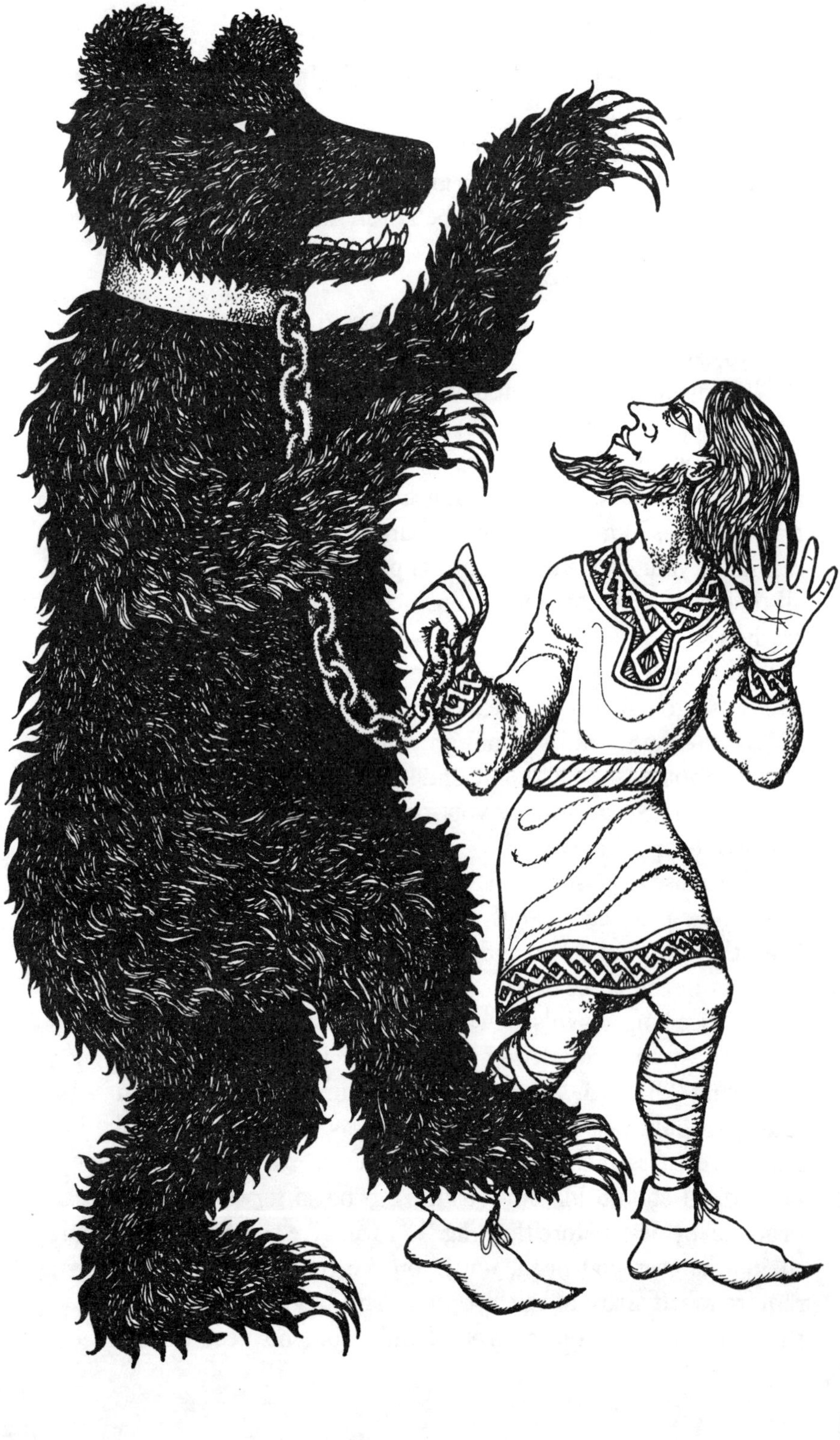

provisioning and your money is all gone, and in that case you get no profit of your bear."

When he looked at it that way, it seemed to him that what the steward said went pretty close to the mark, so that was what they settled on, that he should make over half the beast to Aki, and it was for the king to set a value on the whole.

And now they were to go together to see the king, and so they did, and stood before his table. The king was puzzled who this man, whom he did not know, could be, and, "Who are you?" he asked Authun.

"I am an Icelander, sire," he replied, "and have just come from Greenland, and more recently still from Norway. I had been meaning to present you with this bear, which I purchased with every penny I had, but I am now in something of a quandary, for I own only half of him." And he went on to tell the king what had taken place between him and his steward Aki.

"Is this true, Aki, what he says?" asked the king.

"Yes," he said, "it is."

"And did you think it seemly, when I had raised you up to be a great man, to obstruct and hinder his path when a man was trying to bring me this fine beast, for which he had given his all, when even king Harald, who is our enemy, saw fit to let him go in peace? Think then how honourable this was on your part! It would be only right to have you put to death—and though I will not do that, you shall leave this land without a moment's delay, and never come into my sight again. As for you, Authun, I owe you the same thanks as if you were giving me the whole animal. So stay here with me." He agreed to this, and remained with king Svein for a while.

But after some time had gone by Authun said to the king, "I should like to go away now, sire." The king answered, rather coldly, "What do you want, if you don't want to stay with us?" "I want to go south on a pilgrimage." "If you did not wish to follow so good a course," the king admitted, "I should be displeased by your eagerness to be off." The king now gave him a large amount of silver, and he travelled southwards with the pilgrims to Rome. The king made the arrangements for his journey, and told him to come and see him when he returned.

Now he went his ways until he came south to Rome, and when he had spent as much time there as he wished, he set out on his way back. He fell sick, very sick, and grew woefully thin. All the money the king had given him for his journey was now spent, he took the style of a beggar and begged for his food. He had become bald and quite pitiful to see.

He came back to Denmark at Easter, to the very place where the king was in residence. He did not dare let himself be seen but remained in the church transept, hoping to encounter the king when he went to church that evening. But when he saw the king with his handsomely attired courtiers, again he dare not let himself be seen. And when the king went to the drinking in hall, Authun ate his food outside, as is the custom of pilgrims to Rome before they lay aside their staff and scrip.

And now in the evening, as the king went to evensong, Authun reckoned on meeting him; but however daunting a prospect this had looked before, it had by now grown far worse, for the courtiers were in drink. And yet, as they were going back in, the king noticed a man who he felt sure lacked the confidence to come forward and speak to him, and as the courtiers were entering the king turned back, saying, "Let anyone now come forward who craves audience of me, for I believe there is such a man here present." Then Authun came forward and fell at the king's feet, and the king could hardly recognise him. But as soon as he knew who he was, he took Authun by the hand and welcomed him. "How greatly you are changed," he said, "since last we met," and he led him inside behind him. When the courtiers saw him they laughed at him, but, "You need not laugh at him," said the king, "he has provided for his soul better than you." Then the king had a bath prepared for him and gave him clothes to wear, and Authun remained with him.

One day in spring, so the story goes, the king invited Authun to stay with him for the rest of his days, promising that he would make him his cup-bearer and heap him with honours.

"God reward you, sire," said Authun, "for all the honour you would do me, but what I really have in mind is to return to Iceland."

"That strikes me as a curious choice," said the king.

"I cannot bear, sire," said Authun, "that I should enjoy such honours here with you, and my mother tramp the beggar's path out in Iceland, for by now the provision I made for her before I left home will be at an end."

"That is well spoken, and like a man," replied the king, "and you will prove a man of happy fortune. This is the only reason for your departure which would not displease me. But stay with me now till the ships make ready." And so he did.

One day, towards the end of spring, king Svein walked down to the jetties, where ships were being overhauled in readiness for voyages to many lands, to the Baltic and Germany, Sweden, and Norway. He and Authun came to a very fine ship which men were making ready, and "What do you think of this for a ship, Authun?" asked the king. "Very fine, sire," was his answer. "I am going to give you this ship," said the king, "in return for the bear." Authun thanked him for his gift as well as he knew how.

When time had passed and the ship was quite ready, king Svein had this to say to Authun: "Since you want to be away it is not for me to stop you. But I have heard that your country is ill supplied with havens, the coasts often wide open and dangerous to shipping. Now should you be wrecked and lose both ship and lading, there will be little to show that you have met king Svein and given him a princely gift." With that the king gave him a leather purse full of silver. "You will not be entirely penniless, even if you are shipwrecked, so long as you hold on to this. And yet," said the king, "it may happen that you lose this money too, and you will then reap little benefit from having found king Svein and given him a princely gift." With that the king drew a ring from his arm and gave it to Authun, saying, "Even if you are so unlucky as to suffer shipwreck and lose your money, you will not be penniless should you manage to get ashore, for many carry gold on them in case of shipwreck, and it will be clear that you have met king Svein if you save the ring. But I would urge upon you," said the king, "not to give away the ring unless you consider yourself under a great enough obligation to some great man—but give him the ring, for it well becomes men of rank to accept such. And now, good luck go with you."

Then he put to sea and sailed to Norway, where he had his goods carried ashore—and he needed more help for this than when he was in Norway last. He then went to visit king Harald, to make good the promise he had made him before going to Denmark. He had a courteous greeting for the king, and the king took it affably. "Sit down," he said, "and take a drink with us." And so he did.

"And how did king Svein reward you for the bear?" king Harald asked him.

"By accepting it from me, sire," replied Authun.

"So too would I have rewarded you," said the king. "How else did he reward you?"

"He gave me silver for my pilgrimage," replied Authun.

"King Svein gives many men silver for pilgrimages, and for other things too," said the king, "and they don't have to bring him a grand present for it. What else was there?"

"He offered to make me his cup-bearer," said Authun, "and heap me with honours."

"In that he spoke well," said the king. "Still, he would give you more of a reward than that."

"He gave me a merchant ship and such wares as sell best here in Norway."

"That was handsome of him," said the king, "but so too would I have rewarded you. Did he reward you with anything further?"

"He gave me a leather purse full of silver, saying I should not then be penniless if I held on to it, even though my ship was wrecked off Iceland."

"That was nobly done," said the king, "and something I would not have done. I should have held us quits had I given you the ship. Did he reward you any further?"

"To be sure he rewarded me, sire," said Authun. "He gave me this ring I have on my arm, arguing it might so turn out that I should lose all that money and yet, said he, not be penniless if I held on to the ring. And he charged me never to part with it unless I should consider myself under so great an obligation to some great man that I wanted to give it him. And now I have found him, for you had the opportunity to deprive me of both these things, the bear and my life too; yet you let me go in peace where others might not."

The king accepted his gift graciously, and gave Authun fine gifts in return before they parted. Authun used his money for a passage to Iceland, promptly left for home that summer, and was thought to be a man of the happiest good fortune.

translated by GWYN JONES

The Battle of Stamford Bridge

The Battle of Stamford Bridge, near York, was fought on September 25th, 1066, nineteen days before the Battle of Hastings. The defeat and death of Harald Hardradi (called Sigurdsson in this translation), claimant to the English throne together with Harold Godwinson and Duke William of Normandy, put an end to the Viking domination of Europe. This extract from King Harald's Saga, *written by the Icelandic historian and saga writer Snorri Sturluson (1179–1241), is a rousing mixture of fact and legend. The battle is described from the point of view of the Norwegians, who are thought to have numbered about 9000 men and 300 ships. Harald was joined by Harold Godwinson's own brother, Tostig, who had been deposed as Earl of Northumbria in the previous year for treachery. Tostig was killed in the battle and twenty-four ships were sufficient to carry the Norwegian survivors home.*

On Monday, when King Harald Sigurdsson had taken breakfast, he ordered the trumpets to sound for going on shore. The army accordingly got ready, and he divided the men into the parties who should go and who should stay behind. In every division he allowed two men to land and one to remain behind. Earl Tostig and his retinue prepared to land with King Harald; and, for watching the ships, remained behind the king's son Olaf, the Earls of Orkney, Paul, and Erlend, and also Eystein Orre, a son of Thorberg Arneson, who was the most able and best beloved by the king of all his liegemen, and to whom the king had promised his daughter Maria. The weather was uncommonly fine, and it was hot sunshine. The men therefore laid aside their armour, and went on the land only

The Battle of Stamford Bridge

with their shields, helmets, and spears, and girt with swords; and many had also arrows and bows, and all were very merry. Now as they came near the castle a great army seemed coming against them, and they saw a cloud of dust as from horses' feet, and under it shining shields and bright armour. The king halted his people, and called to him Earl Tostig, and asked him what army this could be. The earl replied that he thought it most likely to be a hostile army; but possibly it might be some of his relations who were seeking for mercy and friendship in order to obtain certain peace and safety from the king. Then the king said: "We must all halt to discover what kind of a force this is." They did so; and the nearer this force came the greater it appeared, and their shining arms were to the sight like glittering ice.

Then said King Harald: "Let us now fall upon some good, sensible counsel; for it is not to be concealed that this is an hostile army, and the king himself without doubt is here."

Then said the earl: "The first counsel is to turn about as fast as we can to our ships to get our men and our weapons, and then we will make a defence according to our ability; or otherwise let our ships defend us, for there these horsemen have no power over us."

Then King Harald said: "I have another counsel. Put three of our best horses under three of our briskest lads, and let them ride with all speed to tell our people to come quickly to our relief. The Englishmen shall have a hard fray of it before we give ourselves up for lost."

The earl said the king must order in this, as in all things, as he thought best; adding, at the same time, it was by no means his wish to fly. Then King Harald ordered his banner Land-ravager to be set up; and Frirek was the name of him who bore the banner.

Then King Harald arranged his army, and made the line of battle long, but not deep. He bent both wings of it back, so that they met together, and formed a wide ring equally thick all round, shield to shield, both in the front and rear ranks. The king himself and his retinue were within the circle; and there was the banner, and a body of chosen men. Earl Tostig, with his retinue, was at another place, and had a different banner. The army was arranged in this way because the king knew that horsemen were accustomed to ride forwards with great vigour, but to turn back immediately. Now the king ordered that his own and the earl's attendants should ride forwards where it was most required. "And our bowmen," said he, "shall be near to us; and they who stand in the first rank shall set the spear-shaft on the ground, and the spear-point against the horseman's breast if he rides at them; and those who stand in the second rank shall set the spear-point against the horse's breast."

King Harold Godwinson had come with an immense army, both of cavalry and infantry. Now King Harald Sigurdsson rode around his array to see how every part was drawn up. He was upon a black horse, and the horse stumbled under him, so that the king fell off. He got up in haste, and said: "A fall is lucky for a traveller."

The English king Harold said to the Northmen who were with him: "Do ye know the stout man who fell from his horse, with the blue kirtle and the beautiful helmet?"

"That is the king himself," said they.

The English king said: "A great man, and of stately appearance is he; but I think his luck has left him."

Twenty horsemen rode forward from the Thingmen's troops against the Northmen's array; and all of them, and likewise their horses, were clothed in armour.

One of the horsemen said: "Is Earl Tostig in this army?"

The earl answered: "It is not to be denied that ye will find him here."

The horseman says, "Thy brother King Harold sends thee salutation, with the message that thou shalt have the whole of Northumberland; and, rather than thou shouldst not submit to him, he will give thee the third part of his kingdom to rule over along with himself."

The earl replies: "This is something different from the enmity and scorn he offered last winter; and if this had been offered then it would have saved many a man's life who now is dead, and it would have been better for the kingdom of England. But if I accept of this offer, what will he give King Harald Sigurdsson for his trouble?"

The horseman replied: "He has also spoken of this, and will give him seven feet of English ground, or as much more as he may be taller than other men."

The Battle of Stamford Bridge

"Then," said the earl, "go now and tell King Harold to get ready for battle; for never shall the Northmen say with truth that Earl Tostig left King Harald Sigurdsson to join his enemy's troops when he came to fight west here in England. We shall rather all take the resolution to die with honour, or to gain England by a victory."

Then the horsemen rode back.

King Harald Sigurdsson said to the earl: "Who was the man who spoke so well?"

The earl replied: "That was King Harold Godwinson."

Then said King Harald Sigurdsson: "That was by far too long concealed from me; for they had come so near to our army that this Harold should never have carried back the tidings of our men's slaughter."

Then said the earl: "It was certainly imprudent for such chiefs, and it may be as you say; but I saw he was going to offer me peace and a great dominion, and that, on the other hand, I would be his murderer if I betrayed him; and I would rather he should be my murderer than I his, if one of two be to die."

King Harald Sigurdsson observed to his men, "That was but a little man, yet he sat firmly in his stirrups."

It is said that Harald made these verses at this time:—

> *Advance! advance!*
> *No helmets glance,*
> *But blue swords play*
> *In our array.*
>
> *Advance! advance!*
> *No mail-coats glance,*
> *But hearts are here*
> *That ne'er knew fear.*

His coat of mail was called Emma; and it was so long that it reached almost to the middle of his leg and so strong that no weapon ever pierced it. Then said King Harald Sigurdsson: "These verses are but ill composed; I must try to make better;" and he composed the following:—

In battle-storm we seek no lee,
With skulking head, and bending knee,
Behind the hollow shield.
With eye and hand we fend the head;
Courage and skill stand in the stead
Of panzer,* helm, and shield,
In Hilda's† deadly field.

Now the battle began. The Englishmen made a hot assault upon the Northmen, who sustained it bravely. It was no easy matter for the English to ride against the Northmen on account of their spears, therefore they rode in a circle around them. And the fight at first was but loose and light as long as the Northmen kept their order of battle; for although the English rode hard against the Northmen, they gave way again immediately, as they could do nothing against them. Now when the Northmen thought they perceived that the enemy were making but weak assaults, they set after them, and would drive them into flight; but when they had broken their shield-rampart, the Englishmen rode up from all sides and threw arrows and spears on them. Now when King Harald Sigurdsson saw this, he went into the fray where the greatest crash of weapons was; and there was a sharp conflict, in which many people fell on both sides. King Harald then was in a rage, and ran out in front of the array and hewed down with both hands; so that neither helmet nor armour could withstand him, and all who were nearest gave way before him. It was then very near with the English that they had taken to flight. So says Arnor, the earl's scald:—

Where battle-storm was ringing,
Where arrow-cloud was singing,
Harald stood there
Of armour bare,
His deadly sword still swinging.
The foemen feel its bite;
His Norsemen rush to fight,

* and † Samuel Laing explains that *panzer* is a coat of mail and that *Hilda* was the goddess of war. Maybe he was thinking of Hild, one of the Valkyries.

> *Danger to share*
> *With Harald there,*
> *Where steel on steel was ringing.*

King Harald Sigurdsson was hit by an arrow in the windpipe, and that was his death-wound. He fell, and all who had advanced with him, except those who retired with the banner. There was afterwards the warmest conflict, and Earl Tostig had taken charge of the king's banner. They began on both sides to form their array again, and for a long time there was a pause in fighting.

But before the battle began again Harold Godwinson offered his brother Earl Tostig peace, and also quarter to the Northmen who were still alive; but the Northmen called out, all of them together, that they would rather fall, one across the other, than accept of quarter from the Englishmen. Then each side set up a war-shout, and the battle began again.

Eystein Orre came up at this moment from the ships with the men who followed him, and all were clad in armour. Then Eystein got King Harald's banner Land-ravager; and now was, for the third time, one of the sharpest of conflicts, in which many Englishmen fell, and they were near to taking flight. This conflict is called Orre's storm. Eystein and his men had hastened so fast from the ships that they were quite exhausted, and scarcely fit to fight before they came into the battle; but afterwards they became so furious that they did not guard themselves with their shields as long as they could stand upright. At last they threw off their coats of ring-mail, and then the Englishmen could easily lay their blows at them; and many fell from weariness, and died without a wound. Thus almost all the chief men fell among the Norway people. This happened towards evening; and then it went, as one might expect, that all had not the same fate, for many fled, and were lucky enough to escape in various ways; and darkness fell before the slaughter was altogether ended.

Styrkar, King Harald Sigurdsson's marshal, a gallant man, escaped upon a horse, on which he rode away in the evening. It was blowing a cold wind, and Styrkar had not much other clothing upon him but his shirt, and had a helmet on his head and a drawn sword in his hand. As soon as his weariness was over, he began to feel cold. A waggoner met him in a lined skin-coat. Styrkar asks him: "Wilt thou sell thy coat, friend?"

"Not to thee," says the peasant. "Thou art a Northman; that I can hear by thy tongue."

Styrkar replies: "If I were a Northman, what wouldst thou do?"

"I would kill thee," replied the peasant; "but, as ill luck would have it, I have no weapon just now by me that would do it."

Then Styrkar says: "As you can't kill me, friend, I shall try if I can't kill you." And with that he swung his sword and struck him on the neck, so that his head came off. He then took the skin-coat, sprang on his horse, and rode down to the strand.

Olaf Haraldsson had not gone on land with the others, and when he heard of his father's fall he made ready to sail away with the men who remained.

translated by SAMUEL LAING

FOLK-TALES

The Pleiades
Denmark

There was once a man and he had six sons. He did not give them, however, any names such as other people have, but called them according to their age, the Oldest, Next to the Oldest, the Next to the Next to the Oldest, the Next to the Next to the Youngest, the Next to the Youngest and the Youngest. They had no other names.

When the Oldest was eighteen and the Youngest twelve, their father sent them out into the world that each might learn a trade. They went together for a short distance until they came to a place where six roads diverged; there they separated and each was to go his own way. But before parting they agreed to meet in two years at that same place and to return to their father together.

On the day appointed they all met and went home to their father who asked each one what he had learned. The Oldest said that he was a ship-builder and could build ships which could propel themselves. The Next to the Oldest had gone to sea and had become a helmsman and could steer a ship over land as well as over water. The Next to the Next to the Oldest had only learned to listen, but that he could do so well that when he was in one country he could hear what was going on in another. The Next to the Next to the Youngest had become a sharpshooter, and he never missed his aim. The Next to the Youngest had learned how to climb, and he could climb up a wall like a fly and no cliff was too steep for him to scale.

When the father had heard what the five brothers could do, he said that it was all very well but that he had expected something more from them. Then he asked what the Youngest had learned; he had great hopes in him for he was his favourite. The Youngest was glad that it was at last his turn to speak, and he answered joyously that he had become a master-thief. When his father heard that, he was furious and exclaimed, "Shame on you, for the disgrace that you have brought upon me and the whole family."

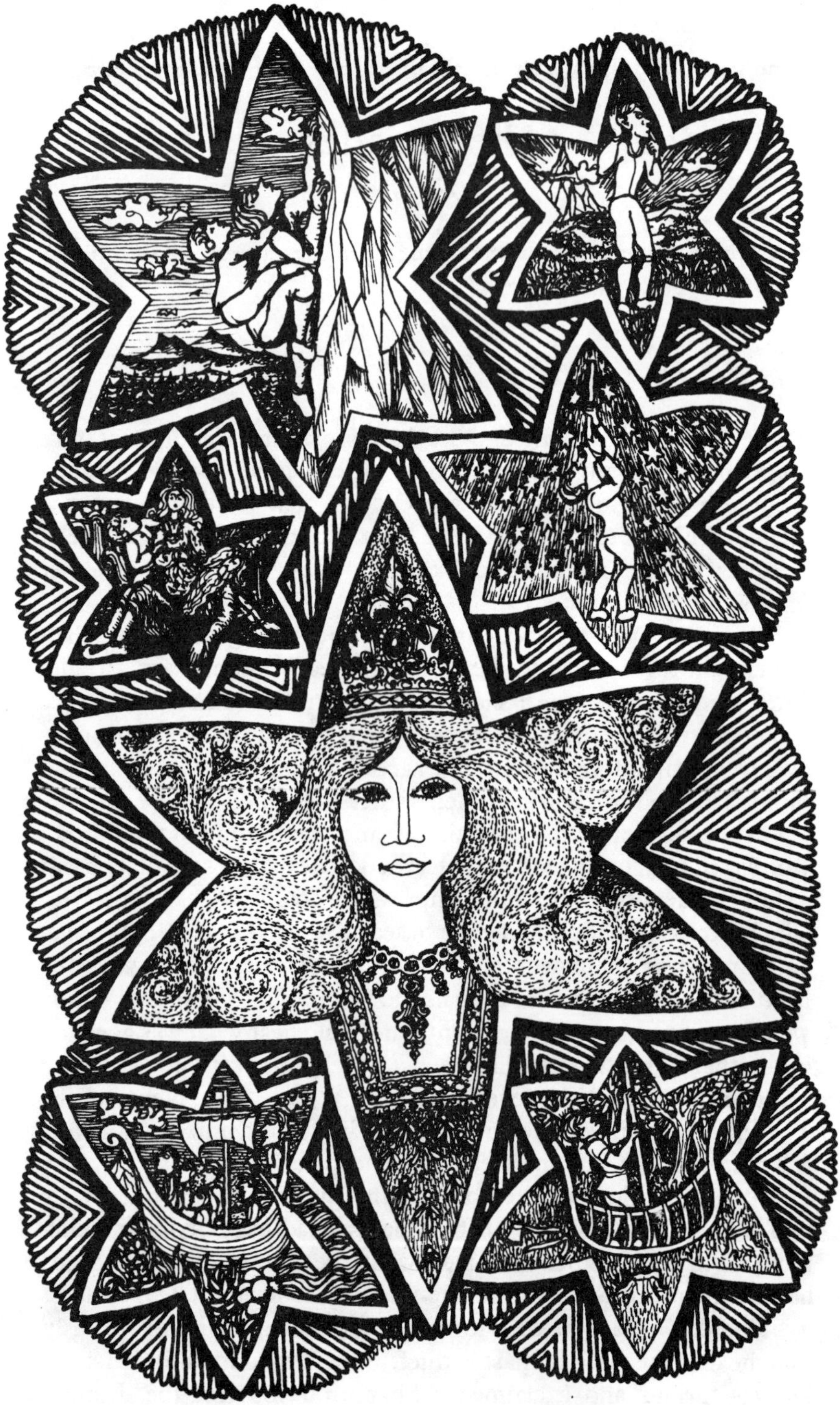

The Pleiades

Now it happened that at this very time the king's beautiful young daughter had been stolen by a wicked wizard, and the king promised the half of his realm and the princess in marriage to the one who should free her from the wizard. When the six brothers heard this they resolved to try their luck. The shipbuilder built a ship that went of itself. The helmsman steered it over land and sea. The listener listened carefully and at last said that he heard the wizard inside a mountain of glass. Thither they sailed. The climber quickly climbed to the top of the mountain and saw the ugly wizard lying sleeping with his head in the lap of the princess. Then he hurried down, and taking the little master-thief on his back, went into the inside of the mountain. The thief stole the princess so cleverly from under the head of the wizard that he did not notice it, but continued to sleep.

As soon as they were on board, the ship sailed away, but the listener had to continue to keep a watch on the wizard. When they were not far from land he said to the others: "Now the wizard is awaking! now he is stretching himself! now he misses the princess! now he is coming!"

Now the king's daughter was beside herself with fear, and declared that they would all die if there were not a sharpshooter on board. The wizard could fly through the air and would soon overtake them; he was also invulnerable except in one small black spot, not larger than a pinhead, in the middle of his chest. Hardly had she finished speaking when they saw the wizard in the distance rushing through the air. The sharpshooter took careful aim, shot, and his bullet struck the little black spot and at once the wizard burst into thousands of fiery pieces, and these we know as meteorites.

At last the six brothers reached home with the princess and brought her to the king. But they were all in love with her, and each one could truthfully say that without his help she could not have been saved. Then the king was distressed, for he did not know to whom he should give his daughter. And the princess was also sad, for she did not know whom she loved best.

But God would not that there should be strife among them, so he sent death to the six brothers and to the king's daughter in one and the same night. Then he made of the seven a constellation which men call the Pleiades. And of these stars the brightest is the princess and the faintest the little master-thief.

collected by SVEND GRUNDTVIG
translated by J. Grant Cramer

How Some Wild Animals Became Tame Ones

Lapland

Once upon a time there lived a miller who was so rich that, when he was going to be married, he asked to the feast not only his own friends but also the wild animals who dwelt in the hills and woods round about. The chief of the bears, the wolves, the foxes, the horses, the cows, the goats, the sheep, and the reindeer, all received invitations; and as they were not accustomed to weddings they were greatly pleased and flattered, and sent back messages in the politest language that they would certainly be there.

The first to start on the morning of the wedding-day was the bear, who always liked to be punctual; and, besides, he had a long way to go, and his hair, being so thick and rough, needed a good brushing before it was fit to be seen at a party. However, he took care to awaken very early, and set off down the road with a light heart. Before he had walked very far he met a boy who came whistling along, hitting at the tops of the flowers with a stick.

"Where are you going?" said he, looking at the bear in surprise, for he was an old acquaintance, and not generally so smart.

"Oh, just to the miller's marriage," answered the bear carelessly. "Of course, I would much rather stay at home, but the miller was so anxious I should be there that I really could not refuse."

"Don't go, don't go!" cried the boy. "If you do you will never come back! You have got the most beautiful skin in the world—just the kind that everyone is wanting, and they will be sure to kill you and strip you of it."

"I had not thought of that," said the bear, whose face turned white, only nobody could see it. "If you are certain that they would be so wicked—but perhaps you are jealous because nobody has invited *you*?"

"Oh, nonsense!" replied the boy angrily, "do as you see. It is your skin, and not mine; *I* don't care what becomes of it!" And he walked quickly on with his head in the air.

The bear waited until he was out of sight, and then followed him slowly, for he felt in his heart that the boy's advice was good, though he was too proud to say so.

The boy soon grew tired of walking along the road, and turned off into the woods, where there were bushes he could jump and streams he could wade; but he had not gone far before he met the wolf.

"Where are you going?" asked he, for it was not the first time he had seen him.

"Oh, just to the miller's marriage," answered the wolf, as the bear had done before him. "It is rather tiresome, of course—weddings are always so stupid; but still one must be good-natured!"

"Don't go!" said the boy again. "Your skin is so thick and warm, and winter is not far off now. They will kill you, and strip it from you."

The wolf's jaw dropped in astonishment and terror. "Do you *really* think that would happen?" he gasped.

"Yes, to be sure, I do," answered the boy. "But it is your affair, not mine. So good-morning," and on he went. The wolf stood still for a few minutes, for he was trembling all over, and then crept quietly back to his cave.

Next the boy met the fox, whose lovely coat of silvery grey was shining in the sun.

"You look very fine!" said the boy, stopping to admire him. "Are you going to the miller's wedding too?"

"Yes," answered the fox; "it is a long journey to take for such a thing as that, but you know what the miller's friends are like—so dull and heavy! It is only kind to go and amuse them a little."

"You poor fellow," said the boy pityingly. "Take my advice and stay at home. If you once enter the miller's gate his dogs will tear you in pieces."

"Ah, well, such things *have* occurred, I know," replied the fox gravely. And without saying any more he trotted off the way he had come.

His tail had scarcely disappeared, when a great noise of crashing branches was heard, and up bounded the horse, his black skin glistening like satin.

"Good morning," he called to the boy as he galloped past, "I can't wait to talk to you now. I have promised the miller to be present at his wedding-feast, and they won't sit down till I come."

"Stop! stop!" cried the boy after him, and there was something in his voice that made the horse pull up. "What is the matter?" asked he.

"You don't know what you are doing," said the boy. "If once you go there you will never gallop through these woods any more. You are stronger than many men, but they will catch you and put ropes round you, and you will have to work and to serve them all the days of your life."

The horse threw back his head at these words, and laughed scornfully.

"Yes, I am stronger than many men," answered he, "and all the ropes in the world would not hold me. Let them bind me as fast as they will, I can always break loose, and return to the forest and freedom."

And with this proud speech he gave a whisk of his long tail, and galloped away faster than before.

But when he reached the miller's house everything happened as the boy had said. While he was looking at the guests and thinking how much handsomer and stronger he was than any of them, a rope was suddenly flung over his head, and he was thrown down and a bit thrust between his teeth. Then, in spite of his struggles, he was dragged to a stable, and shut up for several days without any food, till his spirit was broken and his coat had lost its gloss. After that he was harnessed to a plough, and had plenty of time to remember all he had lost through not listening to the counsel of the boy.

When the horse had turned a deaf ear to his words the boy wandered idly along, sometimes gathering wild strawberries from a bank, and sometimes plucking wild cherries from a tree, till he reached a clearing in the middle of the forest. Crossing this open space was a beautiful milk-white cow with a wreath of flowers round her neck.

"Good-morning," she said pleasantly, as she came up to the place where the boy was standing.

"Good-morning," he returned. "Where are you going in such a hurry?"

"To the miller's wedding; I am rather late already, for the wreath took such a long time to make, so I can't stop."

"Don't go," said the boy earnestly; "when once they have tasted your milk they will never let you leave them, and you will have to serve them all the days of your life."

"Oh, nonsense; what do *you* know about it?" answered the cow, who always thought she was wiser than other people. "Why, I can run twice as fast as any of them! I should like to see anybody try to keep me against my will." And, without even a polite bow, she went on her way, feeling very much offended.

But everything turned out just as the boy had said. The company had all heard of the fame of the cow's milk, and persuaded her to give them some, and then her doom was sealed. A crowd gathered round her, and held her horns so that she could not use them, and, like the horse, she was shut in the stable, and only let out in the mornings, when a long rope was tied round her head, and she was fastened to a stake in a grassy meadow.

And so it happened to the goat and to the sheep.

Last of all came the reindeer, looking as he always did, as if some serious business was on hand.

"Where are you going?" asked the boy, who by this time was tired of wild cherries, and was thinking of his dinner.

"I am invited to the wedding," answered the reindeer, "and the miller has begged me on no account to fail him."

"O fool!" cried the boy. "Have you no sense at all? Don't you know that when you get there they will hold you fast, for neither beast nor bird is as strong or as swift as you?"

"That is exactly why I am quite safe," replied the reindeer. "I am so strong that no one can bind me, and so swift that not even an arrow can catch me. So, goodbye for the present, you will soon see me back."

But none of the animals that went to the miller's wedding ever came back. And because they were self-willed and conceited, and would not listen to good advice, they and their children have been the servants of men to this very day.

retold by ANDREW LANG

The Three Heads of the Well
England

Long before Arthur and the Knights of the Round Table, there reigned in the eastern part of England a king who kept his court at Colchester. He was witty, strong, and valiant, by which means he subdued his enemies abroad, and secured peace among his subjects at home. Nevertheless, in the midst of his glory, his queen died, leaving behind her an only daughter, about fifteen years of age. This lady, from her courtly carriage, beauty and affability, was the wonder of all that knew her; but, as covetousness is said to be the root of all evil, so it happened in this instance. The king, hearing of a lady who had likewise an only daughter, for the sake of her riches had a mind to marry; though she was old, ugly, hooked-nosed, and hump-backed, yet all this could not deter him from marrying her. Her daughter, also, was a yellow dowdy, full of envy and ill-nature; and, in short, was much of the same mould as her mother. This signified nothing, for in a few weeks the king, attended by the nobility and gentry, brought his intended bride to his palace, where the marriage rites were performed. They had not been long in the court before they set the king against his own beautiful daughter, which was done by false reports and accusations. The young princess, having lost her father's love, grew weary of the court, and one day meeting with her father in the garden, she desired him, with tears in her eyes, to give her a small subsistence, and she would go and seek her fortune; to which the king consented, and ordered her mother-in-law to make up a small sum according to her discretion. She went to the queen, who gave her a canvas bag of brown bread and hard cheese, with a bottle of beer. Though this was but a very pitiful dowry for a king's daughter, she took it, returned thanks, and proceeded on her journey, passing through groves, woods, and valleys, till at length she saw an old man sitting on a stone at the mouth of a cave, who said, "Good morrow, fair maiden, whither away so fast?" "Aged father," says she, "I am going to seek my fortune." "What hast thou in thy bag and bottle?" "In my bag I have got bread and cheese, and in my bottle good small beer; will you please to partake of either?" "Yes," said he, "with all my heart." With that the lady pulled out her provisions, and bid him eat and welcome. He did so, and gave her many thanks, saying thus: "There is a thick thorny hedge before you, which will appear impassable; but take this wand in your hand, strike three times, and say, 'Pray, hedge, let me come through,' and it will open immediately; then, a little farther, you will find a well; sit down on the brink of it, and there will come up three golden heads, which will speak: pray do whatever they require." Promising she would follow his directions, she took her leave of him. Arriving at the hedge, and pursuing the old man's directions, it divided, and gave her a passage: then, going to the well, she had no sooner sat down than a golden head came up singing—

> *Wash me, and comb me,*
> *And lay me down softly,*
> *And lay me on a bank to dry,*
> *That I may look pretty*
> *When somebody comes by.*

"Yes," said she, and putting forth her hand, with a silver comb performed the office, placing it upon a primrose bank. Then came up a second and a third head, making the same request, which she complied with. She then pulled out her provisions and ate her dinner. Then said the heads one to another, "What shall we do for this lady who hath used us so kindly?" The first said, "I will cause such addition to her beauty as shall charm the most powerful prince in the world." The second said, "I will endow her with such perfume, both in body and breath, as shall far exceed the sweetest flowers." The third said, "My gift shall be none of the least, for, as she is a king's daughter, I'll make her so fortunate that she shall become queen to the greatest prince that reigns." This done, at their request she let them down into the well again, and so proceeded on her journey. She had not travelled long before she saw a king hunting in the park with his nobles; she would have avoided him, but the king having caught a sight of her, approached, and what with her beauty and perfumed breath, was so powerfully smitten, that he was not able to subdue his passion, but commenced his courtship immediately, and was so successful that he gained her love, and, conducting her to

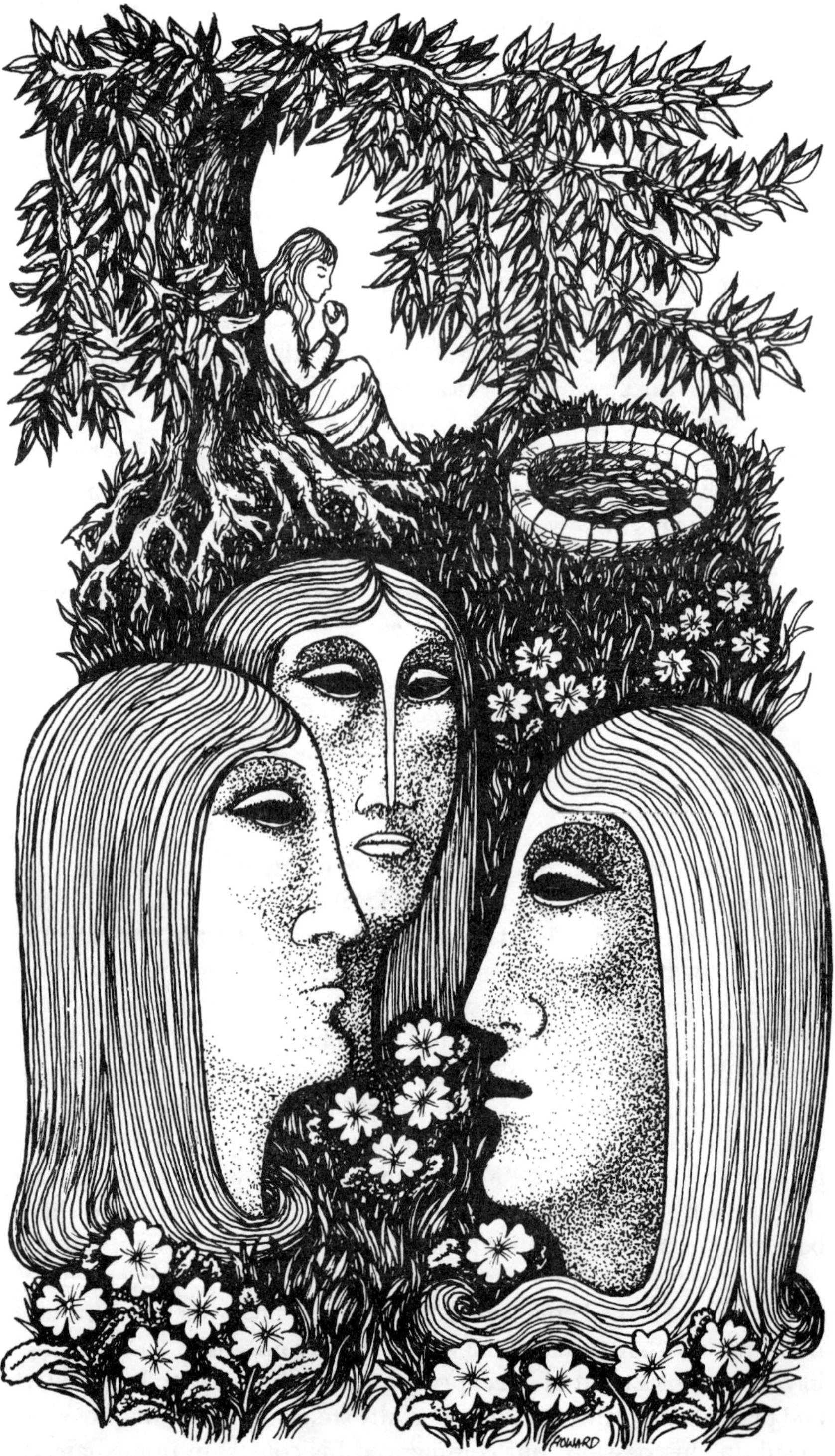
HOWARD

The Three Heads of the Well

his palace, he caused her to be clothed in the most magnificent manner.

This being ended, and the king finding that she was the King of Colchester's daughter, he ordered some chariots to be got ready, that he might pay the king a visit. The chariot in which the king and queen rode was adorned with rich ornamental gems of gold. The king, her father, was at first astonished that his daughter had been so fortunate as she was, till the young king made him sensible of all that happened. Great was the joy at court amongst all, with the exception of the queen and her club-footed daughter, who were ready to burst with malice, and envied her happiness; and the greater was their madness because she was now above them all. Great rejoicings, with feasting and dancing, continued many days. Then at length, with the dowry her father gave her, they returned home.

The deformed daughter, perceiving that her sister had been so happy in seeking her fortune, would needs do the same; so disclosing her mind to her mother, all preparations were made, and she was furnished not only with rich apparel, but sweetmeats, sugar, almonds, &c., in great quantities, and a large bottle of Malaga sack. Thus provided, she went the same road as her sister, and coming near the cave, the old man said, "Young woman whither so fast?" "What is that to you?" said she. "Then," said he, "what have you in your bag and bottle?" She answered, "Good things, which you shall not be troubled with." "Won't you give me some?" said he. "No, not a bit, nor a drop, unless it would choke you." The old man frowned, saying, "Evil fortune attend thee." Going on, she came to the hedge, through which she espied a gap, and thought to pass through it, but, going in, the hedge closed, and the thorns ran into her flesh, so that it was with great difficulty that she got out. Being now in a painful condition, she searched for water to wash herself, and, looking round, she saw the well; she sat down on the brink of it, and one of the heads came up, saying, "Wash me, comb me, and lay me down softly, &c." but she banged it with her bottle, saying, "Take this for your washing." So the second and third heads came up, and met with no better treatment than the first; whereupon the heads consulted among themselves what evils to plague her with for such usage. The first said, "Let her be struck with leprosy in her face." The second, "Let an additional smell be added to her breath." The third bestowed on her a husband, though but a poor country cobbler. This done she goes on till she came to a town, and it being market day, the people looked at her, and seeing such an evil face, fled out of her sight, all but a poor country cobbler (who not long before had mended the shoes of an old hermit, who having no money, gave him a box of ointment for the cure of the leprosy, and a bottle of spirits for a bad breath). Now the cobbler having a mind to do an act of charity, was induced to go up to her and ask her who she was. "I am," said she "the King of Colchester's daughter-in-law." "Well," said the cobbler, "if I restore you to your natural complexion, and make a sound cure both in face and breath, will you in reward take me for a husband?" "Yes, friend," replied she, "with all my heart." With this the cobbler applied the remedies, and they worked the effect in a few weeks, and then they were married, and after a few days they set forward for the court of Colchester. When the queen understood she had married a poor cobbler, she fell into distraction, and hanged herself for vexation. The death of the queen was not a source of sorrow to the king, who had only married her for her fortune, and bore her no affection; and shortly afterwards he gave the cobbler £100 to take the daughter to a remote part of the kingdom, where he lived many years mending shoes, while his wife assisted the housekeeping by spinning, and selling the results of her labour at the country market.

retold by JAMES ORCHARD HALLIWELL

Why the Sea is Salt

Norway

Once on a time, but it was a long, long time ago, there were two brothers, one rich and one poor. Now, one Christmas eve, the poor one hadn't so much as a crumb in the house, either of meat or bread, so he went to his brother to ask him for something to keep Christmas with, in God's name. It was not the first time his brother had been forced to help him, and you may fancy he wasn't very glad to see his face, but he said—

"If you will do what I ask you to do, I'll give you a whole flitch of bacon."

So the poor brother said he would do anything, and was full of thanks.

"Well, here is the flitch," said the rich brother, "and now go straight to Hell."

"What I have given my word to do, I must stick to," said the other; so he took the flitch and set off. He walked the whole day, and at dusk he came to a place where he saw a very bright light.

"Maybe this is the place," said the man to himself. So he turned aside, and the first thing he saw was an old, old man, with a long white beard, who stood in an outhouse, hewing wood for the Christmas fire.

"Good even," said the man with the flitch.

"The same to you; whither are you going so late?" said the man.

"Oh! I'm going to Hell, if I only knew the right way," answered the poor man.

"Well, you're not far wrong, for this is Hell," said the old man; "when you get inside they will be all for buying your flitch, for meat is scarce in Hell; but mind you don't sell it unless you get the hand-quern which stands behind the door for it. When you come out, I'll teach you how to handle the quern, for it's good to grind almost anything."

So the man with the flitch thanked the other for his good advice, and gave a great knock at the Devil's door.

When he got in, everything went just as the old man had said. All the devils, great and small, came swarming up to him like ants round an anthill, and each tried to outbid the other for the flitch.

"Well!" said the man, "by rights my old dame and I ought to have this flitch for our Christmas dinner; but since you have all set your hearts on it, I suppose I must give it up to you; but if I sell it at all, I'll have for it that quern behind the door yonder."

At first the Devil wouldn't hear of such a bargain, and chaffered and haggled with the man; but he stuck to what he said, and at last the Devil had to part with his quern. When the man got out into the yard, he asked the old woodcutter how he was to handle the quern; and after he had learned how to use it, he thanked the old man and went off home as fast as he could, but still the clock had struck twelve on Christmas eve before he reached his own door.

"Wherever in the world have you been?" said his old dame; "here have I sat hour after hour waiting and watching, without so much as two sticks to lay together under the Christmas brose."

"Oh!" said the man, "I couldn't get back before, for I had to go a long way first for one thing, and then for another; but now you shall see what you shall see."

So he put the quern on the table, and bade it first of all grind lights, then a table-cloth, then meat, then ale, and so on till they had got everything that was nice for Christmas fare. He had only to speak the word, and the quern ground out what he wanted. The old dame stood by blessing her stars, and kept on asking where he had got this wonderful quern, but he wouldn't tell her.

"It's all one where I got it from; you see the quern is a good one, and the mill-stream never freezes, that's enough."

So he ground meat and drink and dainties enough to last out till Twelfth Day, and on the third day he asked all his friends and kin to his house, and gave a great feast. Now, when his rich brother saw all that was on the table, and all that was behind in the larder, he grew quite spiteful and wild, for he couldn't bear that his brother should have anything.

"'Twas only on Christmas eve," he said to the rest, "he was in such straits, that he came and asked for a morsel of food in God's name, and now he gives a feast as if he were count or king"; and he turned to his brother and said—

"But whence, in Hell's name, have you got all this wealth?"

"From behind the door," answered the owner of the quern, for he didn't care to let the cat out of the bag. But later in the evening, when he had got a drop too much, he could keep his secret no longer, and brought out the quern and said—

"There, you see what has gotten me all this wealth"; and so he made the quern grind all kind of things. When his brother saw it, he set his heart on having the quern, and, after a deal of coaxing, he got it; but he had to pay three hundred dollars for it, and his brother bargained to keep it till hay-harvest, for he thought, if I keep it till then, I can make it grind meat and drink that will last for years. So you may fancy the quern didn't grow rusty for want of work, and when hay-harvest came, the rich brother got it, but the other took care not to teach him how to handle it.

It was evening when the rich brother got the quern home, and next morning he told his wife to go out into the hay-field and toss, while the mowers cut the grass, and he would stay at home and get the dinner ready. So, when dinner-time drew near, he put the quern on the kitchen table and said—

"Grind herrings and broth, and grind them good and fast."

So the quern began to grind herrings and broth; first of all, all the dishes full, then all the tubs full, and so on till the kitchen floor was quite covered. Then the man twisted and twirled at the quern to get it to stop, but for all his twisting and fingering the quern went on grinding, and in a little while the broth rose so high that the man was like to drown. So he threw open the kitchen door and ran into the parlour, but it wasn't long before the quern had ground the parlour full too, and it was only at the risk of his life that the man could get hold of the latch of the house door through the stream of broth. When he got the door open, he ran out and set off down the road, with the stream of herrings and broth at his heels, roaring like a waterfall over the whole farm.

Now, his old dame, who was in the field tossing hay, thought it a long time to dinner, and at last she said—

"Well! though the master doesn't call us home, we may as well go. Maybe he finds it hard work to boil the broth, and will be glad of my help."

The men were willing enough, so they sauntered homewards; but just as they had got a little way up the hill, what should they meet but herrings, and broth, and bread, all running and dashing, and splashing together in a stream, and the master himself running before them for his life, and as he passed them he bawled out—"Would to heaven each of you had a hundred throats! but take care you're not drowned in the broth."

Away he went, as though the Evil One were at his heels, to his brother's house, and begged him for God's sake to take back the quern that instant; for, said he—

"If it grinds only one hour more, the whole parish will be swallowed up by herrings and broth."

But his brother wouldn't hear of taking it back till the other paid him down three hundred dollars more.

So the poor brother got both the money and the quern, and it wasn't long before he set up a farm-house far finer than the one in which his brother lived, and with the quern he ground so much gold that he covered it with plates of gold; and as the farm lay by the sea-side, the golden house gleamed and glistened far away over the sea. All who sailed by put ashore to see the rich man in the golden house, and to see the wonderful quern, the fame of which spread far and wide, till there was nobody who hadn't heard tell of it.

So one day there came a skipper who wanted to see the quern; and the first thing he asked was if it could grind salt.

"Grind salt!" said the owner; "I should just think it could. It can grind anything."

When the skipper heard that, he said he must have the quern, cost what it would; for if he only had it, he thought he should be rid of his long voyages across stormy seas for a lading of salt. Well, at first the man wouldn't hear of parting with the quern; but the skipper begged and prayed so hard, that at last he let him have it, but he had to pay many, many thousand dollars for it. Now, when the skipper had got the quern on his back, he soon made off with it, for he was afraid lest the man should change his mind; so he had no time to ask how to handle the quern, but got on board his ship as fast as he could, and set sail. When he had sailed a good way off, he brought the quern on deck and said—

"Grind salt, and grind both good and fast."

Well, the quern began to grind salt so that it poured out like water; and when the skipper had got the ship full, he wished to stop the quern, but whichever way he turned it, and however much he tried, it was no good; the quern kept grinding on, and the heap of salt grew higher and higher, and at last down sunk the ship.

There lies the quern at the bottom of the sea, and grinds away at this very day, and that's why the sea is salt.

collected by PETER CHRISTEN ASBJÖRNEN and JÖRGEN I. MOE
translated by Sir George Webbe Dasent

The Bremen Town Musicians
Germany

A donkey had for years faithfully carried his master's sacks of wheat to the mill for grinding. But the donkey was losing his strength and was able to work less and less. His owner had about decided the animal was no longer worth his keep when the donkey, realizing that no kind wind was blowing in his direction, ran away. He took the road to Bremen. Once there, he thought, he would become a town musician. After travelling a while, he came upon a hunting dog lying by the roadside. The dog lay there panting and exhausted as if he had run a great distance.

"What makes you pant so, Catcher?" asked the donkey.

"Oh," said the dog, "I am old and getting weaker each day, and because I can no longer serve my master in the hunt, he wanted to beat me to death, so I've run away. But I don't know how I'm going to earn my bread."

"I'll tell you what to do," replied the donkey. "I'm on my way to Bremen to become a town musician. Come along and you can get a job too. I'll play the lute and you can try the kettle drums."

The dog was delighted and they continued on together. It was not long before they met a cat on the road who looked as mournful as three days of steady rain.

"What crossed your path, Old Whiskerwasher?" inquired the donkey.

"How can I be happy when I've had it up to my ears? I'm getting on in years and my teeth have gone dull. I'd rather sit behind the stove and dream than chase mice and so my mistress wanted to drown me. Well, I managed to get away, but good rat is expensive, and where shall I go?"

"Come with us to Bremen. You know all about night music and you, too, can get a job as a town musician."

The cat thought this a good idea and joined them.

The three fugitives soon came to a farm, where they saw a cock sitting on a gatepost screaming away at the top of his lungs.

"You'll burst our eardrums," the donkey said to the cock. "What's the matter?"

"Here I promised good weather for the holy day because it is the day Our Dear Lady washed the Christ child's shirts and wanted them to dry. But my mistress has no pity on me. Tomorrow is Sunday and guests are coming, and she has told the cook that she wants me in the soup. I'm to have my head chopped off this very evening. That's why I'm screaming as loud and as long as I still can."

"Nonsense," said the donkey. "Come with us. We're off to Bremen. You can find something better to do anywhere than die. You have a good voice, and with your help, if we all make music together, it will surely have style."

The cock agreed to this proposal and the four continued on their way.

Bremen was too far to reach in one day. By evening they had arrived at a forest and decided to spend the night there. The donkey and the dog lay down beneath a huge tree. The cat and the cock, however, made for the branches—the cock flying all the way to the top, where he felt himself safest. But before he went to sleep, he looked about in all directions, and it seemed to him he saw a light in the distance. He called down to his comrades that there must be a house not too far away.

"In that case," said the donkey, "let's get up and go there. The shelter here is pretty flimsy." And since it occurred to the dog that a few bones and a piece of meat would do him good, they all made their way in the direction of the light, which grew brighter and bigger, until they stood before a well-lighted thieves' hideout.

The donkey, as the tallest, went to the window and peered inside.

"What do you see, Greyhorse?" asked the cock.

"What I see," replied the donkey, "is a table loaded with lovely food and drink. And the thieves are sitting around it, enjoying themselves."

"That would be something for us," said the cock.

"Yes, indeed. If only we were inside," said the donkey.

The animals held a conference on how to get the thieves out of the house, and at last worked out a plan. The donkey was to stand on his hind legs with his forelegs on the window sill. The dog was to jump up on the donkey's back, the cat was to climb up on top of the dog, and last of all, the cock was to fly up and seat himself on the cat's head. When they were in position, the signal was given and they began to make music together: the donkey brayed, the dog howled, the cat meowed, the cock crowed. Then they broke through the window and into the room to the accompaniment of crashing glass.

The thieves jumped for fright at the unbearable noise and, convinced that the animals were ghosts, fled into the forest in terror.

The four comrades sat down at the table. They weren't choosy about leftovers and ate everything in sight as if they hadn't touched food in a month. When they had eaten their fill, they put out the lights and each, according to his nature and convenience, found himself a place to sleep.

The donkey lay down on the dung heap, the dog behind the door, the cat on the hearth near the warm ashes, and the cock settled himself on a rafter. And because they were tired out from their long hike, they soon fell asleep.

When midnight had passed, and the thieves saw from a distance that there were no longer any lights on in the house and that all seemed quiet, their chief said, "We shouldn't let them scare us out of our wits."

He ordered one of his men to go back to the house and look around. The messenger, finding all quiet, went into the kitchen to get a light. He mistook the cat's glowing eyes for live coals and struck a match on them. This was no joke to the cat, who sprang at his face, spitting and scratching.

The terrified thief tried to get out the back door, but the dog, who lay there, sprang up and bit him in the leg. As he ran by the dung heap in the yard, the donkey landed him a neat blow with his hind legs; the cock on his roost, awakened by the noise, cried kikeriki.

The thief ran as fast as he could to his chief and said, "There is a terrible witch in the house. She attacked me and scratched my face with her long nails. At the door there is a man with a knife and he stuck me in the leg with it. In the yard there's a black monster, who beat me with a club; and on the roof there sat a judge who cried, 'Bring the scoundrels to me.'

"Then I got away."

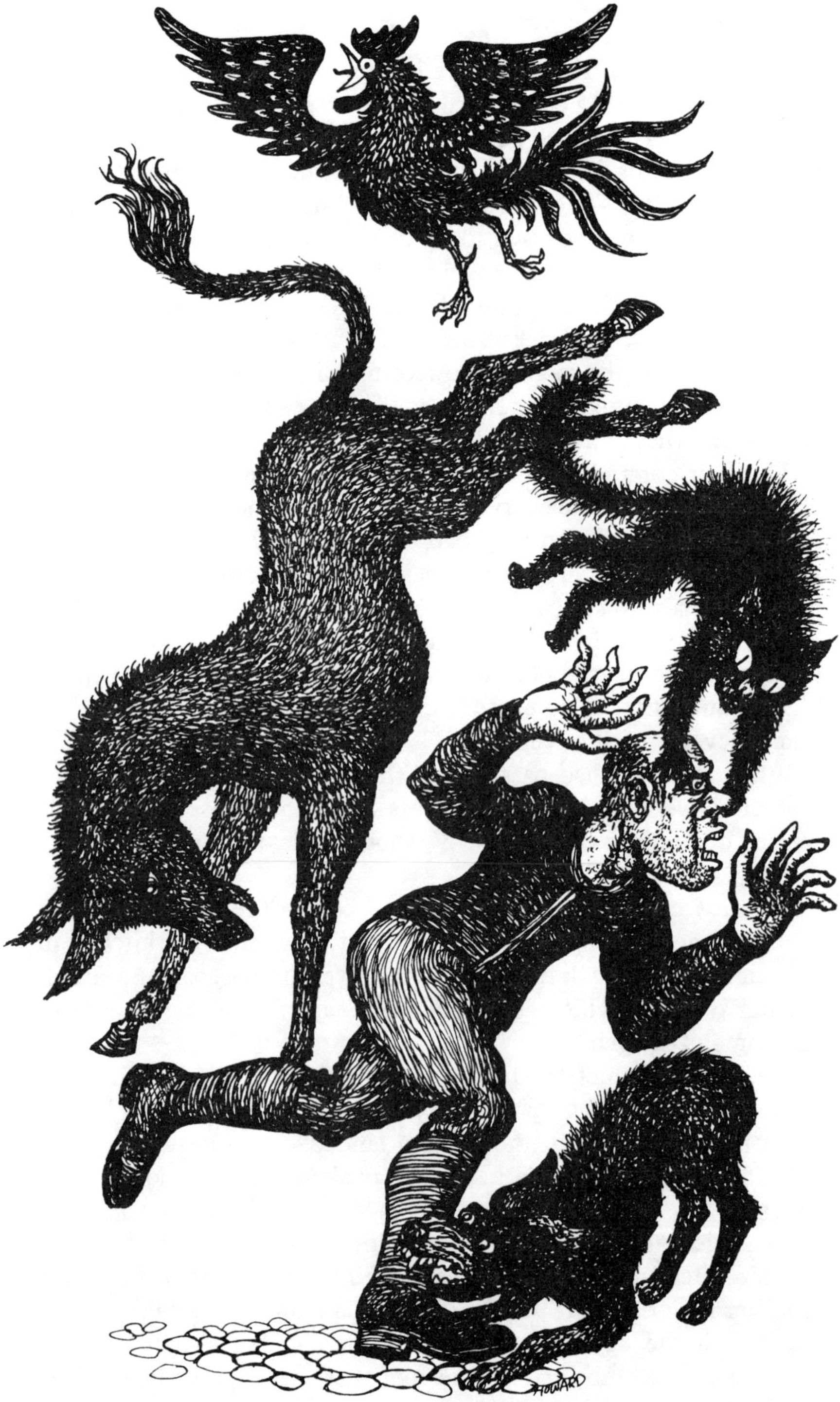
HOWARD

After that the thieves never dared to come near the house, and the four Bremen town musicians felt themselves so much at home they decided to remain for good.

And this tale's still warm from the telling, for I've just heard it.

collected by JACOB and WILHELM GRIMM
translated by Elizabeth Shub

The Wizards of the Vestmanna Isles
Iceland

When the Black Death was raging in Iceland, eighteen wizards gathered, swore friendship with one another, and sailed out to the Vestmanna Isles, intending to ward off death there as long as they could. As soon as they saw by their secret arts that the sickness was abating on the mainland, they wanted to find out whether anyone there was still alive; so they agreed to send one of their company to the mainland, and for this errand they chose one who was neither the most nor the least skilled in their arts. They ferried him to land, and told him that if he was not back before Christmas they would send him a Sending which would kill him. This was early in Advent.

The man went off, walked a long way, and wandered far and wide. But nowhere did he see a living soul; farms stood open, and dead bodies lay about, scattered here and there. Finally he came to one farm whose doors were shut. He was amazed, and now hope stirred in him that he might find some living man. He knocked, and out came a young and pretty girl. He greeted her, but she flung her arms round his neck and wept for joy to see a man, for she said she had thought there was nobody left alive but her. She asked him to stay with her, and he agreed. So now they went indoors and talked; she asked him where he had come from, and where he was going. He told her, and also told her that he would have to be back before Christmas, but all the same she asked him to stay with her as long as he could, and he was so sorry for her that he promised that he would. She told him there was nobody alive in those parts, for she said she had walked a whole week's journey from her house in each direction, and found no one.

Now time slipped by and Christmas drew near, and then the man from the islands wanted to go. The girl begged him to stay, and said that his friends would not be so hard-hearted as to make him pay for

The Wizards of the Vestmanna Isles

it if he stayed with her when she was left all alone in the world. So he let himself be persuaded.

And now Christmas Eve had come, and now he is determined to go, whatever she may say. So then she sees that it's no good pleading any longer, and says: "Do you really think you can get out to the islands tonight? Don't you think you might just as well die here beside me as die somewhere on the way?"

The man realized that the time was too short now, and resigned himself to stay quietly there and wait for death where he was. So the night passed, and he was very gloomy, but the girl was as merry as could be, and asked whether he could see how the men on the Isles were getting on. He said that they were preparing to send a Sending ashore, and that it would arrive that day. Now the girl sat down on the bed beside him, while he lay in bed, a little way behind her. He said that he was beginning to grow sleepy, and that this was due to the Sending's onslaught. Then he fell asleep. The girl sat at the foot of the bed, and she would constantly rouse him a little and make him tell her where the Sending now was. But the nearer it came the deeper he slept, and finally, just after saying that the Sending had reached her farm-lands, he fell into such a deep sleep that she could not wake him again—nor was it long before she saw a russet vapour come into the farmhouse.

This vapour glided gently, very gently, up the room towards her, and then took on human shape. The girl asks the Sending where it is going, and it tells her what its errand is, and tells her to get up off the bed—"for I can't get at him on account of you," it says.

The girl says that in that case it will have to do something for her. The Sending asks what that might be. The girl says it is to let her see how huge it could make itself. The Sending agrees to this, and now it grows so huge that it fills the whole house.

Then the girl says: "Now I want to see how small you can make yourself."

The Sending says it can turn itself into a fly, and with this it changes to the likeness of a fly, for it imagines that now it will be able to slip under the girl's arm and get at the man in bed. But it settles on a marrowbone which the girl was holding and crawls right into it, and the girl sticks a plug in the hole. Then she puts the bone in her pocket with the Sending inside it, and now she wakes the man.

He woke up at once, and was much amazed at being still alive. Then the girl asks him where the Sending is now, and he says he has no idea what has become of it. Then the girl says she had long suspected that those fellows out on the Isles were no great wizards. So now the man was very glad, and they both enjoyed Christmas and were quite contented.

But when New Year drew near, the man began to be silent, and the girl asks what the matter is. He says that the men of the Isles are now busy preparing another Sending, "and they are all of them putting strength into it. It is to come here on New Year's Eve, and there's nothing that can save me then."

The girl said she would not cross that bridge before she came to it— "and you ought not to be afraid of Sendings from those men in the Isles."

She was as merry as could be, so he felt ashamed of showing any weakness.

On New Year's Eve he says the Sending has come ashore— "and it is advancing rapidly, for great strength has been put into it."

The girl tells him to come out with her; he does so, and they walk till they come to a thicket. There she halts, and pulls some branches aside, and there in front of them is a slab of rock. The girl lifts the slab, and there underneath it is an underground chamber. They both go down into it, and a gloomy, ghastly place it is; there is one dim lamp, and it is burning human belly-fat in a human skull. In a bed near this lamp lies an old man, rather ghastly-looking; his eyes are blood-red, and all in all he is horrible enough for the man from the Isles to be quite impressed.

"Well, foster-daughter," says the old man, "there must be something new going on if you are out and about. It's a long while since I saw you. What can I do for you now?"

Then the girl tells him everything that had happened to her, and all about the man, and about the first Sending. The old man asks her to let him see the bone. She does, and he seemed to turn into quite a different person as soon as he was holding it; he turned it round and round in all directions, and stroked it all over.

Then the girl says: "Be quick and help me, foster-father, because my man is beginning to feel sleepy now, and that's a sign that the Sending will soon be here."

The old man takes the plug out of the bone, and out comes the fly. He strokes and pats the fly, and says: "Off you go now, and go to meet any Sendings from the Isles and swallow them up."

Then there was a mighty crash, and the fly zoomed off, and it had grown so huge that one jaw touched the sky and the other scraped the ground; in this way it met all Sendings that came from the Isles, and so the man was saved.

The Wizards of the Vestmanna Isles

So home they went from the underground chamber, the girl and the man from the Vestmanna Isles, and they settled on her farm. They got married soon after, and increased and multiplied and filled the land. And that's as much as I know about this story.

collected by JÓN ÁRNASON
translated by Jacqueline Simpson

Jorinde and Joringel
Germany

There was once an old castle right in the middle of a great, thick forest, and an old woman lived in it all alone; she was a witch. Every morning she changed herself into a cat or a screech-owl, every evening she changed back and looked like a decent human being. She knew how to entice wild animals and birds, and then she slaughtered them, boiled them and roasted them.

When anyone stepped within one hundred paces of the castle, his limbs were locked and he was unable to move an inch until the witch released him; and if a chaste young girl entered this circle, the witch turned her into a bird and stuffed her into a wickerwork cage and carried the cage into one of the castle chambers. She had all of seven thousand such cages, each with its own rare bird, in the castle.

Now there was once a young girl called Jorinde; she was more beautiful than anyone else at all. She and a handsome young man called Joringel had pledged themselves to one another. They were about to be married and were entirely wrapped up in each other. So that they could talk alone together for once in a while, they went walking in the forest.

"Beware!" said Joringel. "Don't go too close to the castle."

It was a lovely evening: the sun glanced between the tree trunks, shafts of light pierced the dark green of the forest, and the turtle-dove sang dolefully from the old hawthorn bushes.

Now and then Jorinde wept. She sat down in the sunlight and moaned; and Joringel moaned too. They felt so dismayed—as if they were about to die. They stared about them, and were lost, and did not know the way home. Half of the sun still stood above the mountain and half was below it.

Jorinde and Joringel

Joringel peered through the undergrowth and saw the old walls of the castle only a few paces away. He was startled and scared to death.

Jorinde sang:

> *My little bird with the little ring red*
> *Sings Sorrow, Sorrow, Sorrow*
> *He sings the little dove will soon be dead,*
> *Sings Sorrow, Sorr . . . tsicuet, tsicuet, tsicuet.*

Joringel looked at Jorinde. Jorinde had been turned into a nightingale and sang "tsicuet, tsicuet". A screech-owl with glowing eyes flew round them three times and three times called "Tu-whit, Tu-whoo."

Joringel could not move; he stood there like a stone, he could not cry or speak or move hand or foot.

Now the sun had gone down. The owl flew into a bush and at once an old woman walked out of it, crooked and yellow and skinny: great red eyes, crooked nose so long that it touched her chin. She murmured, snared the nightingale, and carried it off on her hand.

Joringel was unable to say one word or move one step; the nightingale was gone.

After a long while the hag came back and said in a hollow voice: "Greetings, Zachiel! When the moon shines into the cage, let him loose, Zachiel, at the appointed hour!"

Then Joringel stood free. He fell on to his knees in front of the hag and begged her to give him back his Jorinde. But the witch replied that he would never see her again, and turned her back on him.

Joringel called out after her, he cried, he moaned, but all in vain. "Oh! What will become of me?" Joringel walked away and came at last to a remote village, and there he tended the sheep for a long time. He often walked round the castle but kept his distance from it.

Then one night Joringel dreamed that he found a blood-red flower with a fine large pearl in the middle of it. He picked the flower and went to the castle with it; whatever he touched with the flower was released from its enchantment; and he dreamed that he had won back his Jorinde with it.

As soon as he woke in the morning, Joringel began to search hill and dale for the flower of his dream; he searched for eight days and early on the morning of the ninth day he found the blood-red flower. A heavy dew-drop lay in the middle of it, as large as the finest of pearls.

Joringel carried this flower by day and night until he reached the

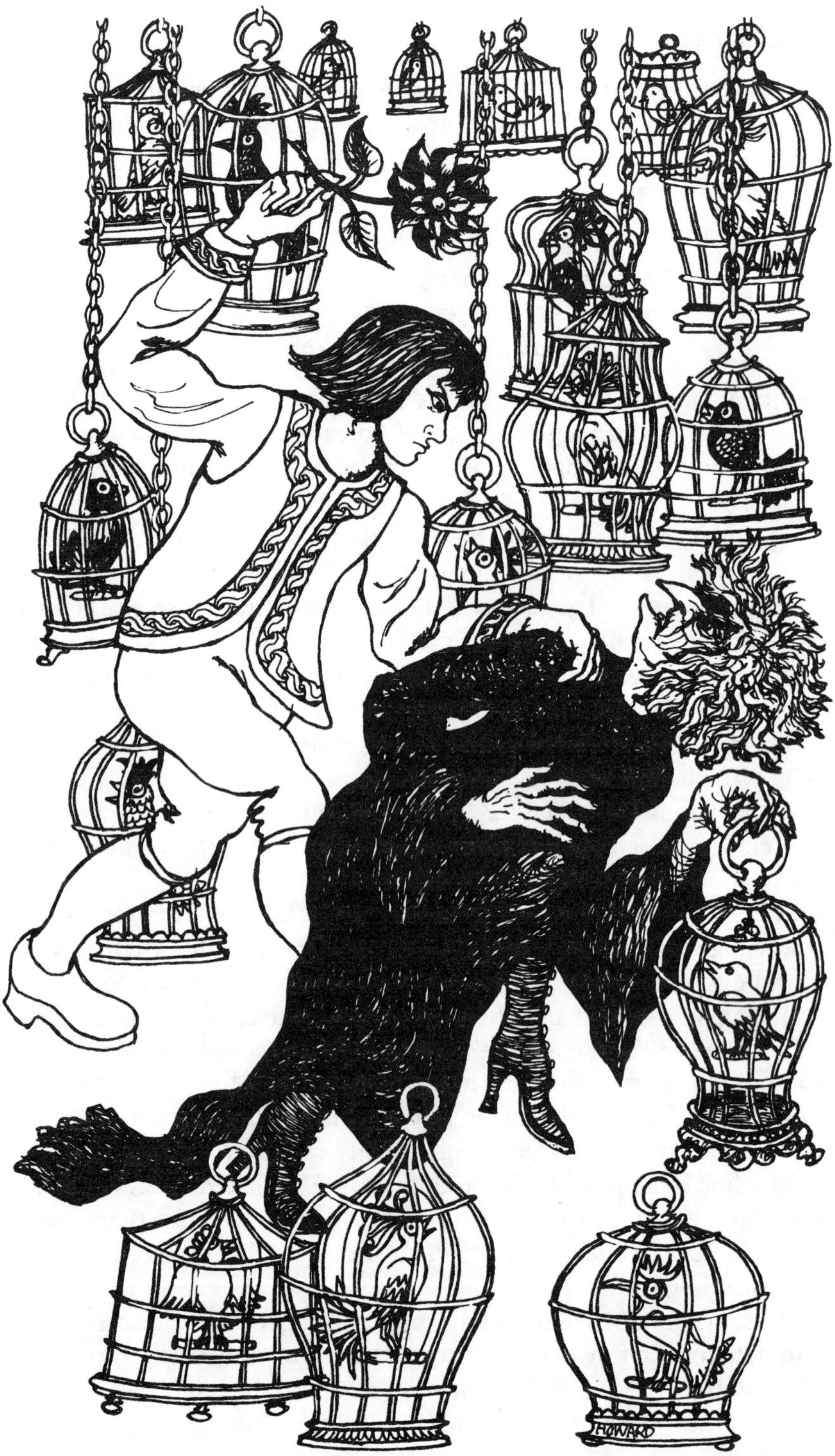
HOWARD

castle. When he stepped within one hundred paces of the castle, his limbs were not locked and he walked straight up to the gate.

Joringel rejoiced. He touched the gate with the flower and it sprang open. He walked through it, into the courtyard, listened, listened for the sound of birdsong; at last he heard it. He went and found the chamber where the witch was feeding the birds in the seven thousand cages.

When she saw Joringel she was angry, very angry; she yelled at him, she fumed and foamed, but she was unable to come within two paces of him.

Joringel took no notice, he went and checked the cages with the birds inside them. But there were many hundreds of nightingales. How would Joringel ever find his Jorinde again?

While he was busy with the cages, Joringel saw the old woman furtively pick up one cage with a bird in it and make for the door. He leaped across the chamber, and with the flower he touched the cage. He touched the hag too, and put an end to her magic powers.

And there stood Jorinde, her arms around his neck, as beautiful as she had been before. Then Joringel turned all the other birds back into young girls; and then he went home with his Jorinde, and they lived happily ever after.

collected by JACOB and WILHELM GRIMM
translated by Hildegund Kübler and Kevin Crossley-Holland

A Stork is not always a Stork
Denmark

Storks are storks, and men are men, and some say that's the end of it. But sometimes storks are men, and men are storks, and this story is the proof of it.

Not so very long ago, on a farm in Denmark, there was a man mowing a field of rye, and as his scythe went forward, a stork kept hopping beside him. This made him very nervous, for he feared he might get a good deep peck. "Be off with you!" he said, and, "Mind your own business, stork!" But it served no purpose, and at last he grew so rattled that he plucked out his short knife and flung it, *zip*, at the stork's head. Luckily he missed, it fell to the ground, and the stork picked it up and flew off.

Soon after this the man who had been mowing felt an urge to go travelling. Try as he would, he could not resist it, so he left the farm and signed for a sailor. Now he would be among icebergs and now off palm-treed coasts; to-day they would sail up steamy rivers, to-morrow down skerried creeks. Nor was he always on sea, for sometimes the urge drove him through jungles and deserts or over frozen plateaux. It was a cruel life he had of it, nor could he tell why. All he knew was that he had to keep going until somewhere, some time, he found something, he knew not what.

After many long years he found himself in Egypt, where he took lodging at an inn. The landlord asked him what he was doing so far from home. "If only I knew!" sighed the traveller, and went on to explain that he had never travelled farther than the nearest farm till after he flung his knife at a stork. "Since then," he said, "I have known not a single day's rest."

The landlord went out from the room, but in a moment or two he returned. "Would this be the knife?" he asked—and it was. "Yes," said the landlord, "and if it hadn't been that I brought up fourteen

A Stork is not always a Stork

children on your father's barn, I should certainly have done you an injury that day."

As soon as the traveller received his knife again, he thought only of home. But first he had to meet the fourteen children, and bonny children they were too, without a feather among them at that moment. He took the next ship back to Denmark, where he told his story to all who would listen. But some said storks are storks, and men are men, and that's the end of it. But most agreed that storks are sometimes men, and men are storks, and reckoned this story the proof of it.

retold by GWYN JONES

Tom Tit Tot

England

Once upon a time there was a woman, and she baked five pies. And when they came out of the oven, they were that overbaked the crusts were too hard to eat. So she says to her daughter:

"Darter," says she, "put you them there pies on the shelf, and leave 'em there a little, and they'll come again."—She meant, you know, the crust would get soft.

But the girl, she says to herself: "Well, if they'll come again, I'll eat 'em now." And she set to work and ate 'em all, first and last.

Well, come supper-time the woman said: "Go you, and get one o' them there pies. I dare say they've come again now."

The girl went and she looked, and there was nothing but the dishes. So back she came and says she: "Noo, they ain't come again."

"Not one of 'em?" says the mother.

"Not one of 'em," says she.

"Well, come again, or not come again," said the woman, "I'll have one for supper."

"But you can't, if they ain't come," said the girl.

"But I can," says she. "Go you, and bring the best of 'em."

"Best or worst," says the girl, "I've ate 'em all, and you can't have one till that's come again."

Well, the woman she was done, and she took her spinning to the door to spin, and as she span she sang:

> "My darter ha' ate five, five pies today.
> My darter ha' ate five, five pies today."

The king was coming down the street, and he heard her sing, but what she sang he couldn't hear, so he stopped and said:

"What was that you were singing, my good woman?"

The woman was ashamed to let him hear what her daughter had been doing, so she sang, instead of that:

> "My darter ha' spun five, five skeins today.
> My darter ha' spun five, five skeins today."

"Stars o' mine!" said the king, "I never heard tell of anyone that could do that."

Then he said: "Look you here, I want a wife, and I'll marry your daughter. But look you here," says he, "eleven months out of the year she shall have all she likes to eat, and all the gowns she likes to get, and all the company she likes to keep; but the last month of the year she'll have to spin five skeins every day, and if she don't I shall kill her."

"All right," says the woman; for she thought what a grand marriage that was. And as for the five skeins, when the time came, there'd be plenty of ways of getting out of it, and likeliest, he'd have forgotten all about it.

Well, so they were married. And for eleven months the girl had all she liked to eat, and all the gowns she liked to get, and all the company she liked to keep.

But when the time was getting over, she began to think about the skeins and to wonder if he had 'em in mind. But not one word did he say about 'em, and she thought he'd wholly forgotten 'em.

However, the last day of the last month he takes her to a room she'd never set eyes on before. There was nothing in it but a spinning-wheel and a stool. And says he: "Now, my dear, here you'll be shut in tomorrow with some victuals and some flax, and if you haven't spun five skeins by the night, your head'll go off."

And away he went about his business.

Well, she was that frightened, she'd always been such a gatless girl, that she didn't so much as know how to spin, and what was she to do tomorrow with no one to come nigh her to help her? She sat down on a stool in the kitchen, and law! how she did cry!

However, all of a sudden she heard a sort of a knocking low down on the door. She upped and opened it, and what should she see but a small little black thing with a long tail. That looked up at her right curious, and that said:

"What are you a-crying for?"

"What's that to you?" says she.

"Never you mind," that said, "but tell me what you're a-crying for."

"That won't do me no good if I do," says she.

"You don't know that," that said, and twirled that's tail round.

"Well," says she, "that won't do no harm, if that don't do no good," and she upped and told about the pies, and the skeins, and everything.

"This is what I'll do," says the little black thing. "I'll come to your window every morning and take the flax and bring it spun at night."

"What's your pay?" says she.

That looked out of the corner of that's eyes, and that said: "I'll give you three guesses every night to guess my name, and if you haven't guessed it before the month's up you shall be mine."

Well, she thought, she'd be sure to guess that's name before the month was up. "All right," says she, "I agree."

"All right," that says, and law! how that twirled that's tail.

Well, the next day, her husband took her into the room, and there was the flax and the day's food.

"Now, there's the flax," says he, "and if that ain't spun up this night, off goes your head." And then he went out and locked the door.

He'd hardly gone, when there was a knocking against the window.

She upped and she oped it, and there sure enough was the little old thing sitting on the ledge.

"Where's the flax?" says he.

"Here it be," says she. And she gave it to him.

Well, come the evening a knocking came again to the window. She upped and she oped it, and there was the little old thing with five skeins of flax on his arm.

"Here it be," says he, and he gave it to her.

"Now, what's my name?" says he.

"What, is that Bill?" says she.

"Noo, that ain't," says he, and he twirled his tail.

"Is that Ned?" says she.

"Noo, that ain't," says he, and he twirled his tail.

"Well, is that Mark?" says she.

"Noo, that ain't," says he, and he twirled his tail harder, and away he flew.

Well, when her husband came in, there were the five skeins ready for him. "I see I shan't have to kill you tonight, my dear," says he; "You'll have your food and your flax in the morning," says he, and away he goes.

Tom Tit Tot

Well, every day the flax and the food were brought, and every day that there little black impet used to come mornings and evenings. And all the day the girl sate trying to think of names to say to it when it came at night. But she never hit on the right one. And as it got towards the end of the month, the impet began to look so maliceful, and that twirled that's tail faster and faster each time she gave a guess.

At last it came to the last day but one. The impet came at night along with the five skeins, and that said:

"What, ain't you got my name yet?"

"Is that Nicodemus?" says she.

"Noo, 't ain't," that says.

"Is that Sammle?" says she.

"Noo, 't ain't," that says.

"A-well, is that Methusalem?" says she.

"Noo, 't ain't that neither," that says.

Then that looks at her with that's eyes like a coal of fire, and that says: "Woman, there's only tomorrow night, and then you'll be mine!" And away it flew.

Well, she felt that horrid. However, she heard the king coming along the passage. In he came, and when he sees the five skeins, he says, says he:

"Well, my dear," says he. "I don't see but what you'll have your skeins ready tomorrow night as well, and as I reckon I shan't have to kill you, I'll have supper in here tonight." So they brought supper, and another stool for him, and down the two sate.

Well, he hadn't eaten but a mouthful or so, when he stops and begins to laugh.

"What is it?" says she.

"A-why," says he, "I was out a-hunting today, and I got away to a place in the wood I'd never seen before. And there was an old chalk-pit. And I heard a kind of a sort of humming. So I got off my hobby, and I went right quiet to the pit, and I looked down. Well, what should there be but the funniest little black thing you ever set eyes on. And what was that doing, but that had a little spinning-wheel, and that was spinning wonderful fast, and twirling that's tail. And as that span that sang:

> '*Nimmy nimmy not*
> *My name's Tom Tit Tot.*'"

Well, when the girl heard this, she felt as if she could have jumped out of her skin for joy, but she didn't say a word.

Next day that there little thing looked so maliceful when he came for the flax. And when night came she heard that knocking against the window panes. She opened the window, and that come right in on the ledge. That was grinning from ear to ear, and Oo! that's tail was twirling round so fast.

"What's my name?" that says, as that gave her the skeins.

"Is that Solomon?" she says, pretending to be afeard.

"Noo, 'tain't," that says, and that came farther into the room.

"Well, is that Zebedee?" says she again.

"Noo, 'tain't," says the impet. And then that laughed and twirled that's tail till you could hardly see it.

"Take time, woman," that says: "next guess, and you're mine." And that stretched out that's black hands at her.

Well, she backed a step or two, and she looked at it, and then she laughed out, and says she, pointing her finger at it:

> 'Nimmy nimmy not
> My name's Tom Tit Tot.'"

Well, when that heard her, that gave an awful shriek and away that flew into the dark, and she never saw it any more.

retold by JOSEPH JACOBS

The Enchanted Apple-tree
Flanders

Once upon a time there lived an old woman whose name was Misery.

Her one and only possession was an apple-tree and even this caused her more pain than pleasure. When the apples were ripe, the village urchins came and stole them off the tree.

This went on year after year, when one day an old man, with a long white beard, knocked at Misery's door. "Old woman," he begged, "give me a crust of bread."

"You, too, are a poor miserable creature," said Misery, who, although she had nothing herself, was full of compassion for others. "Here is half a loaf, take it; it is all I have, eat it in peace, and may it refresh you."

"As you have been so kind," said the old fellow, "I will grant you a wish."

"Oh!" sighed the old woman, "I have only one desire, that is, that anyone who touches my apple-tree may stick to it until I set them free. The way my apples are stolen from me is past all bearing."

"Your wish is granted," said the old fellow, and he went away.

Two days later Misery went to look at her tree; she found hanging and sticking to the branches a crowd of children, servants, mothers who had come to rescue their children, fathers who had tried to save their wives, two parrots who had escaped from their cage, a cock, a goose, an owl, and other birds, not to mention a goat. When she saw this extraordinary sight, she burst out laughing, and rubbed her hands with delight. She let them all remain hanging on the tree some time before she released them.

The thieves had learnt their lesson, and never stole the apples again.

Some time passed by, when one day someone again knocked at old Misery's door.

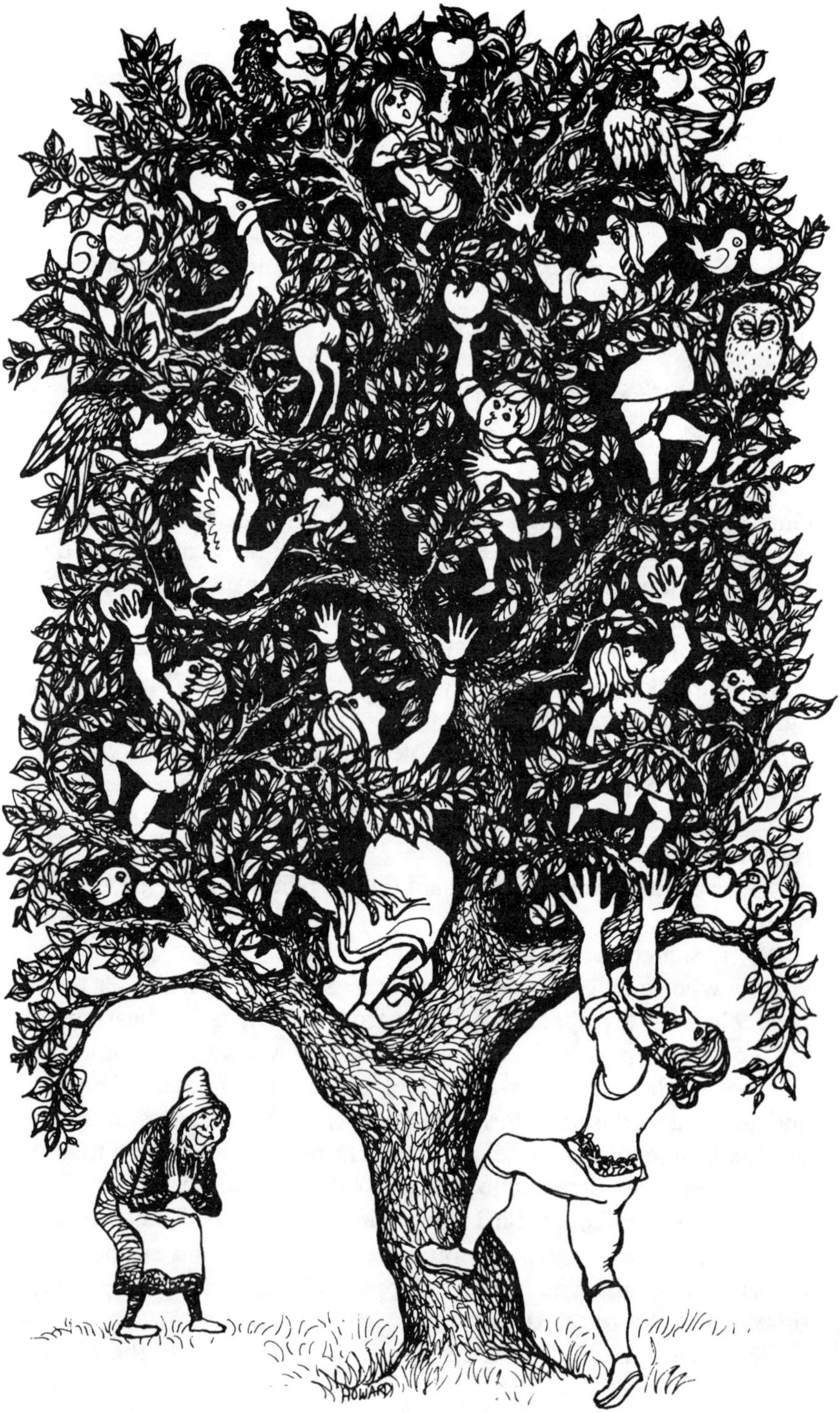
HOWARD

The Enchanted Apple-Tree

"Come in," she cried.

"Guess who I am," said a voice. "I am old Father Death himself. Listen, little mother," he continued. "I think that you and your old dog have lived long enough; I have come to fetch you both."

"You are all-powerful," said Misery. "I do not oppose your will, but before I pack up, grant me one favour. On the tree yonder there grow the most delicious apples you have ever tasted. Don't you think it would be a pity to leave them, without gathering one?"

"As you ask me so graciously, I will take one," said Death, whose mouth was watering as he walked towards the tree. He climbed up to the topmost branches to gather a large rosy apple, but directly he touched it, the wretch remained glued to the tree by his long bony hand. Nothing could tear him off, in spite of his struggles.

"There you are, old tyrant, hanging high and dry," said Misery.

As a result of Death hanging on the tree, no one died. If persons fell into the water they were not drowned; if a cart ran over them they did not even notice it; they did not die even if their heads were cut off.

After Death had hung, winter and summer, for ten long years on the tree, through all weathers, the old woman had pity on him, and allowed him to come down on condition that she should live as long as she liked.

This, Father Death agreed to, and that is why men live longer than the sparrows, and why Misery is always to be found in the world, and will doubtless remain until the end of time.

translated by M. C. O. MORRIS

The Elf Maiden

Lapland

Once upon a time two young men living in a small village fell in love with the same girl. During the winter, it was all night except for an hour or so about noon, when the darkness seemed a little less dark, and then they used to see which of them could tempt her out for a sleigh ride with the Northern Lights flashing above them, or which could persuade her to come to a dance in some neighbouring barn. But when the spring began, and the light grew longer, the hearts of the villagers leapt at the sight of the sun, and a day was fixed for the boats to be brought out, and the great nets to be spread in the bays of some islands that lay a few miles to the north. Everybody went on this expedition, and the two young men and the girl went with them.

They all sailed merrily across the sea chattering like a flock of magpies, or singing their favourite songs. And when they reached the shore, what an unpacking there was! For this was a noted fishing ground, and here they would live, in little wooden huts, till autumn and bad weather came round again.

The maiden and the two young men happened to share the same hut with some friends, and fished daily from the same boat. And as time went on, one of the youths remarked that the girl took less notice of him than she did of his companion. At first he tried to think that he was dreaming, and for a long while he kept his eyes shut very tight to what he did not want to see, but in spite of his efforts, the truth managed to wriggle through, and then the young man gave up trying to deceive himself, and set about finding some way to get the better of his rival.

The plan that he hit upon could not be carried out for some months; but the longer the young man thought of it, the more

The Elf Maiden

pleased he was with it, so he made no sign of his feelings, and waited patiently till the moment came. This was the very day that they were all going to leave the islands, and sail back to the mainland for the winter. In the bustle and hurry of departure, the cunning fisherman contrived that their boat should be the last to put off, and when everything was ready, and the sails about to be set, he suddenly called out:

"Oh, dear, what shall I do! I have left my best knife behind in the hut. Run, like a good fellow, and get it for me, while I raise the anchor and loosen the tiller."

Not thinking any harm, the youth jumped back on shore and made his way up the steep bank. At the door of the hut he stopped and looked back, then started and gazed in horror. The head of the boat stood out to sea, and he was left alone on the island.

Yes, there was no doubt of it—he was quite alone; and he had nothing to help him except the knife which his comrade had purposely dropped on the ledge of the window. For some minutes he was too stunned by the treachery of his friend to think about anything at all, but after a while he shook himself awake, and determined that he would manage to keep alive somehow, if it were only to revenge himself.

So he put the knife in his pocket and went off to a part of the island which was not so bare as the rest, and had a small grove of trees. From one of these he cut himself a bow, which he strung with a piece of cord that had been left lying about the huts.

When this was ready the young man ran down to the shore and shot one or two sea-birds, which he plucked and cooked for supper.

In this way the months slipped by, and Christmas came round again. The evening before, the youth went down to the rocks and into the copse, collecting all the driftwood the sea had washed up or the gale had blown down, and he piled it up in a great stack outside the door, so that he might not have to fetch any all the next day. As soon as his task was done, he paused and looked out towards the mainland, thinking of Christmas Eve last year, and the merry dance they had had. The night was still and cold, and by the help of the Northern Lights he could almost see across to the opposite coast, when, suddenly, he noticed a boat, which seemed steering straight for the island. At first he could hardly stand for joy, the chance of speaking to another man was so delightful; but as the boat drew near there was something, he could not tell what, that was different from the boats which he had been used to all his life, and when it touched the shore he saw that the people that filled it were beings of another world than ours. Then he hastily stepped behind the wood stack, and waited for what might happen next.

The strange folk one by one jumped on to the rocks, each bearing a load of something that they wanted. Among the women he remarked two young girls, more beautiful and better dressed than any of the rest, carrying between them two great baskets full of provisions. The young man peeped out cautiously to see what all this crowd could be doing inside the tiny hut, but in a moment he drew back again, as the girls returned, and looked about as if they wanted to find out what sort of a place the island was.

Their sharp eyes soon discovered the form of a man crouching behind the bundles of sticks, and at first they felt a little frightened, and started as if they would run away. But the youth remained so still, that they took courage and laughed gaily to each other. "What a strange creature, let us try what he is made of," said one, and she stooped down and gave him a pinch.

Now the young man had a pin sticking in the sleeve of his jacket, and the moment the girl's hand touched him she pricked it so sharply that the blood came. The girl screamed so loudly that the people all ran out of their huts to see what was the matter. But directly they caught sight of the man they turned and fled in the other direction, and picking up the goods they had brought with them scampered as fast as they could down to the shore. In an instant, boat, people, and goods had vanished completely.

In their hurry they had, however, forgotten two things: a bundle of keys which lay on the table, and the girl whom the pin had pricked, and who now stood pale and helpless beside the wood stack.

"You will have to make me your wife," she said at last, "for you have drawn my blood, and I belong to you."

"Why not? I am quite willing," answered he. "But how do you suppose we can manage to live till summer comes round again?"

"Do not be anxious about that," said the girl; "if you will only marry me all will be well. I am very rich, and all my family are rich also."

Then the young man gave her his promise to make her his wife, and the girl fulfilled her part of the bargain, and food was plentiful on the island all through the long winter months, though he never knew how it got there. And by-and-by it was spring once more, and time for the fisher-folk to sail from the mainland.

"Where are we to go now?" asked the girl, one day, when the sun seemed brighter and the wind softer than usual.

The Elf Maiden

"I do not care where I go," answered the young man; "what do you think?"

The girl replied that she would like to go somewhere right at the other end of the island, and build a house, far away from the huts of the fishing folk. And he consented, and that very day they set off in search of a sheltered spot on the banks of a stream, so that it would be easy to get water.

In a tiny bay, on the opposite side of the island, they found the very thing, which seemed to have been made on purpose for them; and as they were tired with their long walk, they laid themselves down on a bank of moss among some birches and prepared to have a good night's rest, so as to be fresh for work next day. But before she went to sleep the girl turned to her husband, and said: "If in your dreams you fancy that you hear strange noises, be sure you do not stir, or get up to see what it is."

"Oh, it is not likely we shall hear any noises in such a quiet place," answered he, and fell sound asleep.

Suddenly he was awakened by a great clatter about his ears, as if all the workmen in the world were sawing and hammering and building close to him. He was just going to spring up and go to see what it meant, when he luckily remembered his wife's words and lay still. But the time till morning seemed very long, and with the first ray of sun they both rose, and pushed aside the branches of the birch trees. There, in the very place they had chosen, stood a beautiful house—doors and windows, and everything all complete!

"Now you must fix on a spot for your cow-stalls," said the girl, when they had breakfasted off wild cherries; "and take care it is the proper size, neither too large nor too small." And the husband did as he was bid, though he wondered what use a cow-house could be, as they had no cows to put in it. But as he was a little afraid of his wife, who knew so much more than he, he asked no questions.

This night also he was awakened by the same sounds as before, and in the morning they found, near the stream, the most beautiful cow-house that ever was seen, with stalls and milk-pails and stools all complete, indeed, everything that a cow-house could possibly want, except the cows. Then the girl bade him measure out the ground for a storehouse, and this, she said, might be as large as he pleased; and when the storehouse was ready she proposed that they should set off to pay her parents a visit.

The old people welcomed them heartily, and summoned their neighbours, for many miles round, to a great feast in their honour. In fact, for several weeks there was no work done on the farm at all; and at length the young man and his wife grew tired of so much play and declared that they must return to their own home. But, before they started on the journey, the wife whispered to her husband: "Take care to jump over the threshold as quick as you can, or it will be the worse for you."

The young man listened to her words, and sprang over the threshold like an arrow from a bow; and it was well he did, for, no sooner was he on the other side, than his father-in-law threw a great hammer at him, which would have broken both his legs, if it had only touched them.

When they had gone some distance on the road home, the girl turned to her husband and said: "Till you step inside the house, be sure you do not look back, whatever you may hear or see."

And the husband promised, and for a while all was still; and he thought no more about the matter till he noticed at last that the nearer he drew to the house the louder grew the noise of the trampling of feet behind him. As he laid his hand upon the door he thought he was safe, and turned to look. There, sure enough, was a vast herd of cattle, which had been sent after him by his father-in-law when he found that his daughter had been cleverer than he. Half of the herd were already through the fence and cropping the grass on the banks of the stream, but half still remained outside and faded into nothing, even as he watched them.

However, enough cattle were left to make the young man rich, and he and his wife lived happily together, except that every now and then the girl vanished from his sight, and never told him where she had been. For a long time he kept silence about it; but one day, when he had been complaining of her absence, she said to him: "Dear husband, I am bound to go, even against my will, and there is only one way to stop me. Drive a nail into the threshold, and then I can never pass in or out."

And so he did.

retold by ANDREW LANG

The King o' the Cats
England

One winter's evening the sexton's wife was sitting by the fireside with her big black cat, Old Tom, on the other side, both half asleep and waiting for the master to come home. They waited and they waited, but still he didn't come, till at last he came rushing in, calling out, "Who's Tommy Tildrum?" in such a wild way that both his wife and his cat stared at him to know what was the matter.

"Why, what's the matter?" said his wife, "and why do you want to know who Tommy Tildrum is?"

"Oh, I've had such an adventure. I was digging away at old Mr Fordyce's grave when I suppose I must have dropped asleep, and only woke up by hearing a cat's *Miaou*."

"*Miaou!*" said Old Tom in answer.

"Yes, just like that! So I looked over the edge of the grave, and what do you think I saw?"

"Now, how can I tell?" said the sexton's wife.

"Why, nine black cats all like our friend Tom here, all with a white spot on their chestesses. And what do you think they were carrying? Why, a small coffin covered with a black velvet pall, and on the pall was a small coronet all of gold, and at every third step they took they cried all together, *Miaou*—"

"*Miaou!*" said Old Tom again.

"Yes, just like that!" said the sexton; "and as they came nearer and nearer to me I could see them more distinctly, because their eyes shone out with a sort of green light. Well, they all came towards me, eight of them carrying the coffin, and the biggest cat of all walking in front for all the world like—but look at our Tom, how he's looking at me. You'd think he knew all I was saying."

"Go on, go on," said his wife; "never mind Old Tom."

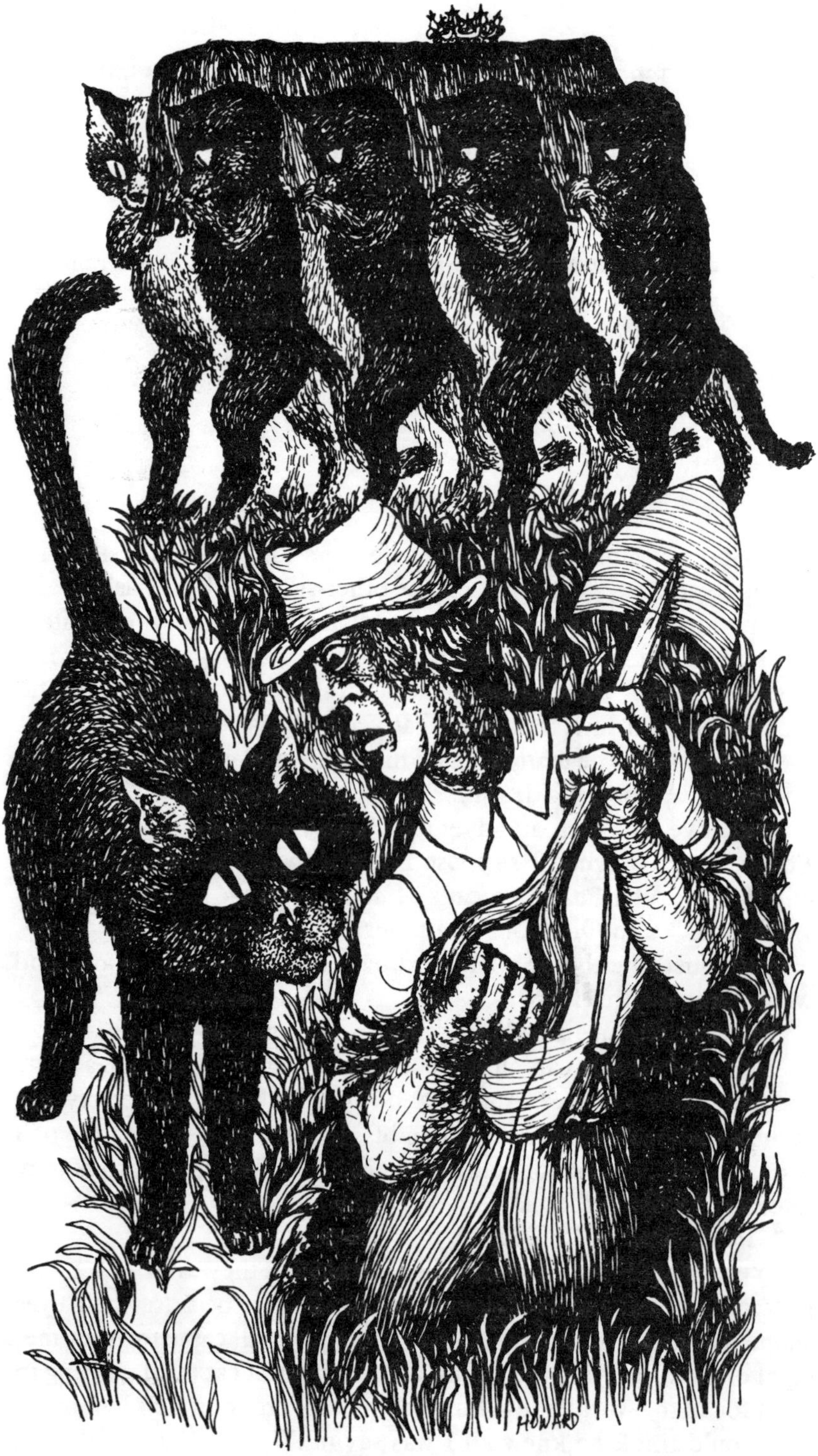
HOWARD

The King o' the Cats

"Well, as I was a-saying, they came towards me slowly and solemnly, and at every third step crying all together, *Miaou*—"

"*Miaou!*" said Old Tom again.

"Yes, just like that, till they came and stood right opposite Mr Fordyce's grave, where I was, when they all stood still and looked straight at me. I did feel queer, that I did! But look at Old Tom; he's looking at me just like they did."

"Go on, go on," said his wife; "never mind Old Tom."

"Where was I? Oh, they all stood still looking at me, when the one that wasn't carrying the coffin came forward and, staring straight at me, said to me—yes, I tell 'ee, *said* to me, with a squeaky voice, "Tell Tom Tildrum that Tim Toldrum's dead," and that's why I asked you if you knew who Tom Tildrum was, for how can I tell Tom Tildrum Tim Toldrum's dead if I don't know who Tom Tildrum is?"

"Look at Old Tom, look at Old Tom!" screamed his wife.

And well he might look, for Tom was swelling and Tom was staring, and at last Tom shrieked out, "What—old Tim dead! then I'm the King o' the Cats!" and rushed up the chimney and was never more seen.

retold by JOSEPH JACOBS

Little Annie the Goose-girl

Norway

Once upon a time there was a King who had so many geese, he was forced to have a lassie to tend them and watch them; her name was Annie, and so they called her "Annie the goose-girl". Now you must know there was a King's son from England who went out to woo; and as he came along Annie sat herself down in his way.

"Sitting all alone there, you little Annie?" said the King's son.

"Yes," said little Annie, "here I sit and put stitch to stitch, and patch on patch. I'm waiting to-day for the King's son from England."

"Him you mustn't look to have," said the Prince.

"Nay, but if I'm to have him," said little Annie, "have him I shall after all."

And now limners were sent out into all lands and realms to take the likenesses of the fairest Princesses, and the Prince was to choose between them. So he thought so much of one of them, that he set out to seek her, and wanted to wed her, and he was glad and happy when he got her for his sweetheart.

But now I must tell you this Prince had a stone with him which he laid by his bedside, and that stone knew everything, and when the Princess came little Annie told her, if so be she'd had a sweetheart before, or didn't feel herself quite free from anything which she didn't wish the Prince to know, she'd better not step on that stone which lay by the bedside.

"If you do, it will tell him all about you," said little Annie.

So when the Princess heard that she was dreadfully downcast, and she fell upon the thought to ask Annie if she would get into bed that

Little Annie the Goose-girl

night in her stead and lie down by the Prince's side, and then when he was sound asleep, Annie should get out and the Princess should get in, and so when he woke up in the morning he would find the right bride by his side.

So they did that, and when Annie the goose-girl came and stepped upon the stone the Prince asked—

"Who is this that steps into my bed?"

"A maid pure and bright," said the stone, and so they lay down to sleep; but when the night wore on the Princess came and lay down in Annie's stead.

But next morning, when they were to get up, the Prince asked the stone again—

"Who is this that steps out of my bed?"

"One that has had three bairns," said the stone.

When the Prince heard that he wouldn't have her, you may know very well; and so he packed her off home again, and took another sweetheart.

But as he went to see her, Annie went and sat down in his way again.

"Sitting all alone there, little Annie the goose-girl," said the Prince.

"Yes, here I sit, and put stitch to stitch, and patch to patch; for I'm waiting to-day for the King's son from England," said Annie.

"Oh! you mustn't look to have him," said the King's son.

"Nay, but if I'm to have him, have him I shall, after all"; that was what Annie thought.

Well, it was the same story over again with the Prince; only this time, when his bride got up in the morning, the stone said she'd had six bairns.

So the Prince wouldn't have her either, but sent her about her business; but still he thought he'd try once more if he couldn't find one who was pure and spotless; and he sought far and wide in many lands, till at last he found one he thought he might trust. But when he went to see her, little Annie the goose-girl had put herself in his way again.

"Sitting all alone there, you little Annie the goose-girl," said the Prince.

"Yes, here I sit, and put stitch to stitch, and patch to patch; for I'm waiting to-day for the King's son from England," said Annie.

"Him you mustn't look to have," said the Prince.

"Nay, but if I'm to have him, have him I shall, after all," said little Annie.

So when the Princess came, little Annie the goose-girl told her the same as she had told the other two, if she'd had any sweetheart before, or if there was anything else she didn't wish the Prince to know, she mustn't tread on the stone that the Prince had put at his bedside; for, said she—

"It tells him everything."

The Princess got very red and downcast when she heard that, for she was just as naughty as the others, and asked Annie if she would go in her stead and lie down with the Prince that night; and when he was sound asleep, she would come and take her place, and then he would have the right bride by his side when it was light next morning.

Yes! they did that. And when little Annie the goose-girl came and stepped upon the stone, the Prince asked—

"Who is this that steps into my bed?"

"A maid pure and bright," said the stone; and so they lay down to rest.

Farther on in the night the Prince put a ring on Annie's finger, and it fitted so tight she couldn't get it off again; for the Prince saw well enough there was something wrong, and so he wished to have a mark by which he might know the right woman again.

Well, when the Prince had gone off to sleep, the Princess came and drove Annie away to the pigsty, and lay down in her place. Next morning, when they were to get up, the Prince asked—

"Who is this that steps out of my bed?"

"One that's had nine bairns," said the stone.

When the Prince heard that he drove her away at once, for he was in an awful rage; and then he asked the stone how it all was with these Princesses who had stepped on it, for he couldn't understand it at all, he said.

So the stone told him how they had cheated him, and sent little Annie the goose-girl to him in their stead.

But as the Prince wished to have no mistake about it, he went down to her where she sat tending her geese, for he wanted to see if she had the ring too, and he thought, "if she has it, 'twere best to take her at once for my queen".

So when he got down he saw in a moment that she had tied a bit of rag round one of her fingers, and so he asked her why it was tied up.

"Oh! I've cut myself so badly," said little Annie the goose-girl.

So he must and would see the finger, but Annie wouldn't take the rag off. Then he caught hold of the finger; but Annie, she tried to pull it from him, and so between them the rag came off, and then he knew his ring.

So he took her up to the palace, and gave her much fine clothes and attire, and after that they held their wedding feast; and so little Annie the goose-girl came to have the King of England's son for her husband after all, just because it was written that she should have him.

collected by PETER CHRISTEN ASBJÖRNSEN and JÖRGEN I. MOE
translated by Sir George Webbe Dasent

The Dead Man's Nightcap
Iceland

On a farm beside a church there lived, among others, a young boy and a girl. The boy made a habit of scaring the girl, but she had got so used to it that she was never frightened of anything, for if she did see something she thought it was the boy trying to scare her.

One day it so happened that the washing had been done, and that among the things there were many white nightcaps, such as were in fashion then. In the evening the girl was told to fetch in the washing, which was out in the churchyard. She runs out, and begins to pick up the washing. When she has almost finished, she sees a white spectre sitting on one of the graves. She thinks to herself that the lad is planning to scare her, so she runs up and snatches the spectre's cap off (for she thought the boy had taken one of the nightcaps) and says: "Now don't you start trying to scare me this time!"

So she went indoors with the washing; the boy had been indoors the whole time. They started sorting out the washing; there was one nightcap too many now, and it was earthy on the inside. Then the girl was scared.

Next morning the spectre was still sitting on the grave, and people did not know what to do about it, as nobody dared take the cap back, and so they sent word all round the district, asking for advice. There was one old man in the district who declared that it would be impossible to stop something bad coming of it, unless the girl herself took the cap back to the spectre and placed it on its head in silence, and that there ought to be many people there to watch.

The girl was forced to go with the cap and place it on the spectre's head, and so she went, though her heart was not much in it, and she placed the cap on the head of the spectre, and when she had done so she said: "Are you satisfied now?"

The Dead Man's Nightcap

But at this the dead man started to his feet, struck her, and said: "Yes! And you, are you satisfied?"

And with these words he plunged down into the grave. The girl fell down at the blow, and when men ran to pick her up, she was already dead. The boy was punished because he used to scare her, for it was considered that the whole unfortunate affair had been his fault, and he gave up scaring people. And that is the end of this tale.

collected by JÓN ÁRNASON
translated by Jacqueline Simpson

The Herd-boy and the Giant
Sweden

There was once a boy who tended goats. One day, when wandering about in the forest, he came to a giant's dwelling, when the giant, hearing a noise and outcry in his neighbourhood, came out to see what was the matter. Now the giant being of a vast stature and fierce aspect, the boy was terrified, and ran away as fast as he was able.

In the evening, when the lad returned with his goats from the pasture, his mother was occupied in curdling. Taking a piece of the new-made cheese, he rolled it in the embers, and put it into his wallet. On the following morning he went, as was his custom, to the pasture, and again approached the giant's abode. When the giant heard the noise of the boy and his goats, he was angry, and rising up, seized a huge piece of granite, which he squeezed in his hand so that the fragments flew about in all directions. The giant then said: "If thou ever comest here again, making an uproar, I will crumple thee as small as I now squeeze this stone." The boy, however, did not allow himself to be frightened, but made a sham also to seize a stone, though he only grasped his cheese that had been rolled in the ashes, and which he pressed till the whey ran out between his fingers, and dripped down on the ground. The boy then said: "If thou dost not take thyself away, and leave me in peace, I will squeeze thee as I now squeeze the water out of this stone." When the giant found that the lad was so strong, he was frightened, and went into his hut. And thus the boy and the giant separated for that time.

On the third day they met again in the forest, and the boy asked whether they should make another trial of strength. The giant consented, and the boy said: "Father, I think it will be a good trial, if one of us can cast your axe so high, that it does not fall down again." The

The Herd-boy and the Giant

giant thought it would. They now commenced the trial, and the giant threw first. He hurled the axe up with great force, so that it rose high in the air; but let him try as he might, it always fell down again. Then said the boy: "Father, I did not think you had so little strength. Wait a moment, and you shall see a better throw." The boy then swung his arm to and fro, as if to cast with the greater force; but, at the same time, very cleverly let the axe slide down into the wallet that he had on his back. The artifice escaped the notice of the giant, who continued expecting and expecting to see the axe come down again, but no axe appeared. "Now," thought he to himself, "this boy must be amazingly strong, although he appears so little and weak." They then again separated, each going his own way.

Shortly after, the giant and the herd-boy met again, and the giant asked the boy whether he would enter his service. The boy consented, left his goats in the forest, and accompanied the giant to the latter's habitation.

It is related that the giant and the boy set out for the purpose of felling an oak in the forest. When they reached the spot, the giant asked the boy whether he would hold or fell. "I will hold," said the boy, but added that he was unable to reach the top. The giant then grasped the tree and bent it to the ground; but no sooner had the boy taken fast hold of it, than the tree rebounded, and threw the lad high up in the air, so that the giant could hardly follow him with his eyes. The giant stood long wondering in what direction the boy had taken his flight; then taking up his axe, began to hew. In a little while the boy came limping up; for he had escaped with difficulty. The giant asked him why he did not hold; while the boy, who appeared as if nothing had happened, in return, asked the giant whether he would venture to make such a spring as he had just made. The giant answered in the negative, and the boy then said: "If you will not venture to do that, you may both hold and fell yourself." The giant let this answer content him, and felled the oak himself.

When the tree was to be carried home, the giant said to the boy: "If thou wilt bear the top-end, I will bear the root." "No, father," answered the boy, "do you bear the top-end, I am able enough to bear the other." The giant consented, and raised the top end of the oak upon his shoulder; but the boy, who was behind, called to him to poise the tree better by moving it more forwards. The giant did so, and thus got the whole trunk in equilibrium on his shoulder. But the boy leaped up on the tree, and hid himself among the boughs, so that the giant could not see him. The giant now began his march, thinking that the boy was all the while at the other end. When they had thus proceeded for some distance, the giant thought it was very hard labour, and groaned piteously. "Art thou not yet tired?" said he to the boy. "No, not in the least," answered the boy. "Surely father is not tired with such a trifle." The giant was unwilling to acknowledge that such was the case, and continued on his way. When they reached home, the giant was half-dead from fatigue. He threw the tree down; but the boy had in the meanwhile leaped off, and appeared as if bearing the larger end of the oak. "Art thou not yet tired?" asked the giant. The boy answered: "Oh, father must not think that so little tires me. The trunk does not seem to me heavier than I could have borne by myself."

Another time the giant said: "As soon as it is daylight we will go out and thresh." "Now I," answered the boy, "think it better to thresh before daybreak, before we eat our breakfast." The giant acquiesced, and went and fetched two flails, one of which he took for himself. When they were about to begin threshing, the boy was unable to lift his flail, it was so large and heavy. He therefore took up a stick, and beat on the floor, while the giant threshed. This escaped the giant's notice, and so they continued until daylight. "Now," said the boy, "let us go home to breakfast." "Yes," answered the giant, "for I think we have had a stiff job of it."

Some time after, the giant set his boy to plough, and at the same time, said: "When the dog comes, thou must loose the oxen and put them in the stall to which he will lead the way." The lad promised to do so; but when the oxen were loosed, the giant's dog crept in under

The Herd-boy and the Giant

the foundation of a building to which there was no door. The giant's object was to ascertain whether his boy were strong enough to lift up the house alone, and place the oxen in their stalls. The boy, after having long considered what was to be done, at length resolved on slaughtering the animals, and casting their carcases in through the window. When he returned home, the giant asked him whether the oxen were in their stalls. "Yes," answered the boy, "I got them in although I divided them."

The giant now began to harbour apprehensions, and consulted with his wife how they should make away with the boy. The crone said: "It is my advice that you take your club and kill him to-night while he is asleep." This the giant thought very sound advice, and promised to follow it. But the boy was on the watch, and listening to their conversation; therefore, when evening came, he laid a churn in the bed, and hid himself behind the door. At midnight the giant rose, seized his club, and beat on the churn so that the cream that was in it was sprinkled over his face. He then went to his wife, and laughing said: "Ha, ha, ha! I have struck him so that his brains flew high up on the wall." The crone was pleased at this intelligence, praised her husband's boldness, and thought they might now sleep in quiet, seeing they had no longer cause to fear the mischievous boy.

Scarcely, however, was it light, when the boy crept out of his hiding-place, went in, and bade the giant-folk good morning. At this apparition the giant was naturally struck with amazement. "What," said he, "art thou not yet dead? I thought I struck thee dead with my club." The boy answered: "I rather believe I felt in the night as if a flea had bitten me."

In the evening, when the giant and his boy were about to sup, the crone placed a large dish of porridge before them. "That would be excellent," said the boy, "if we were to try which could eat the most, father or I." The giant was ready for the trial, and they began to eat with all their might. But the boy was crafty: he had tied his wallet before his chest, and for every spoonful that entered his mouth, he let two fall into the wallet. When the giant had despatched seven bowls of porridge, he had taken his fill, and sat puffing and blowing, and unable to swallow another spoonful; but the boy continued with just as much good will as when he began. The giant asked him how it was, that he who was so little could eat so much. The boy answered: "Father, I will soon show you. When I have eaten as much as I can contain, I slit up my stomach, and then I can take in as much again." Saying these words, he took a knife and ripped up the wallet, so that the porridge ran out. The giant thought this a capital plan, and that he would do the like. But when he stuck the knife in his stomach, the blood began to flow, and the end of the matter was, that it proved his death.

When the giant was dead, the boy took all the chattels that were in the house, and went his way in the night. And so ends the story of the crafty herd-boy and the doltish giant.

retold by BENJAMIN THORPE

The Black Bull of Norroway
Scotland

In Norroway, langsyne, there lived a certain lady, and she had three dochters.* The auldest o' them said to her mither: "Mither, bake me a bannock, and roast me a collop,† for I'm gaun awa' to seek my fortune." Her mither did sae; and the dochter gaed awa' to an auld witch washerwife and telled her purpose. The auld wife bade her stay that day, and gang and look out o' her back door, and see what she could see. She saw nocht the first day. The second day she did the same, and saw nocht. On the third day she looked again, and saw a coach-and-six coming alang the road. She ran in and telled the auld wife what she saw. "Aweel," quo' the auld wife, "yon's for you." Sae they took her into the coach, and galloped aff.

The second dochter next says to her mither: "Mither, bake me a bannock, and roast me a collop, for I'm awa' to seek my fortune." Her mither did sae; and awa' she gaed to the auld wife, as her sister had dune. On the third day she looked out o' the back door, and saw a coach-and-four coming along the road. "Aweel," quo' the auld wife, "yon's for you." Sae they took her in, and aff they set.

The third dochter says to her mither: "Mither, bake me a bannock, and roast me a collop, for I'm awa' to seek my fortune." Her mither did sae; and awa' she gaed to the auld witch-wife. She bade her look out o' her back door, and see what she could see. She did sae; and when she came back said she saw nocht. The second day she did the same, and saw nocht. The third day she looked again, and on coming back said to the auld wife she saw nocht but a muckle Black Bull coming roaring along the road. "Aweel," quo' the auld wife, "yon's for you." On hearing this she was next to distracted wi' grief

* Daughters.
† Minced meat.

and terror; but she was lifted up and set on his back, and awa' they went.

Aye they travelled, and on they travelled, till the lady grew faint wi' hunger. "Eat out o' my right lug'"* says the Black Bull, "and drink out o' my left lug, and set by your leavings." Sae she did as he said, and was wonderfully refreshed. And lang they gaed, and sair they rade, till they came in sight o' a very big and bonny castle. "Yonder we maun be this night," quo' the bull; "for my auld† brither lives yonder"; and presently they were at the place. They lifted her aff his back, and took her in, and sent him away to a park for the night. In the morning, when they brought the bull hame, they took the lady into a fine shining parlour, and gave her a beautiful apple, telling her no to break it till she was in the greatest strait ever mortal was in in the world, and that wad bring her out o't. Again she was lifted on the bull's back, and after she had ridden far, and farer than I can tell, they came in sight o' a far bonnier castle, and far farther awa' than the last. Says the bull till her: "Yonder we maun be the night, for my second brither lives yonder"; and they were at the place directly. They lifted her down and took her in, and sent the bull to the field for the night. In the morning they took the lady into a fine and rich room, and gave her the finest pear she had ever seen, bidding her no to break it till she was in the greatest strait ever mortal could be in, and that wad get her out o't. Again she was lifted and set on his back, and awa' they went. And lang they gaed, and sair they rade, till they came in sight o' the far biggest castle, and far farthest aff, they had yet seen. "We maun be yonder the night," says the bull, "for my young brither lives yonder"; and they were there directly. They lifted her down, took her in, and sent the bull to the field for the night. In the morning they took her into a room, the finest of a', and gied her a plum, telling her no to break it till she was in the greatest strait mortal could be in, and that wad get her out o't. Presently they brought hame the bull, set the lady on his back, and awa' they went.

And aye they gaed, and on they rade, till they came to a dark and ugsome glen, where they stopped, and the lady lighted down. Says the bull to her: "Here ye maun stay till I gang and fight the deil. Ye maun seat yoursel' on that stane, and move neither hand nor fit‡ till I come back, else I'll never find ye again. And if everything round about ye turns blue I hae beaten the deil; but should a' things turn red he'll hae conquered me." She set hersel' down on the stane, and by and by a' round her turned blue. O'ercome wi' joy, she lifted the ae fit

* Ear.
† Eldest.   ‡ Foot.

The Black Bull of Norroway

and crossed it owre the ither, sae glad was she that her companion was victorious. The bull returned and sought for but never could find her.

Lang she sat, and aye she grat, till she wearied. At last she rase and gaed awa', she kendna whaur till.* On she wandered till she came to a great hill o' glass, that she tried a' she could to climb, but wasna able. Round the bottom o' the hill she gaed, sabbing and seeking a passage owre, till at last she came to a smith's house; and the smith promised, if she wad serve him seven years, he wad make her iron shoon, wherewi' she could climb owre the glassy hill. At seven years' end she got her iron shoon, clamb the glassy hill, and chanced to come to the auld washerwife's habitation. There she was telled of a gallant young knight that had given in some bluidy sarks† to wash, and whaever washed thae sarks was to be his wife. The auld wife had washed till she was tired, and then she set to her dochter, and baith washed, and they washed, and they better washed, in hopes of getting the young knight; but a' they could do they couldna bring out a stain. At length they set the stranger damosel to wark; and whenever she began the stains came out pure and clean, but the auld wife made the knight believe it was her dochter had washed the sarks. So the knight and the eldest dochter were to be married, and the stranger damosel was distracted at the thought of it, for she was deeply in love wi' him. So she bethought her of her apple, and breaking it, found it filled with gold and precious jewellery, the richest she had ever seen. "All these," she said to the eldest dochter, "I will give you, on condition that you put off your marriage for ae day, and allow me to go into his room alone at night." So the lady consented; but meanwhile the auld wife had prepared a sleeping-drink, and given it to the knight, wha drank it, and never wakened till next morning. The leelang night the damosel sabbed and sang:

> "Seven lang years I served for thee,
> The glassy hill I clamb for thee,
> The bluidy shirt I wrang for thee;
> And wilt thou no wauken and turn to me?"

Next day she kentna what to do for grief. She then brak the pear, and found it filled wi' jewellery far richer than the contents o' the apple. Wi' thae jewels she bargained for permission to be a second night in the young knight's chamber; but the auld wife gied him

---

* She didn't know where to.   † Shirts.

anither sleeping-drink, and he again sleepit till morning. A' night she kept sighing and singing as before:

> *"Seven lang years I served for thee,*
> *The glassy hill I clamb for thee,*
> *The bluidy shirt I wrang for thee;*
> *And wilt thou no wauken and turn to me?"*

Still he sleepit, and she nearly lost hope a'thegeither. But that day when he was out at the hunting, somebody asked him what noise and moaning was yon they heard all last night in his bedchamber. He said he heardna ony noise. But they assured him there was sae; and he resolved to keep waking that night to try what he could hear. That being the third night, and the damosel being between hope and despair, she brak her plum, and it held far the richest jewellery of the three. She bargained as before; and the auld wife, as before, took in the sleeping-drink to the young knight's chamber; but he telled her he couldna drink it that night without sweetening. And when she gaed awa' for some honey to sweeten it wi', he poured out the drink, and sae made the auld wife think he had drunk it. They a' went to bed again, and the damosel began, as before, singing:

> *"Seven lang years I served for thee,*
> *The glassy hill I clamb for thee,*
> *The bluidy shirt I wrang for thee;*
> *And wilt thou no wauken and turn to me?"*

He heard, and turned to her. And she telled him a' that had befa'en her, and he telled her a' that had happened to him. And he caused the auld washerwife and her dochter to be burnt. And they were married, and he and she are living happy till this day, for aught I ken.

retold by ANDREW LANG

The Ghost and the Money-chest
Iceland

There was once a landlord of a church-farm in the north. He was married and a man of great wealth, but much given to hoarding, so that men were convinced that he must possess a large sum of money. His wife was a good woman and very charitable, but she had little influence over her miserly husband.

One winter the farmer fell ill, and died soon afterwards, and his body was laid out and buried. The estate was now put in order, but no money was found. The widow was asked if she knew of any, but answered not so much as a single shilling, and since men knew nothing but good of her, her word was not questioned. It was the guess of many that he must have buried the money, as was indeed later found to have been the case.

As the winter advanced, people at the church-farm became aware of haunting, and it was the general view that the farmer was walking on account of his hidden money. The haunting increased to such a degree that most of the work-people decided to leave in the spring, and the widow began making preparations to sell the property.

Time passed till the flitting-days arrived. Then a labourer came to the widow and asked to be hired, and she took him. After he had been there a while, however, he too became aware of a considerable amount of haunting. Once he asked his mistress whether her late husband had not possessed a large quantity of money, but as before she replied that she knew nothing of it.

The days now passed until it was market time. The hired man went to market, and among other things he bought a quantity of sheet iron and a length of white linen. And when he got home, he had a shroud sewn of the linen, while from the sheet-iron he made himself a breastplate and iron gloves, for he was a skilful smith.

Time passed, until once more the days grew shorter and the nights dark. Then one evening, when all were asleep, the hired man put on the breastplate and iron gloves, and then the shroud over all, and went out into the churchyard. Going close to the farmer's grave, he walked back and forth there, playing with a silver piece in the palm of his hand.

It was not long before a ghost rose up from the farmer's grave, and coming quickly to the hired man, it asked, "Are you one of us?"

"Yes," answered the hired man.

"Let me feel you," said the ghost.

The hired man now reached out a hand and the ghost felt how cold it was. It said, "True enough, you are a ghost, too. Why are you walking?"

"To play with my silver piece," replied the other.

At this, the ghost hopped over the churchyard wall, and the hired man after it. They went on until they came to the edge of the homefield. Then the ghost turned over a hummock and pulled up its money-chest, and they took to playing with the money. This went on all night, but when dawn began to approach the ghost would have put the money away. Then the other said that he wanted to take a look at the small change, and he began playing with it and scattering it about all over again. Then the ghost said, "I am not sure you are a ghost."

"Oh yes I am," said the other. "Feel for yourself"—and he held out the other hand.

"True enough," said the ghost, and it now began to collect all the money together again. But still the hired man kept throwing it hither and thither.

The ghost now became angry and said that he must be a living man and meant to cheat it, but he denied this. The ghost then clutched him by the chest, and felt the iron plate on him, and how cold it was.

"What you say is true; you are the same as I am," said the ghost. And once again it began to collect its money together. The hired man now dared not but let it have its way, and said, "Let me put my silver piece with your money."

"Certainly," said the ghost, and it now replaced the hummock so that nothing could be seen. After this they returned to the churchyard.

"Where is your hole?" asked the ghost.

"On the other side of the church," replied the other.

"You go into yours first," said the ghost.

"No," said the hired man, "you go first."

They continued to argue about this until dawn. Then the ghost

The Ghost and the Money-chest

jumped into its grave, while the hired man returned to the farmhouse.

He now filled a cask with water and placed it under the platform. Into this he put his garments of the night and also went out and fetched the money-chest, which he put in as well.

The day passed and evening came, and all went to bed. The hired man slept by the door, and the night was not far advanced when the ghost came in, sniffing and snuffing all about, and struck a mighty blow on the edge of the platform, after which it went out, the hired man following.

Men say that he now dealt in such wise with the farmer's grave that the ghost was never seen again.

He had put his garments and the money-chest in water so that the ghost should not be able to smell earth on them.

The hired man married the widow, and they lived together for many years.

And so ends this story.

collected by JÓN ÁRNASON and MAGNÚS GRÍMSSON
translated by Alan Boucher

Mr Miacca

England

Tommy Grimes was sometimes a good boy, and sometimes a bad boy; and when he was a bad boy, he was a very bad boy. Now his mother used to say to him: "Tommy, Tommy, be a good boy, and don't go out of the street, or else Mr Miacca will take you." But still when he was a bad boy he would go out of the street; and one day, sure enough, he had scarcely got round the corner, when Mr Miacca did catch him and popped him into a bag upside down, and took him off to his house.

When Mr Miacca got Tommy inside, he pulled him out of the bag and sat him down, and felt his arms and legs. "You're rather tough," says he; "but you're all I've got for supper, and you'll not taste bad boiled. But body o' me, I've forgot the herbs, and it's bitter you'll taste without herbs. Sally! Here, I say, Sally!" and he called Mrs Miacca.

So Mrs Miacca came out of another room and said: "What d'ye want, my dear?"

"Oh, here's a little boy for supper," said Mr Miacca, "and I've forgot the herbs. Mind him, will ye, while I go for them."

"All right, my love," says Mrs Miacca, and off he goes.

Then Tommy Grimes said to Mrs Miacca: "Does Mr Miacca always have little boys for supper?"

"Mostly, my dear," said Mrs Miacca, "if little boys are bad enough, and get in his way."

"And don't you have anything else but boy-meat? No pudding?" asked Tommy.

"Ah, I loves pudding," says Mrs Miacca. "But it's not often the likes of me gets pudding."

"Why, my mother is making a pudding this very day," said

Mr Miacca

Tommy Grimes, "and I am sure she'd give you some, if I ask her. Shall I run and get some?"

"Now, that's a thoughtful boy," said Mrs Miacca, "only don't be long and be sure to be back for supper."

So off Tommy pelted, and right glad he was to get off so cheap; and for many a long day he was as good as good could be, and never went round the corner of the street. But he couldn't always be good; and one day he went round the corner, and as luck would have it, he hadn't scarcely got round it when Mr Miacca grabbed him up, popped him in his bag, and took him home.

When he got him there, Mr Miacca dropped him out; and when he saw him, he said: "Ah, you're the youngster that served me and my missus such a shabby trick, leaving us without any supper. Well, you shan't do it again. I'll watch over you myself. Here, get under the sofa, and I'll set on it and watch the pot boil for you."

So poor Tommy Grimes had to creep under the sofa, and Mr Miacca sat on it and waited for the pot to boil. And they waited and they waited, but still the pot didn't boil, till at last Mr Miacca got tired of waiting, and he said: "Here, you under there, I'm not going to wait any longer; put out your leg, and I'll stop your giving us the slip."

So Tommy put out a leg and Mr Miacca got a chopper, and chopped it off, and pops it in the pot.

Suddenly he calls out: "Sally, my dear, Sally!" and nobody answered. So he went into the next room to look out for Mrs Miacca, and while he was there Tommy crept out from under the sofa and ran out of the door. For it was a leg of the sofa that he had put out.

So Tommy Grimes ran home, and he never went round the corner again till he was old enough to go alone.

retold by JOSEPH JACOBS

The Woman of the Sea
Shetland

One clear summer night, a young man was walking on the sand by the sea on the Isle of Unst. He had been all day in the hayfields and was come down to the shore to cool himself, for it was the full moon and the wind blowing fresh off the water.

As he came to the shore he saw the sand shining white in the moonlight and on it the sea-people dancing. He had never seen them before, for they show themselves like seals by day, but on this night, because it was midsummer and a full moon, they were dancing for joy. Here and there he saw dark patches where they had flung down their sealskins, but they themselves were as clear as the moon itself, and they cast no shadow.

He crept a little nearer, and his own shadow moved before him, and of a sudden one of the sea-people danced upon it. The dance was broken. They looked about and saw him and with a cry they fled to their sealskins and dived into the waves. The air was full of their soft crying and splashing.

But one of the fairy-people ran hither and thither on the sands, wringing her hands as if she had lost something. The young man looked and saw a patch of darkness in his own shadow. It was a seal's skin. Quickly he threw it behind a rock and watched to see what the sea-fairy would do.

She ran down to the edge of the sea and stood with her feet in the foam, crying to her people to wait for her, but they had gone too far to hear. The moon shone on her and the young man thought she was the loveliest creature he had ever seen. Then she began to weep softly to herself and the sound of it was so pitiful that he could bear it no longer. He stood upright and went down to her.

"What have you lost, woman of the sea?" he asked her.

She turned at the sound of his voice and looked at him, terrified.

The Woman of the Sea

For a moment he thought she was going to dive into the sea. Then she came a step nearer and held up her two hands to him.

"Sir," she said, "give it back to me and I and my people will give you the treasure of the sea." Her voice was like the waves singing in a shell.

"I would rather have you than the treasure of the sea," said the young man. Although she hid her face in her hands and fell again to crying, more hopeless than ever, he was not moved.

"It is my wife you shall be," he said. "Come with me now to the priest, and we will go home to our own house, and it is yourself shall be mistress of all I have. It is warm you will be in the long winter nights, sitting at your own hearth stone and the peat burning red, instead of swimming in the cold green sea."

She tried to tell him of the bottom of the sea where there comes neither snow nor darkness of night and the waves are as warm as a river in summer, but he would not listen. Then he threw his cloak around her and lifted her in his arms and they were married in the priest's house.

He brought her home to his little thatched cottage and into the kitchen with its earthen floor, and set her down before the hearth in the red glow of the peat. She cried out when she saw the fire, for she thought it was a strange crimson jewel.

"Have you anything as bonny as that in the sea?" he asked her, kneeling down beside her and she said, so faintly that he could scarcely hear her, "No."

"I know not what there is in the sea," he said, "but there is nothing on land as bonny as you." For the first time she ceased her crying and sat looking into the heart of the fire. It was the first thing that made her forget, even for a moment, the sea which was her home.

All the days she was in the young man's house, she never lost the wonder of the fire and it was the first thing she brought her children to see. For she had three children in the twice seven years she lived with him. She was a good wife to him. She baked his bread and she spun the wool from the fleece of his Shetland sheep.

He never named the seal's skin to her, nor she to him, and he thought she was content, for he loved her dearly and she was happy with her children. Once, when he was ploughing on the headland above the bay, he looked down and saw her standing on the rocks and crying in a mournful voice to a great seal in the water. He said nothing when he came home, for he thought to himself it was not to wonder at if she were lonely for the sight of her own people. As for the seal's skin, he had hidden it well.

There came a September evening and she was busy in the house, and the children playing hide-and-seek in the stacks in the gloaming. She heard them shouting and went out to them.

"What have you found?" she said.

The children came running to her. "It is like a big cat," they said, "but it is softer than a cat. Look!" She looked and saw her seal's skin that was hidden under last year's hay.

She gazed at it, and for a long time she stood still. It was warm dusk and the air was yellow with the afterglow of the sunset. The children had run away again, and their voices among the stacks sounded like the voices of birds. The hens were on the roost already and now and then one of them clucked in its sleep. The air was full of little friendly noises from the sleepy talking of the swallows under the thatch. The door was open and the warm smell of the baking of bread came out to her.

She turned to go in, but a small breath of wind rustled over the stacks and she stopped again. It brought a sound that she had heard so long she never seemed to hear it at all. It was the sea whispering down on the sand. Far out on the rocks the great waves broke in a boom, and close in on the sand the little waves slipped racing back. She took up the seal's skin and went swiftly down the track that led to the sands. The children saw her and cried to her to wait for them, but she did not hear them. She was just out of sight when their father came in from the byre and they ran to tell him.

"Which road did she take?" said he.

"The low road to the sea," they answered, but already their father was running to the shore. The children tried to follow him, but their voices died away behind him, so fast did he run.

As he ran across the hard sands, he saw her dive to join the big seal who was waiting for her, and he gave a loud cry to stop her. For a moment she rested on the surface of the sea, then she cried with her voice that was like the waves singing in a shell, "Fare ye well, and all good befall you, for you were a good man to me."

Then she dived to the fairy places that lie at the bottom of the sea and the big seal with her.

For a long time her husband watched for her to come back to him and the children; but she came no more.

retold by HELEN WADDELL

Johnnie in the Cradle
Scotland

A man and his wife were not long married, and they had a wee kiddie called Johnnie, but he was always crying and never satisfied. There was a neighbour near, a tailor, and it came to market day, and Johnnie was aye greeting, and never growing. And the wife wanted to get a day at the market, so the tailor said he'd stay and watch wee Johnnie. So he was sitting sewing by the fire, and a voice said: "Is ma mother and ma faither awa'?" He couldn't think it was the baby speaking, so he went and looked out of the window, but there was nothing, and he heard it again. "Is ma mother and ma faither awa'?" And there it was, sitting up, with its wee hands gripping the sides of the cradle. "There's a bottle of whisky in the press," it says. "Gie's a drink." Sure enough, there was one, and they had a drink together. Then wee Johnnie wanted a blow on the pipes, but there was not a set in the house, so he told the tailor to go and fetch a round strae* from the byre, and he played the loveliest tune on the pipes through the strae. They had a good talk together, and the wee thing said, "Is ma mother and ma faither coming home?" And when they came, there he was, "Nya, nya, nya", in the cradle. By this time the tailor knew it was a fairy they had there, so he followed the farmer into the byre, and told him all that had happened. The farmer just couldn't bring himself to believe it; so between them they hit on a contrivance. They let on that a lot of things had not been sold at the market, and there was to be a second day of it, and the tailor promised to come over again to sit by the bairn. They made a great stir about packing up, and then they went through to the barn, and listened through the

* Straw.

keek hole in the wall. "Is ma mother and ma faither gone?" said the wee thing, and the mother could just hardly believe her ears. But when they heard the piping through the cornstrae, they kent it was a fairy right enough, and the farmer went into the room, and he set the gridle on the fire and heated it red hot, and he fetched in a half bagful of horse manure, and set it on the gridle, and the wee thing looked at him with wild eyes. When he went to it to grip it, and put it on the gridle, it flew straight up the lum*, and as it went it cried out, "I wish I had been longer with my mother. I'd a kent her better."

collected by HAMISH HENDERSON

* Chimney.

Peter Bull
Denmark

There once lived in Denmark a peasant and his wife who owned a very good farm, but had no children. They often lamented to each other that they had no one of their own to inherit all the wealth that they possessed. They continued to prosper, and became rich people, but there was no heir to it all.

One year it happened that they owned a pretty little bull-calf, which they called Peter. It was the prettiest little creature they had ever seen—so beautiful and so wise that it understood everything that was said to it, and so gentle and so full of play that both the man and his wife came to be as fond of it as if it had been their own child.

One day the man said to his wife, "I wonder, now, whether our parish clerk could teach Peter to talk; in that case we could not do better than adopt him as our son, and let him inherit all that we possess."

"Well, I don't know," said his wife, "our clerk is tremendously learned, and knows much more than his Paternoster, and I could almost believe that he might be able to teach Peter to talk, for Peter has a wonderfully good head too. You might at least ask him about it."

Off went the man to the clerk, and asked him whether he thought he could teach a bull-calf that they had to speak, for they wished so much to have it as their heir.

The clerk was no fool; he looked round about to see that no one could overhear them, and said, "Oh, yes, I can easily do that, but you must not speak to anyone about it. It must be done in all secrecy, and the priest must not know of it, otherwise I shall get into trouble, as it is forbidden. It will also cost you something, as some very expensive books are required."

That did not matter at all, the man said; they would not care so very much what it cost. The clerk could have a hundred dollars to begin with to buy the books. He also promised to tell no one about it, and to bring the calf round in the evening.

He gave the clerk the hundred dollars on the spot, and in the evening took the calf round to him, and the clerk promised to do his best with it. In a week's time he came back to the clerk to hear about the calf and see how it was thriving. The clerk, however, said that he could not get a sight of it, for then Peter would long after him and forget all that he had already learned. He was getting on well with his learning, but another hundred dollars were needed, as they must have more books. The peasant had the money with him, so he gave it to the clerk, and went home again with high hopes.

In another week the man came again to learn what progress Peter had made now.

"He is getting on very well," said the clerk.

"I suppose he can't say anything yet?" said the man.

"Oh, yes," said the clerk, "he can say 'Moo' now."

"Do you think he will get on with his learning?" asked the peasant.

"Oh, yes," said the clerk, "but I shall want another hundred dollars for books. Peter can't learn well out of the ones that he has got."

"Well, well," said the man, "what must be spent *shall* be spent."

So he gave the clerk the third hundred dollars for books, and a cask of good old ale for Peter. The clerk drank the ale himself, and gave the calf milk, which he thought would be better for it.

Some weeks passed, during which the peasant did not come round to ask after the calf, being frightened lest it should cost him another hundred dollars, for he had begun to squirm a bit at having to part with so much money. Meanwhile the clerk decided that the calf was as fat as it could be, so he killed it. After he had got all the beef out of the way he went inside, put on his black clothes, and made his way to the peasant's house.

As soon as he had said "Good-day" he asked, "Has Peter come home here?"

"No, indeed, he hasn't," said the man; "surely he hasn't run away?"

"I hope," said the clerk, "that he would not behave so contemptibly after all the trouble I have had to teach him, and all that I have spent upon him. I have had to spend at least a hundred dollars of my own money to buy books for him before I got him so far on. He could say anything he liked now, so he said to-day that he longed to see his parents again. I was willing to give him that pleasure, but I was afraid that he wouldn't be able to find the way here by himself, so I made myself ready to go with him. When he had got outside the house I remembered that I had left my stick inside, and went in again to get it. When I came out again Peter had gone off on his own account. I thought he would be here, and if he isn't I don't know where he is."

The peasant and his wife began to lament bitterly that Peter had run away in this fashion just when they were to have so much joy of him, and after they had spent so much on his education. The worst of it was that now they had no heir after all. The clerk comforted them as best he could; he also was greatly distressed that Peter should have behaved in such a way just when he should have gained honour from his pupil. Perhaps he had only gone astray, and he would advertise him at church next Sunday, and find out whether anyone had seen him. Then he bade them "Good-bye," and went home and dined on a good fat veal roast.

Now it so happened that the clerk took in a newspaper, and one day he chanced to read in its columns of a new merchant who had settled in a town at some distance, and whose name was "Peter Bull". He put the newspaper in his pocket, and went round to the sorrowing couple who had lost their heir. He read the paragraph to them, and added, "I wonder, now, whether that could be your bull-calf Peter?"

"Yes, of course it is," said the man; "who else would it be?"

His wife then spoke up and said, "You must set out, good man, and see about him, for it *is* him, I am perfectly certain. Take a good sum of money with you, too; for who knows but what he may want some cash now that he has turned a merchant!"

Next day the man got a bag of money on his back and a sandwich in his pocket, and his pipe in his mouth, and set out for the town where the new merchant lived. It was no short way, and he travelled for many days before he finally arrived there. He reached it one morning, just at daybreak, found out the right place, and asked if the merchant was at home. Yes, he was, said the people, but he was not up yet.

"That doesn't matter," said the peasant, "for I am his father. Just show me up to his bedroom."

He was shown up to the room, and as soon as he entered it, and caught sight of the merchant, he recognized him at once. He had the same broad forehead, the same thick neck, and same red hair, but in other respects he was now like a human being. The peasant rushed straight up to him and took a firm hold of him. "O Peter," said he, "what a sorrow you have caused us, both myself and your mother, by running off like this just as we had got you well educated! Get up, now, so that I can see you properly, and have a talk with you."

The merchant thought that it was a lunatic who had made his way in to him, and thought it best to take things quietly.

"All right," said he, "I shall do so at once." He got out of bed and made haste to dress himself.

"Ay," said the peasant, "now I can see how clever our clerk is. He has done well by you, for now you look just like a human being. If one didn't know it, one would never think that it was you we got from the red cow; will you come home with me now?"

"No," said the merchant, "I can't find time just now. I have a big business to look after."

"You could have the farm at once, you know," said the peasant, "and we old people would retire. But if you would rather stay in business, of course you may do so. Are you in want of anything?"

"Oh, yes," said the merchant; "I want nothing so much as money. A merchant has always a use for that."

"I can well believe that," said the peasant, "for you had nothing at all to start with. I have brought some with me for that very end." With that he emptied his bag of money out upon the table, so that it was all covered with bright dollars.

When the merchant saw what kind of man he had before him he began to speak him fair, and invited him to stay with him for some days, so that they might have some more talk together.

"Very well," said the peasant, "but you must call me 'Father'."

"I have neither father nor mother alive," said Peter Bull.

"I know that," said the man; "your real father was sold at Hamburg last Michaelmas, and your real mother died while calving in spring; but my wife and I have adopted you as our own, and you are our only heir, so you must call me 'Father'."

Peter Bull was quite willing to do so, and it was settled that he should keep the money, while the peasant made his will and left to him all that he had, before he went home to his wife, and told her the whole story.

She was delighted to hear that it was true enough about Peter Bull—that he was no other than their own bull-calf.

"You must go at once and tell the clerk," said she, "and pay him the hundred dollars of his own money that he spent upon our son. He has earned them well, and more besides, for all the joy he has given us in having such a son and heir."

The man agreed with this, and thanked the clerk for all he had done, and gave him two hundred dollars. Then he sold the farm, and removed with his wife to the town where their dear son and heir was living. To him they gave all their wealth, and lived with him till their dying day.

retold by ANDREW LANG

The Juniper Tree
Germany

A long while ago, at least two thousand years, there lived a rich man who had a good and beautiful wife. They loved one another very dearly; but they had no children; and she prayed and longed for a child with a great longing.

Now in the courtyard that lay beneath the windows of the house in which they lived there stood a juniper tree which, however long the night or sharp the frost, was never without its dark-green, needle-pointed leaves. And one sunlit winter's day as she was standing beneath it, paring an apple, she cut her finger, and the drops of blood trickled down from her finger on to the snow.

"Ah!" said she, with a sigh as she gazed at it, "how happy should I be if only I had a child, as white as that snow, as red as that blood!"

As she uttered these words, her heart lightened, a wild joy sprang up in her, and she knew that her wish would come true. The happy days went by. When winter was gone and its snows had melted away, the meadows began to grow green again. April came; the woods and fields were sweet with the flowers of spring; the trees put forth their green leaves; the wild cherries shed their petals upon the ground; and the birds poured out their songs, daybreak to evening, in the woods and groves. Then followed summer. The small spicy flowers of the juniper began to unfold, her heart leapt within her at their fragrance, and she fell on her knees, beside herself for joy. When autumn drew near, ripening fruit hung thick upon the trees; and one still and lovely evening she ate greedily of the juniper berries. But after that she began to be sick and sad and sorrowful. And when the eighth month was passed, she called her husband to her, wept, and said, "If I should die, then I pray thee bury me under this juniper tree."

The Juniper Tree

Not long after this, her child was born—the child of her desire, and lovely; as red as blood, as white as snow; but she herself was weak and wearied out. As soon as she had looked upon it, an exceeding great joy overcame her, and she fainted away and died.

Her husband buried her under the juniper tree, and wept and mourned over her. But in time his grief began to abate, and he to forget. And at length he dried his tears, and took to himself another wife.

Time passed on, and a daughter was born to her; but the child of his first wife was a boy. The mother loved and doted on her daughter, but she hated her stepson. She knew that he would inherit her husband's possessions, and the very sight and thought of him cut her to the heart. And she began to think how she might get everything for her daughter only. So she treated him very harshly, half starved him, never let him rest, and would beat and punish him for no fault and without reason, so that he went continually in fear of her and could find no place in the house to play in, or be at peace. And as time went by her cruelty increased, and she hated him more and more.

Now it happened one day, when the mother was in her store-room, that her little girl ran up to her, and said, "Mother, may I have an apple?"

"Why, yes, my pretty dear," she said; and gave her a ripe rosy apple out of her apple-chest. Now this chest had a heavy and cumbersome lid, and was fitted with a broad sharp lock of iron.

"Mother," said the little girl, "may I have an apple for my little brother too?"

A pang of envy and jealousy went through the woman's breast, but she showed no sign of it. "Yes, indeed, my child," she said. "When he comes in from school, he too shall have an apple."

As she was speaking, she happened to look out of the window and saw the little boy in the distance coming home from school. At sight of him the Evil One entered into her heart. She took back the apple she had given her daughter, threw it into the apple-chest and shut down the lid, telling her that she should have an even sweeter one before she went to bed.

When the little boy came in at the door, she was lying in wait for him, and alone; and she said to him in a small wheedling voice, her face cold and grey with wickedness, "Come in, my dear, and I will give you an apple."

The little boy gazed at her. "Thank you, Mother," he said. "I should like to have an apple. But how strange and dreadful you look!"

It seemed to her that she was compelled to listen to a voice within her. "Look!" she said. "Come with me." And she took him in secret into her store-room, lifted the heavy lid of the chest, and said, "There, you shall choose one for yourself."

So he came near, and as he stooped himself over the edge of the apple-chest to do as she had bidden him, of a sudden and with all her force she let fall the lid with its iron lock upon his neck, and his head fell off among the apples.

When she lifted the lid and saw what she had done, she was stricken with terror, not knowing—when her husband came home—how she should explain this dreadful thing and free herself from it. She sat down to think. And presently she stole upstairs into an upper room, took a white linen handkerchief out of a drawer, and having returned to the chest, set the little boy's head upon his narrow shoulders again, tied the handkerchief round his neck, and carrying him out, seated him on a stool in the yard and put an apple in his hand.

Not long after this her little daughter came running into the kitchen to her mother, who was standing bent double by the fire, stirring the soup in a great caldron that had been prepared for her husband's supper.

"Mother," said she, "little brother is sitting in the garden with an apple in his hand. I asked him to give me a taste, but he didn't answer me. And his face looked so pale and still that I was frightened."

"Nonsense, child!" said her mother. "Go back to him. Speak to him again, and if he refuses to answer you, give him a sound box on the ear. That will call him to his senses."

The child went back, and said, "Brother, please, please give me a taste of your apple." But the mouth answered never a word; so she hit him lightly on the cheek; and immediately his head fell off. At sight of it she was terrified and ran screaming back to her mother, and hid her eyes in her lap. She wept and wept and would not be comforted.

"My dear, my own pretty dear!" cried her mother; "what have you done! Alas, what dreadful thing is this! But hold your tongue. Let nobody hear of it. Leave all to me." And she took the body of the little boy, cut it into pieces, and put them into the caldron.

When her husband came home and sat down to supper, he asked her, "Where is my son?"

She made no answer, as if she had not heard; and served up a great bowl of black soup upon the table. And the girl sat silently weeping.

The Juniper Tree

"I asked," said the man again, "where is my son?"

"Your son?" said the woman. "A friend of his mother's came and has taken him away to stay with his great-uncle."

"Taken him away!" said her husband. "But he did not even stay to bid goodbye to me."

"He begged me to let him go," said the woman. "He cried to go. Again and again I said, 'No; your father will miss you.' He would not listen. He is a stubborn child. But, why trouble? He will be well taken care of."

"Ay," said her husband; "but I am grieved to think of it. He should not have gone away without wishing me goodbye." He turned away from her. "Weep no more, child," he said to his daughter. "Your brother will come back again."

With that he began to eat. But he stayed sad and sorrowful, and as he ate, his misery increased with his hunger and it seemed he could never be satisfied. His supper done, he went out alone, his mind tormented with dread and horror. And his wife took the great caldron and in the dusk of the evening emptied out what was in it on the stones of the yard—soup, bones and all.

But her little daughter had been watching all that she did; and on seeing this, went softly upstairs and fetched a brightly coloured silk handkerchief, which her father had given her, from out of a drawer. With this she crept downstairs again and out into the garden. There she wrapped up the bones in her handkerchief, as if in a shroud, and, weeping bitterly, carried them out into the yard and laid them under the juniper tree.

And in the quiet of the evening the juniper tree began to bestir itself, and its branches to sway gently to and fro, to open out their bushy-green leaves, and as gently bring them together again, like a child softly clapping its hands for gladness. At the same time a little cloud, as it were, seemed to arise from out of the midst of the tree, and within the cloud there burned a radiance as of a fire. And there fluttered up from out of the fire a bird marvellous in beauty, which mounted into the air and, singing wildly and sweetly, flew away. When the bird had vanished into the evening, the branches of the juniper tree became still and dark again; and the bones that had lain at the foot of the tree were there no longer. At this the little girl was comforted, and her heart leapt for joy. It was as if she knew that her brother who had been dead was now alive again. She went merrily into the house, sat down to her supper, and ate.

The night went by; and early the next morning the bird that had soared up from out of the tree came flying over the village and

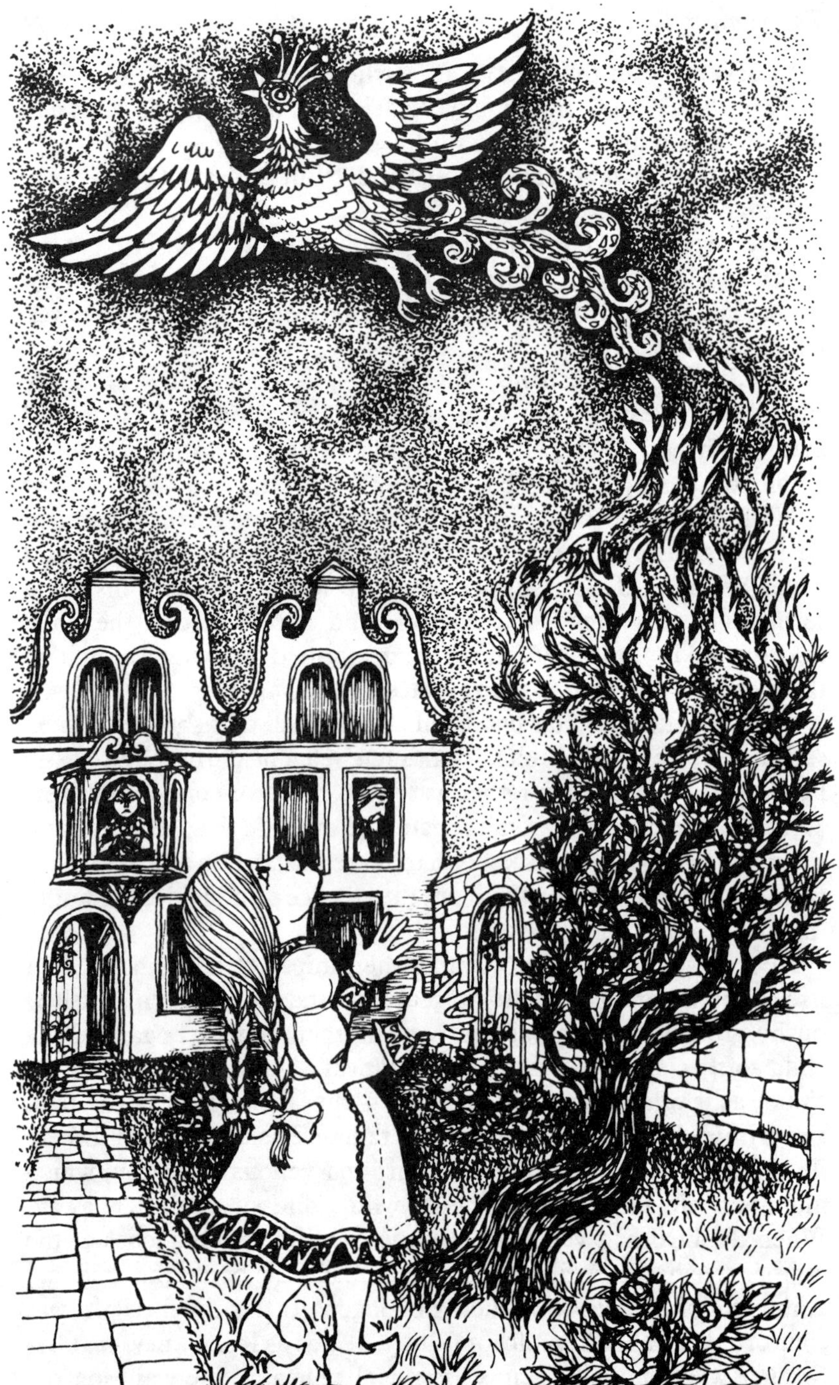

The Juniper Tree

alighted on the roof of the house of a goldsmith. And there it began to warble and sing.

> *"My mother slew her little son;*
> *My father thought me lost and gone:*
> *Out in the dusk on the darkening stones*
> *She flung in hatred my poor bones.*
> *My gentle sister pitied me,*
> *And laid me under the juniper tree;*
> *Now, now I wander merrily,*
> *Over hill and dale I fly.*
>   *Soo-eet, soo-eet—*
>   *Ki-weet, ki-weet:*
> *Oh, what a happy bird am I!"*

Now the goldsmith in his apron was sitting in his workshop fitting together the last links of a slender gold chain. When he heard the strange bird singing on the housetop he rose from his stool so suddenly that one of his slippers fell off. Without staying to put it on again, his chain in one hand, his pincers in the other, he ran out into the street and gazed up at the bird, its bright feathers burnished with the shining of the sun. And he said to the bird, "A marvellous sweet song that was, my pretty bird. Pray sing it to me again and I shall hear every single note of it."

"Nay," answered the bird. "I may not sing twice for nothing. But give me that chain of gold, and I will sing again gladly."

It swooped down from the roof, and perching on the goldsmith's shoulder sang its song again, took the slender chain of gold in its claw, and flew away, until it came to the house of a cobbler who was sitting within mending a shoe.

At sound of its first few notes, the cobbler was spellbound; he called his wife and his children, boys and girls, to come and listen; and there they all stood in the sunny street, their eyes fixed on this strange bird, that had now fallen silent. "A marvellous sweet song, that was," he said. "Pray, pretty bird, sing it all over again."

"Nay," answered the bird; "I may not sing twice for nothing."

At this the cobbler bade his wife run upstairs to the garret. "On the topmost shelf of the cupboard," he told her, "you will find a pair of small red shoes of the finest leather ever made. Bring them down to me."

At sight of the shoes, the bird came near, took them dangling in its other claw, returned to the gable of the cobbler's house, and repeated its song.

And when the song was over, with the golden chain in its one claw, the red shoes in the other, it flew away, far away, until it came to a mill, where on a green bank beside the mill-dam sat a miller with his men hicking and hacking at a new mill-stone. *Hick-hack, hick-hack* went their mallets and chisels: *Klippity-klop, klippity-klop* went the old mill-wheel. And the bird, having perched on the branch of a linden tree that stood near at hand, began to sing.

> "*My mother slew her little son* . . ."

The miller stopped working to listen:

> "*My father thought me lost and gone* . . ."

One of his men began listening:

> "*Out in the dusk on the darkening stones*
> *She flung in hatred my poor bones* . . ."

And another:

> "*My gentle sister pitied me,*
> *And laid me under the juniper tree* . . ."

And yet another:

> "*Now, now I wander merrily,*
> *Over hill and dale I fly.*
> *Soo-eet, soo-eet—*
> *Ki-weet, ki-weet:*
> *Oh, what a happy bird am I!*"

Now all had stopped working and were listening. And the miller—beside himself with delight at the song and at the bird itself, with its sunlit shimmering feathers, red and emerald, the bright golden ring about its neck, and eyes which glittered like dark clear waterdrops as it gazed down on them—besought it with tears in his own to sing again.

"Nay," answered the bird; "I may not sing twice for nothing. Give me that nether mill-stone and I will most gladly."

To the amazement of the miller, the bird flew down among them, and when he and his men had heaved up the heavy mill-stone upon its edge, it thrust its gentle head through the hole which they had pierced in the middle of the stone, and flew back again into the linden tree. There it repeated its song.

The Juniper Tree

When its last note had died away and the dull *klippity-klop, klippity-klop* of the mill-wheel was heard again, it spread its wings, and—the mill-stone about its neck, the chain of gold in one claw, the red shoes in the other—it flew and flew until it came and alighted on the roof of the house in the courtyard of which stood the juniper tree from whence it had sprung. There it stayed silent a while.

And the three of them—the man and his wife and the little girl—were sitting within the house at meat.

"I know not why," said the father; "but I feel lighter in spirit than for many hours past. It may be because the sun is shining; it may be a friend is coming, bringing good news."

At this moment, the bird flew down from the roof of the house and perched above its porch.

"Good news, forsooth!" cried the woman. "Or *evil*. You must be mad, husband. There is thunder in the air; it's growing dark. I am in a fever; my teeth keep chattering; my heart is like lead in my body."

She tore open her bodice with a shuddering sigh.

But the little girl sat listening, the tears from her eyes dropping slowly down upon her plate, half for joy and half for sadness; for the bird above the porch had begun to sing—although the words of its song came but faintly to the ears of those who were sitting within the house.

At its close, the man rose from his chair. "Never in all the days of my life," he said, "have I heard bird sing a song so strange and so marvellous sweet as that. I must go out and see. It may be, if we do not scare it away, it can be enticed to sing again."

"Go out! No!" said the woman. "I entreat you not to leave me. There is dread and danger in the air. The blood in my veins runs like fire. I am sick, and must die."

But he was gone, and the bird had begun to sing again:

> *"My mother slew her little son;*
> *My father thought me lost and gone..."*

With these words, the bird so let fall the golden chain dangling from its claw that it encircled his neck. Filled with delight, he hastened back into the house.

"See," he said, "what this magical and marvellous bird has given me, a necklet of the finest gold!"

At this, the little girl also got up from her stool and ran out. And the bird had been singing on:

> *"Out in the dusk on the darkening stones*
> *She flung in hatred my poor bones.*
> *My gentle sister pitied me,*
> *And laid me under the juniper tree...."*

At this, the bird let fall the bright red-leather shoes at her feet. She ran back, wild with joy.

"Look, look, dear father," she cried; "see what the bird has brought for me!"

> *"Now, now I wander merrily,*
> *Over hill and dale I fly.*
> *Soo-eet, soo-eet—*
> *Ki-weet, ki-weet:*
> *Oh, what a happy bird am I!"*

The song had come to an end, and again there was silence both in the house and out. At this, the woman could endure herself no longer. Her face was grey and drawn with misery.

"I cannot breathe," she said. "It is as though the world were coming to an end. O, where to hide myself! I must be gone."

But as she stepped beyond the threshold of the house and out from the porch, the bird let fall the mill-stone upon her, and without sigh or sound, she fell dead in the shadow of the juniper tree.

At noise of her fall, the father and the little girl ran out of the house; and lo, there, under the juniper tree, stood the little boy, come back from his enchantment. He leapt into his father's arms. They wept together for joy, the man and his two children, and returned into the house.

collected by JACOB and WILHELM GRIMM
retold by Walter de la Mare

Toller's Neighbours
Denmark

Once upon a time a young man and a young girl were in service together at a mansion down near Klode Mill, in the district of Lysgaard. They became attached to each other, and as they both were honest and faithful servants, their master and mistress had a great regard for them, and gave them a wedding dinner the day they were married. Their master gave them also a little cottage with a little field, and there they went to live.

This cottage lay in the middle of a wild heath, and the surrounding country was in bad repute; for in the neighbourhood were a number of old grave-mounds, which it was said were inhabited by the Mount-folk; though Toller, so the peasant was called, cared little for that. "When one only trusts in God," thought Toller, "and does what is just and right to all men, one need not be afraid of anything." They had now taken possession of their cottage and moved in all their little property. When the man and his wife, late one evening, were sitting talking together as to how they could best manage to get on in the world, they heard a knock at the door, and on Toller opening it, in walked a little little man, and wished them "Good evening." He had a red cap on his head, a long beard and long hair, a large hump on his back, and a leathern apron before him, in which was stuck a hammer. They immediately knew him to be a Troll; notwithstanding he looked so good-natured and friendly, that they were not at all afraid of him.

"Now hear, Toller," said the little stranger, "I see well enough that you know who I am, and matters stand thus: I am a poor little hill-man, to whom people have left no other habitation on earth than the graves of fallen warriors, or mounds, where the rays of the sun never can shine down upon us. We have heard that you are come to live here, and our king is fearful that you will do us harm, and even destroy us. He has, therefore, sent me up to you this evening, that I should beg of you, as amicably as I could, to allow us to hold our dwellings in peace. You shall never be annoyed by us, or disturbed by us in your pursuits."

"Be quite at your ease, good man," said Toller, "I have never injured any of God's creatures willingly, and the world is large enough for us all, I believe; and I think we can manage to agree, without the one having any need to do mischief to the other."

"Well, thank God!" exclaimed the little man, beginning in his joy to dance about the room, "that is excellent, and we will in return do you all the good in our power, and that you will soon discover; but now I must depart."

"Will you not first take a spoonful of supper with us?" asked the wife, setting a dish of porridge down on the stool near the window; for the Man of the Mount was so little that he could not reach up to the table. "No, I thank you," said the mannikin, "our king is impatient for my return, and it would be a pity to let him wait for the good news I have to tell him." Hereupon the little man bade them farewell and went his way.

From that day forwards, Toller lived in peace and concord with the little people of the Mount. They could see them go in and out of their mounds in daylight, and no one ever did anything to vex them. At length they became so familiar, that they went in and out of Toller's house, just as if it had been their own. Sometimes it happened that they would borrow a pot or a copper-kettle from the kitchen, but always brought it back again, and set it carefully on the same spot from which they had taken it. They also did all the service they could in return. When the spring came, they would come out of their mounds in the night, gather all the stones off the arable land, and lay them in a heap along the furrows. At harvest time they would pick up all the ears of corn, that nothing might be lost to Toller. All this was observed by the farmer, who, when in bed, or when he read his evening prayer, often thanked the Almighty for having given him the Mount-folk for neighbours. At Easter and Whitsuntide, or in the Christmas holidays, he always set a dish of nice milk-porridge for them, as good as it could be made, out on the mound.

Once, after having given birth to a daughter, his wife was so ill that Toller thought she was near her end. He consulted all the cunning people in the district, but no one knew what to prescribe for her recovery. He sat up every night and watched over the sufferer, that he might be at hand to administer to her wants. Once he fell asleep, and on opening his eyes again towards morning, he saw the room full of the Mount-folk: one sat and rocked the baby, another was busy in cleaning the room, a third stood by the pillow of the sick woman and made a drink of some herbs, which he gave his wife. As soon as they observed that Toller was awake they all ran out of the room; but from that night the poor woman began to mend, and before a fortnight was past she was able to leave her bed and go about her household work, well and cheerful as before.

Another time, Toller was in trouble for want of money to get his horses shod before he went to the town. He talked the matter over with his wife, and they knew not well what course to adopt. But when they were in bed his wife said: "Art thou asleep, Toller?" "No," he answered, "what is it?" "I think," said she, "there is something the matter with the horses in the stable, they are making such a disturbance." Toller rose, lighted his lantern, and went to the stable, and, on opening the door, found it full of the little Mount-folk. They had made the horses lie down, because the mannikins could not reach up to them. Some were employed in taking off the old shoes, some were filing the heads of the nails, while others were tacking on the new shoes; and the next morning, when Toller took his horses to water, he found them shod so beautifully that the best of smiths could not have shod them better. In this manner the Mount-folk and Toller rendered all the good services they could to each other, and many years passed pleasantly. Toller began to grow an old man, his daughter was grown up, and his circumstances were better every year. Instead of the little cottage in which he began the world, he now owned a large and handsome house, and the naked wild heath was converted into fruitful arable land.

One evening just before bed-time, someone knocked at the door, and the Man of the Mount walked in. Toller and his wife looked at him with surprise; for the mannikin was not in his usual dress. He wore on his head a shaggy cap, a woollen kerchief round his throat, and a great sheep-skin cloak covered his body. In his hand he had a stick, and his countenance was very sorrowful. He brought a greeting to Toller from the king, who requested that he, his wife, and little Inger would come over to them in the Mount that evening, for the king had a matter of importance, about which he wished to talk with him. The tears ran down the little man's cheeks while he said this, and when Toller tried to comfort him, and inquired into the source of his trouble, the Man of the Mount only wept the more, but would not impart the cause of his grief.

Toller, his wife and daughter, then went over to the Mount. On descending into the cave, they found it decorated with bunches of sweet willow, crowsfoot, and other flowers, that were to be found on the heath. A large table was spread from one end of the cave to the other. When the peasant and his family entered, they were placed at the head of the table by the side of the king. The little folk also took their places, and began to eat, but they were far from being as cheerful as usual; they sat and sighed and hung down their heads; and it was easy to see that something had gone amiss with them. When the repast was finished, the king said to Toller: "I invited you to come over to us because we all wished to thank you for having been so kind and friendly to us, during the whole time we have been neighbours. But now there are so many churches built in the land, and all of them have such great bells, which ring so loud morning and evening, that we can bear it no longer; we are, therefore, going to leave Jutland and pass over to Norway, as the great number of our people have done long ago. We now wish you farewell, Toller, as we must part."

When the king had said this, all the Mount-folk came and took Toller by the hand, and bade him farewell, and the same to his wife. When they came to Inger, they said: "To you, dear Inger, we will give a remembrance of us, that you may think of the little Mount-people when they are far away." And as they said this, each took up a stone from the ground and threw it into Inger's apron. They left the Mount one by one, with the king leading the way.

Toller and his family remained standing on the Mount as long as they could discern them. They saw the little Trolls wandering over the heath, each with a wallet on his back and a stick in his hand. When they had gone a good part of the way, to where the road leads down to the sea, they all turned round once more, and waved their hands, to say farewell. Then they disappeared, and Toller saw them no more. Sorrowfully he returned to his home.

The next morning Inger saw that all the small stones the Mount-folk had thrown into her apron shone and sparkled, and were real precious stones. Some were blue, others brown, white, and black, and it was the Trolls who had imparted the colour of their eyes to the stones, that Inger might remember them when they were gone; and all the precious stones which we now see, shine and sparkle only because the Mount-folk have given them the colour of their eyes, and it was some of these beautiful precious stones which they once gave to Inger.

retold by **BENJAMIN THORPE**

Door Prayer at Evening
Iceland

Guard the door, good Lord, this night,
Gracious, by thy Cross its might:
Windows, walls, roofs, floors and houses,
As thy darkness round us closes,
Here the Holy Ghost do dwell,
Fend us from the Fiend of Hell,
And all his imps be barred as well.

God keep the door and Crux the lock, Mary Maiden all within and Michael Angel all without; may none break down the goodman's door.

Out Gurg,
In Jesus.
Out Gassagull,
In God's angel,
Out Regarist,
In Jesus Christ.
Out Maledictus,
In Benedictus.

Into God's keeping we commend us all, and good night.

collected by JÓN ÁRNASON and MAGNÚS GRÍMSSON
translated by Alan Boucher

Bibliography

Collectors, authors, translators and books represented in this anthology

Heroic Legends

CROSSLEY-HOLLAND, KEVIN (translator). *Beowulf.* With an introduction by Bruce Mitchell. Macmillan, London, 1968. Reissued by D. S. Brewer, Cambridge, 1977.

MORRIS, WILLIAM. *The Story of Sigurd the Volsung and the Fall of the Niblungs.* Ellis and White, London, 1877.

PICARD, BARBARA LEONIE. *German Hero-Sagas and Folk-Tales.* Oxford University Press, London, 1958.

WEBER, HENRY, JAMIESON, R. and W. S. [Walter Scott] (translators). *Illustrations of Northern Antiquities.* Edinburgh, 1814. (In this book Germanic material predominates, but there are also translations from Icelandic, including the passage by Walter Scott included in this anthology.)

Sagas

GATHORNE-HARDY, G. M. (translator). *The Norse Discoverers of America: The Wineland Sagas.* Oxford University Press, London, 1921.

JONES, GWYN (translator). *Eirik the Red and other Icelandic Sagas.* Oxford University Press, London, 1961.

KERSHAW, N. (later Chadwick) (translator). *Stories and Ballads of the Far Past.* Cambridge University Press, Cambridge, 1921.

LAING, SAMUEL (translator). *The Heimskringla, or Chronicle of the Kings of Norway.* Longmans, London, 1844. (*Part One: The Olaf Sagas.* Revised by Jacqueline Simpson. J. M. Dent, Everyman's Library, London, 1964. *Part Two: Sagas of the Norse Kings.* Revised by Peter Foote. J. M. Dent, Everyman's Library, London, 1961).

MAGNUSSON, MAGNUS and PÁLSSON, HERMANN (translators). *King Harald's Saga*. Penguin, Harmondsworth, 1966.
Njal's Saga. Penguin, Harmondsworth, 1960.
The Vinland Sagas. Penguin, Harmondsworth, 1965.

Folk-Tales

ASBJÖRNSEN, PETER C. and MOE, JORGEN I. *Popular Tales from the Norse*. Edmonston and Douglas, Edinburgh, 1859. Reissued by The Bodley Head, London, 1969.

BOSSCHÈRE, JEAN DE and MORRIS, M. C. O. *Christmas Tales of Flanders*. Heinemann, London, 1917. Reissued by Dover Publications, New York, 1972.

BOUCHER, ALAN. *Ghosts, Witchcraft and the Other World* (Icelandic folktales I) Iceland Review Library, Reykjavik, 1977. These are translations of material collected by Jón Árnason and Magnús Grímsson. The second and third volumes, also translated by Alan Boucher, are *Elves, Trolls and Elemental Beings* and *Adventures, Outlaws and Past Events*.

BRIGGS, KATHARINE M. *A Dictionary of British Folk-Tales*. Four volumes. Routledge and Kegan Paul, London, 1970–1.

CUTT, NANCY and W. TOWRIE. *The Hogboon of Hell and other Strange Orkney Tales*. André Deutsch, London, 1979.

GRIMM, JACOB and WILHELM. *About Wise Men and Simpletons*. Translated by Elizabeth Shub. Hamish Hamilton, London, 1972.

GRUNDTVIG, SVENDT. *Danish Fairy Tales*. Translated by J. Grant Cramer. Four Seas Company. 1919. Reissued by Dover Publicatons, New York, 1972.

HALLIWELL, JAMES ORCHARD. *Popular Rhymes and Nursery Tales of England*. John Russell Smith, London, 1849. Reissued by The Bodley Head, London, 1970.

JACOBS, JOSEPH. *English Fairy Tales*. David Nutt, London, 1890.
More English Fairy Tales. David Nutt, London, 1894.
These two volumes were combined and reissued under the title *English Fairy Tales* by The Bodley Head, London, 1968.

JONES, GWYN. *Scandinavian Legends and Folk-Tales*. Oxford University Press, London, 1956.

LANG, ANDREW. *The Fairy Tale Books of Many Colours*. This twelve-volume series of translations and retellings of the folk-tales of the world was published by Longmans, Green in London between 1888 and 1910 and reissued by Dover Publications, New York, between 1965 and 1968.

MARE, WALTER DE LA. *Animal Stories*. Faber and Faber, London, 1939.

SIMPSON, JACQUELINE. *Icelandic Folktales and Legends*. B. T. Batsford, London, 1972. This book consists of translations of folk material collected by Jón Árnason.

THORPE, BENJAMIN. *Yule-Tide Stories: A Collection of Scandinavian and North-German Popular Tales and Traditions*. Henry G. Bohn, London, 1853.

WADDELL, HELEN. *The Princess Splendour and Other Stories*. Longman, London, 1969.

WAHLENBERG, ANNE. *Great Swedish Fairy Tales*. Translated by Holger Lundbergh. Chatto and Windus, London, 1973.